UNTIL WE ARE FREE

REFLECTIONS ON BLACK LIVES MATTER IN CANADA

EDITED BY RODNEY DIVERLUS, SANDY HUDSON, AND SYRUS MARCUS WARE

Printed and bound in Canada at Friesens. The text of this book is printed on 100% post-consumer recycled paper with earth-friendly vegetable-based inks.

COVER ART: Photo by Paige Galette
COVER AND TEXT DESIGN: Duncan Campbell, University of Regina Press
COPY EDITOR: Marionne Cronin
PROOFREADER: Kristine Douaud

"All Power to All People?: Black LGBTI2QQ Activism, Remembrance, and Archiving in Toronto" by Syrus Marcus Ware was originally published in TSQ: Transgender Studies Quarterly, Volume 4:2, pp. 170–80. (c) 2017 Duke University Press. All rights reserved. Republished by permission of the copyright holder, Duke University Press. www.dukeupress.edu.

Library and Archives Canada Cataloguing in Publication

TITLE: Until we are free : reflections on Black Lives Matter in Canada / edited by Rodney Diverlus, Sandy Hudson, and Syrus Marcus Ware.

NAMES: Diverlus, Rodney, 1990- editor. | Hudson, Sandy, 1985- editor. | Ware, Syrus Marcus, editor.

DESCRIPTION: Includes bibliographical references.

IDENTIFIERS: Canadiana (print) 20190224347 | Canadiana (ebook) 20190224363 | ISBN 9780889776944 (softcover) | ISBN 9780889777361 (hardcover) | ISBN 9780889776968 (PDF) | ISBN 9780889776982 (HTML)

SUBJECTS: LCSH: Black lives matter movement—Canada. | LCSH: Blacks—Canada—Social conditions. | LCSH: Blacks—Civil rights—Canada. | LCSH: Blacks—Political activity—Canada. | LCSH: Race discrimination—Canada. | LCSH: Canada—Race relations. | CSH: Black Canadians—Social conditions. | CSH: Black Canadians—Civil rights. | CSH: Black Canadians—Political activity.

CLASSIFICATION: LCC FC106.B6 U58 2020 | DDC 305.896/071—dc23

10 9 8 7 6 5 4 3 2

University of Regina Press, University of Regina
Regina, Saskatchewan, Canada, S4S 0A2
TEL: (306) 585-4758 FAX: (306) 585-4699
WEB: www.uofrpress.ca

We acknowledge the support of the Canada Council for the Arts for our publishing program. We acknowledge the financial support of the Government of Canada. / Nous reconnaissons l'appui financier du gouvernement du Canada. This publication was made possible with support from Creative Saskatchewan's Book Publishing Production Grant Program.

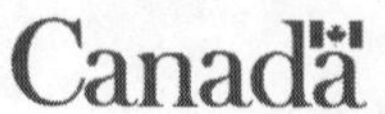

For our Ancestors,
whose struggle we continue
until we are free.

For our Elders,
whose fight we continue
until we are free.

For Andrew Loku, Jermaine Carby, Sumaya
Dalmar, Abdirahman Abdi, Pierre Coriolan,
Amleset Haile, Kwasi Skene-Peters, Alex Wetlauffer,
and the unnamed, whose lives we will continue
to honour until we are free and ever after.

For our children and our grandchildren,
whose futures we will defend
until we are free.

For all of us in the now,
may we all be free.

There can be no future where white supremacy thrives at the expense of Black humanity, and with this orientation, we will continue to fight for true liberation until the day that each of us experience it. All Black life.

Until we are all free.

—THE EDITORS

CONTENTS

PART III: CREATIVE ACTIVISMS: ARTS IN THE MOVEMENT

PART IV: THEORIZING BLACKNESS: CONSIDERATIONS THROUGH TIME AND SPACE

PART V: AND BEYOND: BLACK FUTURITIES AND POSSIBLE WAYS FORWARD

INTRODUCTION

THE YEAR 2055 C.E.—AN IMAGINED FUTURE

It is summer and the heat waves of years ago are now our coldest experiences. The temperatures have climbed to highs that sound like they are lifted from science fiction novels. Except in the winters; those of course have gotten considerably cooler since the jet stream rerouted. I scan the horizon for the nearest shade and set off from my shelter. This weekly water-sourcing trek was always daunting, but summer treks seemed particularly dangerous. If it wasn't the heat, it was the violence on the roads, always worse in summer when more people were out travelling. At my current pace, I imagine I'll reach the shade in the next ten minutes, and it's not a moment too soon. Heat blisters have begun to erupt on my shoulders, joining the scabs of past others.

It has been five minutes. Three minutes to go. Thirty seconds . . .

I'm sweating profusely by the time I reach the shade under one of the few trees left in this region. Under one of the few trees left anywhere, really. I sit down for a moment, opening my water flask. I drink, aggressively at first, but soon at an even pace. I remember an earlier time in our movement, before the temperatures rose in that dramatic upswing, when the world had more people, more animals. More life. I remember life before the droughts, fires, and class wars. Before the race wars. A time before end and destruction. I remember writing about our activisms, documenting the experiences we were having as Black activists in the movement for Black lives in Canada. I remember gathering with a host of Black Canadian theorists, artists, and authors, all of whom had been writing about Black activism during this moment in this northern part of Turtle Island. I remember sharing what they wrote in a collection, an assemblage of stories that wove a complex yarn about the meaning of Blackness in Canada, about the ways that we were fighting to survive and to thrive. I keep a copy of these pages, weather-worn, torn, and crumpled from a life on the road in my shoulder bag, and I read them over and over. It's amazing to me to remember a time when there were still prisons and carceral spaces, borders and confinement. To remember a time of trepidation.

In these tattered pages are words by El Jones and Randy Riley about the injustices that Black people faced in the criminal (in)justice system. In this collaborative essay the authors consider the jury system in Canada and its implicit anti-Blackness and the results for Black prisoners and ex-prisoners. These coils contain stories told by Syrus Marcus Ware and Giselle Dias (Niigaanii Zhaawshko Giizhigokwe) on building abolitionist counters to these systems of violence across the northern part of Turtle Island. They discuss abolitionist struggles over the past twenty years in Ontario, considering the changes to movement-building and the deepening of Black and Indigenous solidarity organizing over those two decades. There are transcribed conversations like the one of Rodney Diverlus interviewing Patrisse Khan-Cullors and Janaya Khan on understanding the Black Lives Matter movement as global and beyond concepts of borders. Or Rodney and Sandy Hudson's retelling of the movement's origins in what was Canada. In this text they reminisce about the beginning days of Black Lives Matter. Robyn Maynard and Leanne Betasamosake Simpson explore Black and Indigenous life on Turtle Island. As a chunk, these texts speak about carceral violence. And it closes with a chapter by Sandy Hudson exploring borders, and in particular how Black identities disrupt imperialism and colonialism globally. Hudson argues for a dismantlement of borders, both physical and conceptual, as a central tenet of Black liberation.

I love handling these pages, feeling their smoothness in parts and deep creases in others. I remember buying paper—going into virtually any store and purchasing compressed processed trees. Sitting here under this tree in a barren landscape, trees have never seemed more treasured and necessary. Maybe this is part of why I keep these pages with me; they are a memory of another time, but also now my responsibility to keep and treasure, protected and safe.

I take a deep drink of water. I flip through the pages. The middle section of the manuscript explored creative activisms. I loved reading this section. As an artist, I related to the writings of Ravyn Wngz and Syrus Marcus Ware about the role of the arts in the broader movement for Black lives. I loved the poetry of Naila Keleta Mae, her words dancing through an understanding of a life lived complexly, imbued with Blackness and its countless other intersections. The Afrofuturistic ideas of Camille Turner, who writes about her performance/installation project, Afronautics Research Lab. I finish it off with a text from Rodney Diverlus dissecting the choreographic and movement elements of Black Lives Matter—Toronto, and Black-centric curated protest as a modality for mass mobilization. Shifting on the ground to ensure I was maximizing my shade coverage, I began to read. Sitting and reading was a luxury afforded to few and was a dangerous pursuit—who knew what could come up on you while you were lost in a book? But I knew this route well and my shady spot was less travelled and as safe as safe could be in these times.

I've read this thousands of times, but my eyes raced across the pages finding new gems and new insights with each read. I reread Sara Jama's writing about disability and Blackness, rooting these considerations in her personal experiences of activism and of disability. The complex and challenging text exploring Blackness in the atmosphere by Dana Inkster deconstructs Black noise, both conceptually and from the personal. I read and reread QueenTite's explorations of the experiences of first-generation Canadians living in the Prairies. And that of Paige Galette, weaving a story of migration and survival, of finding community and ultimately finding home in the northern part of Turtle Island. I soaked up OmiSoore Dryden's retelling of the racial impacts of discrimination in blood donation. My eyes skim the titles, "Black and Muslim," by Gilary Massa, a deep examination of the ways that she grew to understand her Blackness and Muslim identity, and the ways that those two experiences intersected and interlocked.

And we wrote about the future! The future I'm now living. Syrus Marcus Ware looked forward by looking back at Black LGBTTI2QQ activism in Toronto. Leroi Newbold wrote about children in the movement—both their participation in activism and the activism created specifically for, by, and/or about them.

We wrote about our future and it was beautiful. But nothing ever written could compare to this future that I get to experience. We live mostly underground and are safer than we were under draconian rule and an anti-Black police state. Policing was one of the first things to go in our post-revolutionary society. We inherited a host of environmental problems, but we are working hard to find solutions, working in labs below the heat-crusted earth, calculating our way out of this climate-change spiral.

Black people did, eventually, "win." We won our freedoms, our right to self-determination. We set up free communities. And we will continue to win, when we find a way to live on this changed planet.

I looked up. The sun was shifting in the sky. I feared I'd lingered a little too long to continue on my journey but resolved to pick up my pace and make it to the water treatment plant before the sun sets. I take a tube of sun ointment from my bag and slather it over my blisters. I gather my papers and place them back in my bag, a safe reminder of another time.

PART I

FRAMING OUR OWN STORY: BLACK LIVES MATTER IN CANADA, THEN AND NOW

1

THE ORIGIN STORY OF BLACK LIVES MATTER CANADA

SANDY HUDSON AND RODNEY DIVERLUS

Black Lives Matter—Toronto's origin story is equal parts rapid response, solidarity actions, community-driven rage, and timing. It's a story of happenstance, momentum, and seizing a once-in-a-generation opportunity. It's a story that has been told by several outside of the organization based on what they think they know and what they have been able to surmise based on their observations. But for this project we give you our origin story from the vantage point of the creators and document for all of you what is possible when a community comes together in rage and in a commitment to liberation.

FRAMING THE MOMENT: A PRELUDE

On July 13, 2013, the world watched with bated breath as George Zimmerman was acquitted in Sanford, Florida, for the murder of Trayvon Martin. A jury found no fault in Zimmerman, the cretin who shot the unarmed teenager. That night we watched the news as it broke. In our respective homes we scoured the Internet and digested think pieces, commentary, tweets, and spent the night taking in the collective shock felt across the globe. Flurries of texts were exchanged with our friends. Our people were in a state of shock.

It was common knowledge that, historically, police were rarely, if ever, found guilty when they killed Black people. But surely, we all thought, this case would be different. For many of us in our twenties, this was the first time that we witnessed sustained public interest in addressing anti-Black violence. Most of us were young children when Rodney King's beating was headline news, and twenty-two years later, we hoped something would be different; we longed for justice.

We saw ourselves in Trayvon. We too could have been Trayvon. He deserved better. He deserved life. The day after, sleep-deprived and numb, there was a small community gathering and vigil held in Riverdale Park in Toronto. The invitation was kept mostly to extended social media networks, and for many of us following the case, coming together was the only thing we could do. Strangers came together to hold space and time for Trayvon, for our children.

In the year following Trayvon's shooting, the case had gone from an issue localized within the Black American community to headline-grabbing news. The injustices in the Trayvon Martin case were being discussed across media platforms, trickling up to the Canadian news cycle. This case captured the public's attention and triggered a global discourse on anti-Black violence not seen in a generation. Suddenly there were think pieces on the disproportionate rate of police violence against Black people that exposed the reality of how many of us were dying at the hands of police. With America's anti-Black and deeply racist dirty laundry aired out, a global audience of Black and non-Black people tweeted, shared, wrote, and reflected on the case and, more broadly, the realities of living while Black.

This was never just about Trayvon Martin and Zimmerman. The fervour on both sides of the debate was indicative of a more complex system of issues impacting Black people in the United States, Canada, and throughout the African diaspora. Cultural commentators were making the links between Martin and the legacy of North America's chattel slavery; Jim Crow laws in the United States continued investment in prison cages, disenfranchisement, and the "wars" on drugs, gangs, and guns—the accepted rhetoric for what is really a war on Black people. Zimmerman represented the deep-seated anti-Black attitudes enshrined in North American culture; he was the new face of white supremacy.

Black people in Canada are familiar with these realities. We too experience anti-Blackness across institutions. Police violence and anti-Black attitudes are realities that define the Black experience in Canada. We all remember our parent's conversations with us about racism when we were children. These conversations are repeated at dinner tables across the diaspora: "Work twice as hard as your white friends to get half of what they will get." "Be alert and careful around the police; they are not your friends." To be Black means having a deep understanding of the precarity of living in societies built on anti-Blackness, thriving off the exploitation, control, and disposal of our whole selves.

On the day of the Zimmerman verdict, there was rage. We were heartbroken, disillusioned, stunned; we grieved for Martin's family and community, our respective families, our communities.

We sat in the grass and listened to speaker after speaker draw on their experiences with anti-Blackness; some of us familiar, many of us strangers. The reality was that the analysis was there, the anger was there. We knew that police violence was not relegated to the United States. We knew about the impacts of anti-Black violence in our own communities. Mothers spoke for their sons and, sadly, we knew that Martin's fate could also be ours. We knew the crux of the issues but lacked the vehicle through which we could harness and channel our rage. After the vigil we dispersed back to our respective communities.

While we sat in the park, grappling with the verdict, Alicia Garza, 4,000 kilometres away in Oakland, California, was also reflecting on this moment. Sitting at a local bar with friends,[1] she wrote an open letter of love to Black people, in which she said, "Black people. I love you. I love us. Our lives matter, Black Lives Matter."[2] Patrisse Khan-Cullors took the last three words and put a hashtag on it: #BlackLivesMatter. Unbeknownst to them, they were about to create a global movement.

Over the next year, #BlackLivesMatter grew from a viral hashtag to an online platform. Garza and Khan-Cullors, along with New York organizer Opal Tometi, went on to create the skeletal framework for the Black Lives Matter organization. The platform captured a global community's imagination and became a viral space to house our collective rage. For the next year, activists, community members, media, pundits, and politicians alike would use #BlackLivesMatter as a lens through which to understand the political, cultural, and historical moment of the day. Those three words captured what many of us couldn't articulate, a rallying cry heard by Black people across the globe.

One year later it is August 2014, and once again the death of an unarmed Black American teenager grabbed international headlines. Mike Brown was killed by police officer Darren Wilson on August 9, 2014, in Ferguson, Missouri.[3] Akin to Martin, Brown's killing sparked a fury of rallies and protests. The small town of Ferguson became ground zero for an uprising. With Trayvon Martin's murder still fresh in our collective memory, Black communities across North America reached their boiling point. At the time Black Lives Matter, a loose coalition of American freedom fighters, organized a Freedom Ride to Ferguson. Busloads of freedom fighters descended onto Ferguson to lend solidarity and support to the Black people of Ferguson, then engaged in continuous protests. On some of these buses were Torontonian Black and non-Black activists, educators, students, community organizers, and general community folks who were compelled to do something. The coming months brought more actions, more think pieces, and more people utilizing Black Lives Matter as a mantra to rally behind.

In mid-November a global call for solidarity came from the activists on the ground in Ferguson. A grand jury was deliberating on whether charges would be laid against Officer Darren Wilson in Mike Brown's murder. In anticipation of an indictment, communities were encouraged to host solidarity actions twenty-four hours after the jury delivered their decision.

FROM SEED TO FRUIT: CAPITALIZING ON A MOMENT

On November 17, 2014, Sandy Hudson sent a message to a cluster of organizers within the city of Toronto:

> Friends, a no-indictment decision for Darren Wilson in the murder of Mike Brown is expected any day now. I am wondering if anyone is aware of solidarity actions being planned in Toronto. If not, I think we should do what we can to plan something.

One by one, with no questions asked, voices of affirmation rang in. Many of us were eager to take action, eager to harness our growing rage. We began brainstorming and discussing options. Included in that message were other Black people in Toronto we had organized with in the past, including some who would go on to be core organisers of Black Lives Matter—Toronto: Yusra Khogali, Janaya Khan, Pascale Diverlus, and many other comrades and community leaders. Off the bat, it became important for us to create not just a space for solidarity, but one that centred the experience of Black communities in Canada, that uplifted the local stories not grabbing headlines. We wanted to create a space where all our issues, be it carceral violence or the terrorizing of our communities by TAVIS—the Toronto Anti-Violence Intervention Strategy—could be challenged. We were enraged by the homicide of Jermaine Carby, a twenty-four-year-old Black man from Brampton, Ontario, who was killed by Peel Regional Police officer Ryan Reid.[4] We were seeking to rupture the violent way that Canada attempts to absent us; it was a radical, geographic shift in our understandings of Blackness in the Americas.

But the radical, geographic shift was not a new one. It was informed by the internationalist insistences of our ancestors, who insisted upon a global refusal to succumb to anti-Blackness and white supremacy in the abolitionist organizing of the emancipation struggle, the pan-African internationalism of the mid-century anti-colonial struggles, and the movement to end the Apartheid regime in South Africa.

On November 24, 2014, a Missouri grand jury announced that charges would not be laid against Darren Wilson for the killing of Mike Brown.[5] The jury had decided that there was no "probable cause," effectively determining that Mike Brown's killing was justified, not even worthy of a trial.

Huddled in the Black Coalition for Aids Prevention offices in Toronto, we watched the press conference and ensuing news coverage of the decision. Eerily silent, our collective hearts had sunk. Fixated on our screens we watched live as the streets of Ferguson were engulfed in Black people's rage. Fires lit from the tears of a community reeling from death; the Ferguson uprising had begun.

We knew it was time to take to the streets. The rage we felt in that room was nothing compared to what was being felt in Black families' living rooms across the world. We gathered to plan what we thought would be a modest vigil—surely no larger than 150 in attendance—to publicly mourn the injustice of Ryan Reid's killing of Jermaine Carby and the injustice of Darren Wilson's killing of Michael Brown in Ferguson, Missouri.

We were a new collective. Some of us had never organized anything before and were learning on the spot how to care for one another in this space of mourning. We spent the entire night planning and curating a Black Lives Matter rally. We called ourselves "Black Lives Matter—Toronto Coalition" and sent out a public call for action for the following night across the street from the United States consulate. That night we coordinated logistics, content, media, and the nuts and bolts of an action. We taught one another how to create a child-friendly, accessible, spiritual event with consideration for all the people who may attend. With no money, we gathered handwarmers, gloves, food, public transportation funds, candles, legal support, performances, spiritual leaders, and childminders to make sure our community was cared for in the space.

In an effort to build the links between the police violence that happens here and elsewhere, we invited the family of Jermaine Carby to speak. Accessibility was an important consideration for our action. It was important to have Black ASL interpreters, access vehicles, and various modalities to plug into the action. As a group, most of us were queer or trans, many first generation or migrants, from various backgrounds and experiences. It was important for us to cultivate a space in which all Black people could come with their full selves: their grief, their rage. These are central tenets that would go on to form the founding principles of Black Lives Matter—Toronto.

We debated many key details of the action, challenging ourselves to establish a shared set of values as a loose collective of people. We struggled with whether to identify this as a "peaceful" demonstration, in an attempt to reject the media's and public's hierarchization of resistance, with some being seen as palatable and others as inappropriate. Many of our Black comrades in cities across North America are called violent, thugs, and terrorists, simply for engaging in direct action. We believed that the radical Black tradition transcends the Western, white framing of "peace."

We shared a simple call-out with a message to white allies that would prove controversial:

> WHITE/NON-BLACK ALLIES
>
> While we appreciate the solidarity shown by White and Non-Black POC, we want to remind folks of some things:
>
> - Please refrain from taking up space in all ways possible. Remember that you are there in support of Black folks, so should never be at the centre of anything
> - Refrain from speaking to the media. Black voices are crucial to this
> - Stand behind Black folks or between us and the police
> - If you see a cop harassing a Black person, come in and engage (chances are they are least likely to arrest you).

The call was widely criticized by media internationally, in a raw reminder that the dominant society is more interested in how we mourn and the spectacle of our mourning than in what we mourn and the conditions of our lives.

Overnight, our call was shared widely, and the next day, November 25, a shocking number of over 3,000 Black Torontonians and allies stood in snow, freezing rain, and below-freezing temperatures chanting "Black Lives Matter," "Hands up; don't shoot," and a slew of affirmations. We reflected, chanted, sang, and held space together. We heard from local families impacted by violence, paid our respects to those we had lost, and shared space as a community in pain.

We had organized our action and engaged in a media cycle of interviews. It became clear that our city was desperately longing for Black mobilization on the violence that our communities face at the hands of the state. We were flooded with emails and requests for support, many from families who had experience police brutality locally. When we saw the response by the community, we held a reflection meeting and decided we could not ethically end our mobilizing after this one event. There were so many organizers in the city of Toronto who were doing excellent work, but there had been a dearth of Black-specific radical mobilizing since the 1990s. Our OGs[6] had fought for us through the Black Action Defense Committee, the Black Women's Collective, Aya Men, POWA, etc.; it was time for us to do the same.

We committed to continuing the fight that our OGs and ancestors had continued for centuries. We wondered to ourselves, would the founders of Black Lives Matter allow for a chapter outside of the United States? Would they commit to a global orientation for the movement? Within days of our first action, we connected with Patrisse Khan-Cullors. After a discussion of shared principles, we agreed that our fight is the same.

And so we demonstrated.

DIRECT ACTION: BEGINNINGS ON THE ROAD TO A CONTINUED ABOLITIONIST MOVEMENT

We held a die-in for Eric Garner at Yonge and Dundas Square. We held rallies at the United States consulate and at the Toronto Police Service Headquarters. We held vigils. We supported families and community members struggling through loss. We deepened our commitment to Black art, ensuring that the artists' role of imagining our liberated future was essential to all our organizing. We gave ourselves to our community in any way we could in the fight against state violence.

And then, on July 5, 2015, the police in Toronto killed Andrew Loku.

Our response to this horror is told in the chapter written by Janaya Khan and is a tribute to the relationship we have with Tamil organizers in Toronto. After consulting with our Tamil comrades, we worked with Andrew Loku's community to build a vigil in tribute to his life and a demonstration in fury at his murder. We decided we would shut down the Allen Road expressway that cuts through the city, its southernmost exit a few blocks away from Andrew Loku's home, a major police station, and Toronto's Eglinton West neighbourhood, also known as Little Jamaica. Our intention was to make it impossible for the media and politicians to ignore Andrew's killing.

We created five different highly confidential plans for our action, knowing that it would be quite risky. None of these plans materialized the way we planned, but because of our organizing skill we were able to bring both the north- and southbound traffic on the Allen to a halt for hours, demanding justice for Andrew Loku. Hundreds joined us, marching with us from the vigil to the expressway and spilling out from the homes, shops, and eateries along Eglinton West. We were undeniable, and we forced the media and the government to pay attention.

About a year later, we were still organizing for Andrew Loku; when the Special Investigations Unit, Ontario's supposed police watchdog, quietly announced late on a Friday night that they would not recommend that charges be laid against Andrew Doyle, the police officer who killed Andrew within seconds of arriving at his apartment building to investigate a noise complaint. We cancelled our weekend plans, provided support to Andrew's community, and organized late into the night, planning a public day-long arts-focused action and a secret demonstration to follow: a tent city. We planned to camp outside of Toronto City Hall to again force the media to pay attention to a story that the state had tried to bury.

During the day, we danced, sang, chanted, and created. The arts were essential to our work, as Syrus Marcus Ware and Ravyn Wngz explain in their chapter. As night fell, we set up our tents, lit a fire, and announced our intention to stay. The hundreds in the crowd were supportive, and dozens stayed with us late into the night. It didn't take long for dozens of police on horseback to show up, likely two for every protestor, in full riot gear. As the police advanced on us, telling the white man who was serving as our liaison that they intended to break us up physically and arrest us, we had a decision to make. Would we stay and defy them, or would we shut down our tent city protest a mere three hours after it had begun?

We were nervous about our inability to keep everybody safe. City Hall was not lit well at night. We were set up quite a distance away from the street, and we weren't visible in a way that would keep us safe. But the crowd that had stayed with us was insistent: they wanted to stay until we saw some sort of movement from media and decision makers about Andrew Loku. As we grappled with the risks of staying, someone made an outlandish suggestion: if the police want us to move, let's move; let's move straight to the Toronto Police Service Headquarters.

The suggestion seemed outlandish, riskier, more dangerous. But when we thought about it and analyzed it there were a plethora of reasons why the police station was a safer place for us to be, not least of which was its proximity to the street and how well lit we would be. Our liaison delivered word to the police: they had won; we were dispersing. And while they started to go back to their divisional police stations, we scattered as though we were headed in different directions and all quickly relocated to the Toronto Police Service Headquarters, a story elaborated on in Janaya Khan's chapter. The action blew up in ways we could not have foretold. We had support from all over the country and beyond, with American reinforcements arriving midweek to help us with the logistics. We had hot meals delivered five times a day from a local caterer. We had a health centre, a kitchen, an entertainment space, and day-long programming for children and adults alike. We took care of street-involved people around us. We resolved conflicts as they arose. We were surrounded by art and creation—all day, every day. And we won several victories in our refusal to leave that space.

While Tent City was a catalyst for so many different victories and initiatives for Black people in the city of Toronto, the most victorious thing we did in the two weeks that Tent City lasted was to completely imagine a new way of organizing society. We also encouraged our community and others to understand and believe that we have it within us to create a better world. There's no one we can rely on to do it for us. We had to be the visionaries, and we could be bold and unapologetic in bringing our visions to life.

Being attentive to the ways we could build our community was a part of Tent City and was an essential part of our Love is the Cure project. When we heard that one of the most important avenues for Black artist education in the city was unable to keep its doors open for lack of grants, we refused to accept its closure as a foregone conclusion. We supported D'bi Young's Watah School by fundraising through a night of performance followed by a party. We showcased some of Toronto's brightest young Black talents, D'bi Young's performing arts students, and auctioned off the works of Black visual artists to raise the funds necessary to keep the Watah School alive.

It was a beautiful night in support of building community and supporting crucial community-based arts education in Toronto.

We all agree that education is of primary importance in the work that we do. The Black Lives Matter—Toronto Freedom School and the Canadian Freedom Intensive are two of our most important initiatives aimed at combatting the absence of Blackness in traditional education; providing affirming, queer-positive education for our young people; providing an avenue for children to be involved in the movement; and providing political education to adults. At the Freedom School, modelled after the Freedom School of the Black Panthers, children learn, through a trans-feminist lens, about Black Canadian and diasporic history and to engage in political resistance to anti-Black racism and state. At the Canadian Freedom Intensive, participants learn skills for Black-affirming struggle, including critical media analysis, healing, and arts and political education. Through this work we are building a movement that will outlast those of us who are nurturing it in this present moment.

Our work is always focused on and central to our community, no matter who or what we are being told is more important to attend to. In 2016, we were named the Honoured Group at the Toronto Pride Parade.

In perhaps our most controversial action, we shut down the Pride Parade in a refusal to be used as a cover for the way Pride Toronto was hurting so many within the queer and trans community, including Black, deaf, Indigenous, disabled, sex-working, and brown queer and trans people.

We halted the parade, right in front of Prime Minister Justin Trudeau's float. As we sat on the street and waited for the executive director of Pride to come and meet us and hear our demands, two representatives of the Prime Minister came to approach us. We are here to hear your demands, they told us. They said that they knew we had words for the Prime Minister and that, while he wouldn't meet us during the parade, they would take back our concerns and a meeting could be set up later.

We were both confused and tickled. Here was the Prime Minister of Canada, attending the Pride Parade of which we were the honourees, thinking that our action was about him. We laughed and told his representatives that this was not about Justin Trudeau. We had no desire to meet with him. They were confused. Surely we wanted to speak with him about something. He was ready to acquiesce; we just needed to get the parade going again. Again we laughed and refused and waited for the executive director of Pride to capitulate to the demands the queer and trans community had been making of Pride for years.

What those representatives clearly did not know is that we maintain a principle that we will never meet with politicians privately. We know that game. They make promises in private that never materialize in public in order to placate a group enough that it will no longer engage in disruptive and embarrassing protest. We have never met with politicians privately, and each time they ask we insist on and create a public forum where our community can speak truth to power directly, and where politicians are forced to reckon with our communities as a whole.

We started to grow throughout Canada, with Black Lives Matter—Vancouver securing, as we did, a ban on police in uniform at Pride. After the police killing of Pierre Coriolan, Black Lives Matter—Montreal shut down the main stage at the Montreal Jazz Festival, forcing attendees and police to contend with the brutality the Montreal police perpetrate upon Black Montreal. Black Lives Matter—Ottawa organized actions across the country when police officers Daniel Montsion and Dave Weir brutally beat Abdirahman Abdi to death with their bare hands. We began to work on migration issues across Canada, protesting the unjust deportation of Beverly Braham, a pregnant woman who was advised not to fly by her doctors, the unconscionable largest mass arrest in Canadian history of Haitian and Nigerian migrants crossing the border and seeking asylum, and the deportation order against Abdoul Abdi of Nova Scotia. After Pride and the first year of our Freedom School summer program for children, Black Lives Matter—Toronto's influence on the movement internationally was undeniable. Our Freedom School's Black-artist-created educational resources are now distributed globally. And radical Black queer and trans organizers were demanding better from Pride organizations across the world, shutting down Pride parades that refused to honour their humanity. We worked with community partners to remove police officers from Canada's largest school board, which has since sparked campaigns in communities across North America.Our community's influence on the global movement was palpable.

This was our beginning, the origin of Black Lives Matter in Canada. From a Facebook thread to today, our lives have not been the same since. Indeed, Black Toronto has never been the same. Building on the momentum from those first years, government legislation has been passed, policies implemented, organizations started, funds announced, positions created, awards distributed, reviews and assessments made, organizations shifted, legal challenges litigated, and a community reawakened. Most significantly, though, anti-Black racism is now a national discourse.

We write this because we know much has been written about us, but not from our mouths. We wrote this origin story to give context to moments past and present. For both of us, recounting the past five years and putting them to paper was a process of ritual. Of gratitude.

What we know as the diaspora outside the imperial centre is that we cannot live lives in liberation without a reorganization of the global system. In some ways, this has been Canada's Black Lives Matter movement's most important contribution: our insistence on a global orientation that rejects the exceptionalism of the imperial centre. When our liberation is won, there can be no imperialist states exerting oppression upon Black people throughout the globe. There can be no capitalist one percent determining the impoverishment of our lives. There can be no heteropatriarchy and cisnormativity stifling our identities and expression. There can be no ableism and ageism that denies humanity to our youth, elders, and those our current society constructs as disabled. There can be no colony on stolen land in which Black people are constructed as subhuman and in excess and are therefore incarcerated, killed, or left to die at a port of entry.

There can be no white supremacist future where whiteness thrives at the expense of Black humanity. And with this orientation, we will continue to fight for true liberation, until the day that we all experience it.

Until we are all free.

All Black life.

NOTES

1 https://www.usatoday.com/story/tech/2015/03/04/alicia-garza-black-lives-matter/24341593/.

2 https://www.thelily.com/for-alicia-garza-co-founder-of-black-lives-matter-activism-begins-in-the-kitchen/.

3 https://www.usatoday.com/story/news/nation/2014/08/14/michael-brown-ferguson-missouri-timeline/14051827/.

4 Peel Region is a suburban region just outside of Toronto that includes the cities of Brampton and Mississauga and the Town of Caledon.

5 https://www.vanityfair.com/news/daily-news/2014/11/ferguson-grand-jury-verdict-darren-wilson.

6 Activist elders.

PART II

CARCERAL VIOLENCE: BLACKNESS, BORDERS, AND CONFINEMENT IN CANADA

2

MANY A THOUSAND GONE

RANDOLPH RILEY AND EL JONES

INTRODUCTION

EL JONES

1. In the Nova Scotia Archives you can hear William Riley, recorded by Helen Creighton in 1943. He sings the song "No More Auction Block." "No more auction block for me," the lyrics go. "Many a thousand gone." William Riley sings the songs carried out of enslavement by the "freedom runners" (as Sylvia Hamilton names them) to Nova Scotia. During the recording he is overcome by emotion. "It makes my heart ache just to sing it," he says. "Don't sing if it's that much effect on you," his daughter Rose soothes him.[1] But of course he keeps singing because if our ancestors didn't sing through pain, none of us would be here. And this is our liberation, that even as we sing of freedom, the suffering of our ancestors rises in us. And in 2018 I will sit in a courtroom and watch his great-great-grandson be convicted (wrongfully) of murder by an all-white jury. The auction block never went away. It makes my heart ache just to write it. Many a thousand gone.

2. I first meet Randy when I am teaching in the African Canadian Transition Program at the Nova Scotia Community College. He is about twenty. In my class, he writes two papers. The first is on

money and the banking system, and the second is on Christianity and Africa. He prints copies of the papers and hands them out to the class and teachers and staff in the program and then to his friends and his neighbourhood. Later, in jail, he asks me if I still have a copy of his papers and if I can send them in to him. He wants to show the guys inside so they can discuss some ideas. I no longer teach in the program, and although I tear apart my boxes hoping that I've saved something, they're gone.

3. I see Randy a couple of days before he is arrested, on the Commons; it is a summer evening. He tells me he's been swimming in the river, tells me about pushing the raft downstream and swimming to it. His girlfriend is expecting another child. For years after, when I think of him I think of the sunlight glinting off him, a river running, and a raft, drifting away.

4. My mother never pierced our ears as babies because keloids run in her family. When you injure the skin, she tells us, the flesh keeps growing, a reaction to healing that never stops. Maybe it comes from slavery, someone else tells me. Maybe we survived because our bodies grew a protective cover. Maybe this is what survival looks like, a wound growing outwards. You cut it away, it comes back. Even our healing is another hurting. This is a metaphor I am using now to tell you about loss and about Black love through prison walls. "Even with all this pain," I write to him after the verdict, "I would not exchange our friendship to not be going through this." We find ways to grow around the wound that is always there in the flesh of Black life.

5. And in five years, his mother dead, his cousin dead, him nearly dead one night from a stabbing, and all while innocent, all while waiting for trial. How do we quantify that? What is the statistic for never having held your youngest daughter? What mathematical proof is there to show Black pain? "Many thousand," sang William Riley, a number beyond numbers, because there is no way to count what happens to us.

6. Randy hears iZrEAL Jones on the radio a couple of years into his remand. He calls us the next time we are on CKDU and asks us if we can do a show educating the guys inside about Black history and

culture. Todd McCallum joins us as our resident historian. We call the show *The Black Power Hour* (BPH.) People inside call in to discuss topics, or to share poetry and rap, or to request music. Sometimes white people call the show to complain about the language in the songs. We tell them prison is the obscenity. Claims of offense and obscenity are always used to silence Black voices. Say "fuck the police," and you get investigated. Shoot Black kids and you walk away without even being charged.

Randy gets transferred to a jail across the province where phone calls are seven dollars for twenty minutes for the long distance call, plus service charges. He organizes a petition and challenges the province about exploitative phone charges. When members of Black Lives Matter—Toronto come to Halifax to give a lecture, we circulate the petition at the event and it gets hundreds of signatures. And I purchase a phone with a local number. We fight for justice and we work around injustice, always.

We present Randy's work in New York, at the Beyond the Bars conference at Columbia University, and at Black Studies conferences, and in talks across Canada. On the phone we write together, discuss essays and lectures, talk about the news, talk about life. The phones are recorded and monitored—even if we wanted to we couldn't talk about his case. He is always in a positive mood, always building, always looking forward. His voice is with me wherever I go, connected through the phone. This is all I can do for him; I can't get his body out, so I record his voice, try to have it heard beyond bars.

"Do Black lives matter in prison?" I ask people inside. "What does Black Lives Matter mean there?" When I ask Matthew Smith, who fearlessly gives me testimony for the Senate hearing on the human rights of prisoners, he reflects: "The world is a prison for Black people."

7. Randy's mother dies after a long illness. We had to fight for him to be taken to the hospital to visit her, scared as the days go by that it will be too late. When he does visit her, the sheriffs tell him that since he is in leg shackles, it will be easiest if he sits in a wheelchair as they transport him to her bedside.

The morning of the funeral he calls and says he's not going to come. The sheriffs won't bring him his clothes; they are making him come to the funeral in orange. "Do you think nobody in the community has seen someone come from jail at a funeral," we say to him. It won't matter. Come. In the Cherrybrook church, Randy stands up to speak. He is in cuffs and shackles. They won't let him come to the front, but a microphone is passed to him. "I'm sorry to come before you like this," he begins, and there, in his childhood community, where he grew up, the church turns to him. "We love you," people call out. After he speaks, the community gets to their feet and applauds him, welcomes him home. And there is no stopping the love. People shout out to him, line up to hug him, to touch him, to cry with him. The sheriffs, sensing that there is no resisting, don't even stop us from touching him. He holds his children. The community opens its arms to him, lets the prison know that they cannot shame us or separate us, that he is their child. In that Black church, in the heart of a historical Black community, as one, we resist the prison-industrial complex through the force of Black love.

8. The verdict takes five days. The courthouse is freezing cold. By the end of the weekend, in a deserted courthouse, we are lying on the floor and on the hard benches. We are in limbo. I think about the name we gave to our ritual dance, now entertainment on cruise ships. In the crowded hold of the slave ships, our bodies were twisted into the small space. The slave goes down, down into the hold, contorting his body under the stick of slavery. And then he jumps up, liberated.

Downstairs, in the cells, Randy is waiting alone. On the fourth day, his lawyer comes upstairs with a note written on a napkin. He hands it to Randy's oldest aunt. Calling us together, she reads his message:

> April 15/18
>
> Family:
>
> Keep your heads high up there, and don't stress over what is now taking place. We must remain in good spirits and synchronize our hearts and our minds, for there is power in the unseen! It is our duty to remain strong, no matter the outcome. We've seen the evidence and we know what a just decision should be. What I wanted most from this trial was to have you all see my name cleared of this, and that has been accomplished. I'm grateful for that. You no longer have to doubt your nephew, cousin, brother, or

friend. Now that you all know what's right, I'm happy!

Love all y'all
Thx for the continued support.

We are all crying. The media waiting there for the verdict turn away uncomfortably, aware they are watching something unbearably painful and private. We never stop being spectacle, here under the white gaze of lawyers, judges, jury, media, who write how he is "staring" at the witnesses, who see threat on Black faces just for having eyes and directing them somewhere, and who then pretend that Black skin doesn't matter here.

9. The foreperson reads the verdict wrong. "Not guilty, first degree," she intones. We are hugging and crying. And then the clerk starts panicking. Read everything in the box, the judge instructs. Start again.

This time she reads, "Guilty, second degree murder." Coming out of the courtroom, his sister gives the finger to the cameras stuck in her face. Tears streaming, she tells the truth. This is a racist system. We can't get justice. A white cameraman argues with her; white people aren't racist he says. Even here, even now, we can't even grieve in peace. We have to come back to the courtroom to hear the sentencing recommendations the white jurors make. The reporters sit awkwardly. One of them asks me, are you okay, and I break down. "How can I be okay?" My hands are lifted to the sky, to the salvation our grandmothers pray for that doesn't come for us. "How can we be okay when you do this to us day after day?" Randy's aunts surround me, make a barrier with their arms, hold me. "Give us some dignity," they condemn the reporters. We are Black flesh, growing around a wound.

10. "What does justice look like?" I ask Randy after he reads me the chapter he wrote for this book. "I think we should end the chapter there," I say. Randy writes back, *what does justice feel like?* This chapter, put together over jail phones that cut out, through lockdowns, written in pen across pads of paper, recorded over calls and transcribed. This is how we speak justice. The family and friends spread out on the floor of the freezing courthouse lobby, refusing to believe the lie that we wouldn't be here if we hadn't done something. This

is our bodies showing up for justice. William Riley, historian of our suffering. That is what justice sounds like, remembering our dead and speaking for them even when it hurts.

Why do you do this, people in prison always ask me; why do you bother fighting for people? Do you think you can win? And yes, I say, yes we can—not all at once, not all the time, and sometimes just the small things. This love, in the pews of the Cherrybrook Baptist Church, in the arms of the community, in the voice over the phone, in walking step by step through suffering and not looking away, in Randy asking how I am through the worst oppression, our tears, our anger, this is how justice feels, this is where we begin to liberate ourselves. This is why we wrote this chapter together, because we are not supposed to reach through the steel doors and the locks, because we are supposed to feel shame, because Black love exists, and it matters.

It makes my heart ache just to feel it.

• • •

THE MISSISSIPPI OF CANADA

RANDOLPH RILEY

The Nova Scotian Black experience is a story of strength, determination, and perseverance. It is the story of a people who have overcome harsh conditions in a place where we have been accepted yet also neglected. The struggles of pains from our past are the reason for our hard faces and passive resistance towards those that govern our lives.

The story of the Black Nova Scotian is unlike any other. To give you some insight into our plight, I must first give you some context. When you consider that Nova Scotia still has the largest Indigenous Black population per capita in Canada, it was almost inevitable that it would have an intense racial divide. We are also home to the largest Black community in the country, North Preston. According to Bridglal Pachai's book, *Beneath the Clouds of the Promised Land*, the settlement of North Preston was initially surveyed in 1784. The extent of the land was some 56,722 acres, or 22,975.6 hectares. North Preston's population flourished from 924 in 1860 to approximately 5,000 strong today, becoming the hub of Blackness in Nova Scotia. Today, one of the community's main priorities is gaining land titles to some lots that are without. When the land was distributed in the colonial days titles were usually withheld, and the situation remains unresolved to this day. This fight is as old as the community itself and has lately received some media attention.

The struggle for land title in North Preston is known all throughout Black Nova Scotia, in part because we are all too familiar with the story of Africville, the shoreline Halifax community demolished in 1964. Land titles played a big role in how the community was taken from its residents and destroyed, to only end up building a dog park in its place. The community of Africville fought the same fight that North Preston is fighting today, but lost and was bulldozed to the ground. The land title saga was the reason why the city could bulldoze without consideration of its residents. Although the residents could trace their land back to their ancestors, without titles the province felt they had a right to displace community residents without care for their arguments. The first land titles acquired in Africville were in the names of a William Brown and William Arnold in 1848. In 1851 Africville had 54 residents. When the residents were being relocated in 1964 the population was 400. The people of Africville were placed into housing projects throughout the city's north end without compensation for their property or belongings. When the bulldozers showed up, they destroyed houses belonging to some folks who were at work and unaware the city had come to bulldoze, who lost everything in the wreckage. The story of the 125-year history of Africville will always be a thorn in the side of this province.

Despite the fact that Black communities in Nova Scotia are so homogenous and unified, Black Nova Scotians are still disenfranchised and without equal opportunity. Since the 1950s Black politicians have represented themselves as participants in the fight for equality, but still, not much has changed when it comes to racial relations in this province. A lot of Black firsts in this country come from this province, but no matter the position gained over the years, inequality is still an issue and racism is still alive and rampant. The racial divide in Nova Scotia has hindered justice and worsened inequalities since my ancestors came to this province. The lack of diversity and inclusion of other ethnic backgrounds in the institutions that hold this province together has caused it to develop white superiority in these establishments, placing the voices and lives of other nationalities in an inferior state.

The fight for equality remains an uphill battle. The blatant racism of the province's institutions is the core reason why Black Nova Scotians from these strong, durable, long-lasting communities are not reaching society's heights. Community members feel left out and the gap in opportunities is widely felt. Assuredly there is a racial component to this. The indifference of white politicians tasked with overseeing and supporting the Black communities is appalling. The lack of funding in our schools, the unemployment rates, and the socioeconomic issues Black folks grapple with is an underlying hindrance to equal opportunity to succeed in this white world of exclusive membership.

At the beginning of 2018, the statue of the eighteenth-century British general Edward Cornwallis was finally removed from a public park in Halifax after years of repeated protest demanding its removal. Cornwallis is considered one of the founding fathers of the province. He is most known, though, for placing a bounty on the scalps of the Mi'kmaq Indigenous peoples. Although this controversial figure's statue was finally taken down, the ideology he promoted is still seen and felt. It was less than ten years ago that a large cross was lit on fire on the lawn of an interracial couple.

CURRENTLY INCARCERATED, WRONGFULLY CONVICTED

The ideology of Cornwallis was recently resurrected at my first-degree murder trial in April of this year, 2018, where I myself, a member of the predominantly Black community of Lake Loon, was wrongfully convicted by an all-white jury. Again, the racial component was prevalent throughout the whole trial, from the reporters to the Crown prosecutors and the jury. In their closing arguments, the prosecutor repeatedly spoke of the victim as *a white man*—almost pleading to the jury to convict me based on race. This miscarriage of justice resulted in me being convicted of second-degree murder, something I was never charged with. My lawyer and everyone in attendance could see there was no evidence to support the conviction. Discussing this afterwards, no matter how we looked at the evidence, there was no way it could even make second degree murder a possibility. This tells you that I was found guilty, why?—Because the jury felt I "probably" did it, because I "looked guilty," or because I was Black and the victim was white. It is so obvious that race played a major role in the wrongfulness of this conviction.

As you may know, the jury process is already under scrutiny due to the recent decision to acquit the killer of Indigenous youth Colten Boushie in Saskatchewan. Here in Nova Scotia, my first question is: how, in the province with the largest Black Indigenous population in the country, are all-white juries even possible? It's to the point where we know that members of communities of colour aren't being called for jury duty all across the country. When the topic is the jury, the term "peer" seems as if it lacks meaning or force. On a panel of jurors, the defendant should be able to identify and relate to some members as a right. It should not be left up to chance and a few peremptory challenges.

Cases involving a jury should be handled with the utmost caution. A defendant's freedom is on the line, and the court entrusts twelve people to make this decision. These are people with little or no direct knowledge of the law, who live life day to day as speculators. Although judges instruct juries not to speculate, it is hard—nearly impossible—to prevent this when the average citizen, including myself, are engrained in speculation.

My second question: why are the most serious charges in the Criminal Code the only ones left up to a jury to decide when we are all aware of the existence of racial bias? From my experience with the justice system, I suspect the majority of wrongful convictions probably happen in cases that are left up to juries, and I firmly believe that, in my case, if the panel had consisted of twelve people of any other race, I would have been found not guilty. The historical reverberations of white supremacy are still present today in juries selected from people who, for example, believe media reports about all of North Preston being criminals and then are in the position to judge Black people from these communities. Being Black, I was fully conscious of the odds stacked against me when the selection of the jury was complete.

The judge is assigned to uphold the law and ensure that justice is served. Yet during a jury trial, the judge becomes nothing more than a referee. If a jury comes back with a verdict that has no evidence to support it, how can a judge, the highest authority in the court, not have a right to intervene and instruct the jury on its unreasonable verdict? Because judges lack this power, I am in jail for a crime I not only didn't commit but had no knowledge of having even taken place. In 2018, how can this be? I feel now, after the more than five years I've spent on remand, that I'm being held captive—enslaved like Solomon Northup from the book *Twelve Years a Slave*. In my opinion, court testimony proved that I'm innocent, yet I am still incarcerated. This issue is bigger than my own case because injustices like this are happening all over Canada. How can an all-white jury be considered fair and impartial when, historically, this is one group of people that have hated, enslaved, lynched, and that now imprison my people?

This history alone should be enough to prove the unfairness and warrant a diverse jury panel.

The white folks of today don't all carry the hatred of their ancestors towards people of colour, but I think it can be agreed that, in sum, there is still racism and a white supremacist assumption of Black guilt that inherently fosters the stigma against Blackness. In no way can it be argued that this unjust verdict which now disrupts and destroys my life and the lives of my family was based on evidence. Rather, it was clearly based on race.

THE PARTY

Since its founding in Oakland, CA, in the 1960s, the Black Panther Party for Self Defense has advocated for Black people to be tried fairly in court by a diverse jury. In the BPP's original Ten-Point Program, in the section entitled "What We Believe," point nine states:

> We want all Black people when brought to trial to be tried by a jury of their peer group or people from their communities as defined by the US constitution. The 14th amendment of the US constitution gives a man a right to be tried by a jury of his peer group. A peer is a person from a similar economic, social, religious, geographical, environmental, historical and racial background. To do this, the court would be forced to select a jury from the Black community from which the Black defendant came. We have been and are being tried by all White juries that have no understanding of the "average reasoning man" of the Black community.[2]

From the outset, the Party demanded that we be tried by a jury of our peers because the white race cannot be tasked with judging us impartially or equally. Since birth we have been indicted because of our Black skin. We have not been seen as equals in the Americas. We are not seen as human, but as a threat.

Here in Nova Scotia, just weeks ago, another Brother of mixed African and Indigenous heritage before the court for a hearing witnessed the Crown prosecutor dismiss his Indigenous roots despite having a Gladue report in front of him—further re-traumatizing him by refusing to acknowledge his systemic oppression at the hands of the government which disenfranchised Indigenous people and alienated many African Nova Scotians from their Mi'kmaq heritage. In this case, the young Brother was charged with uttering threats because he was seen on video punching a photocopied picture of a staff member he was accused of assaulting while in segregation serving forty-one days at the notorious Central Nova Scotia Correctional Facility. The crown requested that he serve one year for punching the picture; the judge disagreed and sentenced him to five months in jail. Five months in jail for punching a picture . . . I almost didn't believe it when he told me.

They think this is trivial, but denying our ancestral heritage and wrongfully convicting us because we are Black is monumental, and it's happening every day in this country.

WHAT DOES JUSTICE FEEL LIKE?

After what I thought was the end of this piece, El suggested that I consider the question, *what does justice look like?* I have struggled with this concept for the better part of the day with the deadline for this chapter looming. Since I believe myself to be a realist, and since we obviously are nowhere near a paradisiacal utopian state of justice, I've chosen to reword this fundamental question, and ask, *what does justice feel like?* Few of us can unilaterally say that we've seen justice in action—but we have all felt injustice and inherently know when it's happening, even when a process to adjust or alleviate said injustice does not exist.

So, *what does justice feel like?* It doesn't feel like police who have carte blanche in Canada and who can victimize Black and Brown people all over the country and be given the benefit of the doubt just because they are armed with a badge. It doesn't feel like sitting in that correctional facility for five years waiting to clear my name, only to have an all-white jury disregard common sense and the rule of law and come back with an unjust and absurd verdict based on prior preconceived notions about Black people and questionable evidence. Justice does not feel like the tragic sagas of Andrew Loku, Olando Brown, Abdirahman Abdi, or Sammy Yatim. It definitely doesn't feel like the cell I currently occupy or the refusal to allow me and my Brothers to receive literature during Ramadan despite numerous and repeated requests. No, justice is not that.

But it looks splendid on paper.

The inquiry into missing and murdered Indigenous women sounded and looked fine before the government went largely over-budget, paraded families on a pedestal, and avoided accountability for their specific role in victimizing the community. They were subsequently given millions of dollars more and the deadline to produce the inquiry's report was extended. All the while, Indigenous women and girls like Tina Fontaine continue to be victimized and their killers are still acquitted. These case files look fine when they profess words such as "due process," "constitutional freedoms," "presumption of innocence," "trial by a jury of your peers," "right to life, liberty, and etc." On paper, and in theory, these concepts sound just fine but what happens to justice when we can visibly see Sandra Bland being harassed and profiled and carted off and jailed to her death despite her protests? Why does justice not ring true when Eric Garner, with numerous broken bones in his back, dying of asphyxiation, repeats "I can't breathe"? What is the perception of justice when the jury comes back with a not guilty verdict in police brutality trials, or when prosecutors can have or spend unlimited resources trying these trumped-up charges?

If you have time and read the Justice Center's *Access To Justice Report*, you will overwhelmingly hear that the people most dependent upon justice and similar systems think that justice is out of their reach, is only for the rich, and that authority figures get away with all types of professional infractions and misconduct. This also is not what justice looks like.

Justice to me feels like getting help when the need is required, despite skin colour. Justice to me is all-inclusive and non-combative and is a search for the truth and a balanced approach with a non-adversarial demeanour. Justice has numerous paths, so justice is tackling racism, poverty, inequity, and illiteracy before you open up a hundred-million-dollar jail to house mostly minorities from at-risk communities. Justice to me feels like taking into account that Black and Indigenous people only occupy 5 to 6 percent of any province yet are overrepresented in judicial systems and occupy nearly 40 to 50 percent of some jails.

That is what justice looks like to me.

> "If you want to judge a nation, visit its jails. A nation should not be judged on how it treats it highest citizens, but on how it treats its lowest ones." —Nelson Mandela

EDITORS' NOTE: *Thank you to Ashley Avery for transcribing Randy Riley's chapter. Randolph Riley would like to send a shout-out to Maurice Pratt for his thoughts and assistance on what justice feels like. Thank you to Matthew Smith for his contributions. And many thanks to Reed "iZrEAL" Jones and Todd McCallum, the Black Power Hour radio team.*

NOTES

1 'Auction Block,' from William Riley, then Mrs. Nina Bartley, Cherry Brook, Halifax County, Nova Scotia, sound recording, Rec. no. 80, Loc. no. AR 5036, AC 2222, MF no. 289.19, Helen Creighton fonds, Nova Scotia Archives.

2 Black Panther Party Program, quoted in Joshua Bloom and Waldo E. Martin, Jr., "The Correct Handling of a Revolution," in *Black Against Empire: The History and Politics of the Black Panther Party* (Oakland: University of California Press, 2013), 72.

REFERENCES

Bloom, Joshua, and Waldo E. Martin, Jr. "The Correct Handling of a Revolution." In *Black Against Empire: The History and Politics of the Black Panther Party*, 65–98. Oakland: University of California Press, 2013.

3

REVOLUTION AND RESURGENCE: DISMANTLING THE PRISON INDUSTRIAL COMPLEX THROUGH BLACK AND INDIGENOUS SOLIDARITY

SYRUS MARCUS WARE AND GISELLE DIAS
(NIIGAANII ZHAAWSHKO GIIZHIGOKWE)

Turtle Island has been the site of decades of prisoners' justice organizing, stretching coast to coast to coast. What follows is a consideration of abolition, the movement for Black lives, Indigenous resurgence, and Black and Indigenous solidarity. This is a recorded conversation between two prisoners, justice activists, and long-time abolitionists: Syrus Marcus Ware and Giselle Dias (Niigaanii Zhaawshko Giizhigokwe, Metis, Red River, Manitoba)—both long-time prison organizers and co-founders of both the Prisoners Justice Action Committee (PJAC) and the Prisoners Justice Film Festival (Toronto and London, ON).

WHAT DOES ABOLITION MEAN TO YOU?

SYRUS: For me, true abolition would only come through a revolutionary process where everything would change. Because if we think about getting rid of the idea of punishing the soul or punishing the body as a way of dealing with conflict, then actually everything changes because that's such the root of how we handle difficulties in our society. So abolition is, yes, the closing and ending of our reliance on the prison-industrial complex as a way of handling our conflict, but it's also an entirely new way of being and relating to each other in the world. A new possibility of the way the communities function, the way that schools would look, the way that community centres would look, the role of collective work in society.

All of that would change through an abolitionist process because we would be more interdependent. I think that, to me, that's what abolition is sort of heading towards.

GISELLE: I think that when I first started talking about abolition in the late 1990s, the focus was on decarceration strategies and finding alternatives to incarceration through transformative justice practices. But that analysis started to expand when I began understanding that abolition is beyond simply abolishing police, prisons, and courts. When I began to understand the expansiveness of other carceral spaces then it became clear that abolition meant abolishing the structures that maintain the prison-industrial complex (white supremacy, colonialism, racism, sexism, homophobia, transphobia, ableism, etc.). It was through a conversation with you that I began to see abolition as a revolutionary struggle.

In the past few years as I've started to learn Anishinaabe teachings and read Indigenous writers, I have started to look at decolonization and resurgence as abolition.

SYRUS: How do you think activism/organizing around abolition has changed or shifted over the time you have been doing this activism?

For me, it makes me think about organizing in the late '90s and the early 2000s, and every conversation in groups of people working on prisoners' justice or whatever had to be . . . we had to have this belaboured conversation about reform or abolition. Whereas now I think there's a lot more people who are interested in the idea or interested in talking about abolition that maybe makes that pressing question—reform versus abolition—less pressing. I don't know.

GISELLE: Yeah. It's so interesting because there are lots of people who are calling themselves abolitionists, but I'm not sure where or how they're thinking about it.

I also think people have learned from the work, the analysis that people have been developing about the PIC over a long time and they are able to get closer to where we are now from the very beginning of their work.

SYRUS: But this is the thing . . . I have these questions about the rapid development of an interest in abolition without the development of . . . Like, where would one go to learn about abolition if they were just coming to this conversation? There isn't necessarily a place to get all the info. We're all just figuring out our analysis and our understanding of what it could look like because we've spent so many years having to debate about *why* abolition that we haven't necessarily had as much time to be able to dream about *how* abolition.

One of the things that I've learned so much from you, Giselle, is that over the years . . . you've just had such a long tenure doing this organizing and doing this activism. And I've learned so much from you about the prison system in Canada and about, yeah, thinking radically about abolition as being connected to Indigenous resurgence, as being connected to Black liberation.

I wonder if you could maybe talk a little bit about your experiences of Black and Indigenous solidarity in doing this organizing against the prison-industrial complex?

GISELLE: I have also learned so much from you over the years and I think even this conversation is developing our analysis further, which will affect how we continue to organize. Especially if our focus is on Black liberation, Indigenous Nation-building, and Black and Indigenous solidarity. This is a new conversation for me about the prison-industrial complex because I haven't actually read much about this nor have I had the opportunity to really talk about it in a meaningful way since I started coming to an understanding of my own identity as an Indigenous woman and starting to learn teachings.

Over time I have started to learn what it means to me to be a Metis woman. I have had to try and reconcile what it means to be the colonized and colonizer. My ancestors travelled the globe to ensure my presence in the world and I have had to try and understand what that means in terms of my place, purpose, and identity. This continues to be a decolonizing, indigenizing, and anti-colonial practice for me.

Several years ago I started going to ceremony and introducing Spirit into my work and it has completely changed abolition for me. I think when you and I were organizing together there was Spirit in our work but not necessarily ceremony.

SYRUS: Yes.

GISELLE: Yeah, and I'm sure for you something else has changed for you over the years because it seems there is a different Spirit in your work now.

SYRUS: Yeah, my work shifted so radically when I started anchoring it around the survival of all of my people, so that then my work became about resiliency, it became about support, it became about love in a way that I think it probably always initially in a deep-rooted way was there but it became much more articulated that that was what I wanted to do. My project in this lifetime was figuring out how we were all going to make it. So all of my artistic projects, all of my activist projects have been trying to get closer to this understanding of how we all get to make it. So, to me, that totally shifts my understanding of both the urgency of abolition but also what kinds of things we're thinking about and talking about when we think about abolition.

GISELLE: Yeah, that totally makes sense to me. I know for me that when I started intentionally grounding my life, activism, and organizing in Spirit and ceremony the shift was so significant to me. Learning about my own identity as a Metis woman is about resurgence. Organizing started to involve sitting in circle, smudging, and prayer. It started to ground my work on abolition and even changed how I talked about transformative justice.

When I used to talk about transformative justice it was just about circle processes, whereas when I started to hear other Indigenous people talk about transformative justice, it was partly a journey into their identity, into their culture, into their spirituality, into knowing who they were, about being grounded in ceremony, in language, in land.

My thinking around transformative justice was so linear. It started to become very exciting for me to think that each time we step into ourselves as Indigenous people we're engaging in resurgence of our Spirits, hearts, minds, and bodies, which is now how I am starting to see as a move towards abolition.

And as Indigenous people continue or start to reclaim identities and teachings and participate in land-based ceremony we are moving towards abolition. Understanding my identity has completely changed the way I thought about abolition. Instead of as a process of tearing down, which I think we need to do, and resisting, which I think we need to do, there's something underneath that which is about the survival and resurgence of Indigenous people.

SYRUS: Yes, and this building up—the building up and the creating from the ground up: building the kinds of structures, the kinds of ways of relating to each other, the kinds of ways of being and knowing that we want to have as an abolitionist process so that the walls are coming down but there's already a garden that's been built in place, so that we have something ready. I think that drives my work so much. I'm so interested in that and that's part of what, to me, has been so beautiful about the movement for Black lives, and being involved in this direct action group, Black Lives Matter—Toronto, and the ways that we've . . . yes, definitely, absolutely called attention to the power structures that are existing in society that are replicating into Blackness and try to tear those down or unsettle them or disrupt them.

But at the same time, we're doing this through building community, through educating our communities around disability justice, through cross-coalition work, through Black and Indigenous solidarity, so that all of the work that we're doing is starting to build the kind of world, the networks that we want to be living in anyways so that, at the end of the day, when the last walls of the last police station come down, great, we're already living this beautiful free life. And that, to me, is really exciting.

GISELLE: Yeah, I think this is what's so great about the conversation we are having now . . . we can start talking about abolition from where we are at in the present. We have known each other so long, been a part of each other's life and work and watched each other's organizing grow, that we get to have conversations like this.

SYRUS: This is what's so exciting, and I remember when we started PJAC in 2004 or whatever, so much of what we were trying to do was to get the larger public to have a conversation about abolition. So that's why we did the film festivals, that's why we did so much public-facing shit, because we were trying to make it at least part of the dinner table conversation of the average population. But now it's just such a different conversation. And to be able to build on the organizing that's happened over the last twenty-five and thirty years, plus all of this new energy and new excitement from an emerging generation of people growing up with abolition as a norm of something to think about. That's just the basis of a general political teaching that you would learn in any type of basic—I don't know—when you're first getting involved in activism. Abolition is something that we're working towards. Get on board. That's exciting, that then there's a whole bunch of new ideas and new ways of thinking about it. So this feels like a really fruitful time.

And we are at this moment where we're in the end of capital—this late-capital, pre-environmental-devastation moment where everything is about to shift. And we're on this precipice and so the opportunity to think that the world could change dramatically is right there. I think there's so many things that are working in our favour that would help us to make the kind of big changes that we need to make.

GISELLE: When PJAC started I think what we did really well was cross-movement building and this really informed how we did the Prisoners' Justice Film Festival that we had in London. People who weren't talking about abolition started talking about abolition and it was amazing. And the connections and relationships we've built with each other to support each other's movements was so important.

SYRUS: Yeah, and the work around immigration detention, psychiatric detention, all of those cross-coalitions where they were these organizations and groups that were already working on those issues coming together with prison abolitionists to have this broader conversation about what it means to stop jailing and then creating carceral spaces for human beings, things that are alive. That's just really exciting. And I think, for me, that work was one of the first times where I was involved in organizing and a lot of the people I was organizing with where Black, Indigenous, and racialized people. A lot of the activism and organizing that I had done before that was usually dominated by white voices. It felt really different. Abolition as a conversation allowed us to have a different starting point and we came together in different ways. For me, that was really unique.

GISELLE: Yeah, and it was an opportunity for me to learn about other movements because I'd been focused on abolition and prisoners' rights for so long that it expanded my mind to think about other movements and how they intersected with the prison-industrial complex.

And then because of PJAC it influenced how I organized when I moved to London, ON. It really shifted who I was able to pull together because there wasn't any formal anti-PIC organizing in the city, but there were people who easily saw how their movements were connected to the PIC.

When I was organizing with Sâkihitowin Awâsis from Atlohsa Native Family Services, she wanted to show a film on resurgence and it just clicked. I was like, "Oh, of course that's abolition."

There was a similar moment for me that I had when you were talking about revolution during one of our PJAC meetings in my apartment and I was like, "Oh, of course this is the revolution. Abolition is a revolutionary movement!"

And when Kyisha Williams asked the question, "how do we reproduce the PIC in our everyday lives?" she pushed me to think more broadly and introspectively.

I think these are examples of how Black and Indigenous solidarity can deepen our work through conversation and relationships.

SYRUS: Oh my gosh!

GISELE: After watching shorts at the PJFF in London from The Ways by Wisconsin Media Lab on *Manoomin: Food that Grows on Water*, learning the language, *Clan Mother*, and the *Powwow Trail,* I was like, "Of course, resurgence is part of abolition."

SYRUS: That is abolition.

GISELLE: Yeah. The amazing thing is that we had done film showings on Indigenous peoples' experiences of incarceration, land defense, solidarity with Palestine, and those have always been clear connections to the prison-industrial complex. But Awasis saw the connection to resurgence so quickly even though she hadn't been doing "formal" anti-prison organizing for very long. It was really humbling for me to learn such a big teaching after having done this work for so long.

But now that I'm thinking about resurgence as abolition I am trying to consider how do we integrate land into the conversation about abolition? I feel like it's really been missing. Conversations about ongoing colonization and the over-incarceration of Indigenous people have routinely been a part of the conversations on abolition but I think abolition has to be even more clearly connected to land in analysis and practice. Returning land has to be a part of abolition conversations.

SYRUS: There's a scholar, Tiffany King, who is a dear friend and just a brilliant academic . . . brilliant thinker, rather, and she wrote in her PhD thesis about this theory of Black fungibility. So she directly connects Black and Indigenous solidarity and some of the tensions between Black and Indigenous communities to this process of creating fungible Black people, where Black people were treated as interchangeably as seeds, used and physically planted as seeds, to terraform the land in order to change it for the process of colonization. So, in order to rid Indigenous people of land, Black people were bred, exchanged, sold, bought at market, exactly the same way that seeds were, planted in the same way that seeds were. If they grew, they grew. If they didn't, they didn't. And they were replaceable because it doesn't matter if all of your tomato seeds grow from your plant packet, you already have more than enough, right?

So, it was just like that concept of Black fungibility helps me so much to understand why Black lives are so disposable in North America and on Turtle Island—

GISELLE: Yeah. I think this is part of why reparations for Black people in the South is so complicated for Black and Indigenous relationships. How do we begin to incorporate reciprocal relationship and balance with the land in our conversations about abolition?

SYRUS: Yeah. I mean it's really complicated for Black people who were brought here. Like, in my family history we were brought here, were bred here. We were sold here. There's really nowhere else to go back to. We were here for generation after generation, brutalized on this place, you know? And so on the one hand, we, of course, give all the land back of 100 percent and where do we . . . what does that then mean for us, and how do we kind of plan for what this could look like. I mean, there's absolutely no conversation about reparations in Canada because Canada can't even admit that it had slavery here, even though it did. But this is something that we're not taught. This is something that we're actively taught the opposite of, actually.

Canada as the safe haven. Canada as the end point of the Underground Railroad. Canada as the saviour, even though there was slavery here and brutal segregation here and brutality here that continues to this day with the carding of Black people and the targeting of Black people and the over-policing of Black that results in an overpopulation of Black people in the prison system in Canada. It's unbelievable.

GISELLE: Yeah. I think that all of that makes it so much more complicated. Also there's so many Indigenous nations with different teachings, language, culture, or ceremony. Nations need time, space, land, resources to build our own governing structures and economies without ongoing colonial violence.

So there's all the work that needs to be done in Indigenous communities with people who still don't have access to clean water, housing, or land. Indigenous people are still forced to live on reserves, in poverty, where the suicide rates are so high amongst youth. These issues, the issue of over-incarceration of Indigenous people and murdered and missing Indigenous women and girls are—all have to be a part of the conversation within abolition.

We need to learn to hold these complexities in our organizing. And I don't think the term "abolition" is right any more. Abolition is too limited a word to describe some of the things we're talking about. I am sure there is a word in Cree or Anishinaabemowin or another Indigenous language that would be more descriptive of what we are talking about.

When people start looking at prisons and how it intersects with every movement, it just becomes clear that abolition has the potential to be a goal we're all working towards if we want to make systemic changes.

SYRUS: Yeah. Totally. That kind of leads into this question about what some of the barriers are to doing this work.

GISELLE: I think we've talked about the complexity of some of the land issues being, I can't remember how you framed it, fungibility?

SYRUS: Yeah. Fungibility.

GISELLE: So, as we talk about fungibility we are talking about the complexity of the conversations about land within abolition. At the same time colonization, capitalism, and racism has created so much lateral violence within Indigenous communities and between Indigenous and Black communities.

I remember reading an article in Upping the Ante where Patricia Monture said something like, "Indigenous people on reserves are just trying to survive; they don't have time to be starting anti-prison movements."[1] Is that something that is being talked about in BLM—Toronto?

SYRUS: Yeah. Yeah. People are just stuck in certain communities. The conditions are so difficult that the prospect of living a full, long life seems so improbable, you know? People are really on a "just try to make it" kind of reality. I think that that's true for a lot of Black people living across Turtle Island because of the way the anti-Blackness is playing out that reduces people's economic opportunities and job prospects and affects where they're able to live. It just affects so many things, right? Not to mention the real potential for a fatality if they have an encounter with the police. So, it's pretty intense.

GISELLE: Yeah. It seems here that as we are talking about abolition we are expanding the term to include ways of strengthening our communities to find alternative economies, to find ways of living together, and revive ways of living in relationship to Mother Earth. Indigenous people have been in these processes for so long. In a conversation with Cara Fabre we started to talk about decolonizing abolition so that we can expand the ways of taking about abolition to include some of these things, which is why I think we need to consider changing the term "abolition."

More recently we can look at Standing Rock, which was such a great example of Indigenous nations across Turtle Island and the world coming together. So there are clearly a lot of barriers, but it is also clear that people are finding ways through those barriers and are doing the work really intentionally through relationships.

In London the PJFF received funding to build an anti-PIC campaign. To ground the work we engaged Black and Indigenous people to talk about what we wanted to do together. We engaged ceremony and Spirit work from the very beginning.

SYRUS: That sounds so dreamy.

GISELLE: Right? The project that we worked on in London with Black, Indigenous, and people of colour were almost all people who had loved ones in prison or had been incarcerated. About fifteen of us gathered in circle to come up with an idea of what we might do together. At first we would just gather and talk about experiences of what loving someone inside is like or what it's like having been incarcerated. And you know after three meetings, the decision was we'll just keep doing this. We'll just keep meeting and supporting each other, and in my colonized activist mind I'm like, "That's it? This is what we're going to do?" I had envisioned a campaign against the expansion of Elgin-Middlesex Detention Center. I think my reaction to feeling like "that's it?" made me start thinking about how to decolonize activist culture.

SYRUS: Oh, I love it.

GISELLE: Yeah. So, really thinking about how do we decolonize activist culture so that we're being good to each other and knowing that they ways in which we can contribute is enough. I have always felt that I am not doing "enough," and that can wreak havoc on my mental health. We need to honour our gifts, honour each other's gifts, recognize those gifts, and lift up those gifts. Then we encourage each other to live those gifts that have been given to us by the Creator.

And I think that's part of abolition. It's the way that we honour each other and the way that we be in community with each other and the way that we respond to each other. We also need to be accountable to each other.

SYRUS: Yeah. I feel that within activism right now, that organizing that I've been involved in, that there's absolutely a sense of the need for community accountability and the need for us to show up for each other, to show up for each other because there's so much stuff that's happening on a daily basis, the kind of microaggressions of living in an anti-Black world. It's just super intense, you know?

So people are just figuring out ways to kind of be there for each other and witness and support each other through this life. I think that that's an exciting thing about right now, and I guess when we were younger I remember we used to talk about dreaming about what the world would look like without prisons and how nice it would be to have a chance to imagine what that could actually look like and how frustrating it was to always have to, instead, answer questions like, but what about . . . ?, and all the ways that you kind of get derailed from having a conversation about abolition.

But I feel like now we're in a place where we can think even beyond that question, and we can start to imagine the future, I think as you frame it, like, the future of anti-prison-industrial-complex organizing within Black and Indigenous communities, like, the way that you sort of talk about that I think is a really beautiful thing that we actually get to imagine that right now. We get to imagine what the future might look like for the ways that our communities could work together to dismantle this fucking thing.

GISELLE: Yeah. And to name and honour the ways we're contributing, right? I think there's a naming process that needs to go on, as well, of being like, this is anti-prison work or this is anti-PIC work. Even this conversation we are having now is abolition work. We need to know it and name it as we're doing it. This will help us integrate it into our consciousness, which will help remind us that this is what we're striving for, this is what we're doing. So often those interactions go unnamed, unacknowledged because it's either natural to us or we're doing something because we're passionate about it. But I think, actually, there's something about naming abolitionist strategies as they're happening to bring it to consciousness.

SYRUS: What about this idea that people still seem to have that the Canadian prison system is so much better than the

United States' one? Like, how are we still talking about that in 2018?

GISELLE: I think, for you and I who have been doing this work for so long, those conversations are so uninteresting and limiting. When you think about the world through a structural violence framework, trying to determine whether the Canadian prison system is "better" than the US system seems . . . I don't know what. And yet, for people starting to just learn about the PIC or for people doing time, these questions are important. How do you talk about it?

SYRUS: I don't know. I mean, to me, it even seems too reductive. What is the Canadian prison system, anymore? Like, I don't even think I know what that is anymore. It's like everything. It's not just carceral spaces to me. It's the way that, you know, as Yusra Khogali describes, the schools have become prisons; the way that there's police, there's wardens, there's school resource officers. There's restricted movements. There's a sense of being captive. There's rampant anti-Blackness. It's just like so what isn't part of the carceral space? That would maybe be easier to name because there's not that many things, I think.

GISELLE: It's so true! And I think that's why abolition—again, I don't know how we name it or how we—maybe abolition will stay for a while longer, but it is everything. And so when I hear people talking about their movements, and it's so clear to see how it intersects with the PIC, even if they're not naming as such, right? Even if the work they're doing is abolitionist, and they don't necessarily realize that's abolitionist because they don't have the knowledge of what abolition is and what anti-PIC work is.

I'd love for you—to hear more about the ways that Black Lives Matter is doing is abolitionist work. How is it talked about?

SYRUS: Yeah. I think we definitely talk about it as abolitionist, but it's interesting how in the actual practice of it—for example, we had this whole thing a couple of years ago where we had this chant that someone had come up with that said, "Indict! Convict! Send that killer cop to jail! The whole, damn system is guilty as hell!" So when I joined the team, I was like, I actually can't say that. I actually can't say that. I'm not—we are not going to gain liberation through indicting people or sending people to jail. We're just not. That's just not a goal that I have.

So—although I agree with the last part, the whole damn system is guilty as hell. So, we ended up actually changing the lyrics. We actually changed it to be a more abolitionist phrase. I think now it says . . . I actually can't even remember what it is, but we've changed the lyrics now so that it says something different. And it's exciting to think about how to make our practices more abolitionist through the little daily choices that we make, like something as simple as a chant, you know?

GISELLE: Yeah. And I think about the most recent case with Colten Boushie and how that unfolded and how some of the conversation became "we need more Indigenous people on juries." And I was like, this can't be the solution to what's going on. And, of course, we want retribution. Of course. I don't even know how to talk about this sometimes.

I really think the conversations that pointed out that property is considered more important than the lives of Indigenous people and that it is a continuation of colonization and the displacement of Indigenous people from the land were essential. However, I didn't hear too much about the complexity of how do we attend to the outcome of the Colten Boushie case while at the same time holding up abolition principles. I know that some of us want white people to experience the type of violence that the state enacts on BIPOC. I don't know how to talk about that in an abolition framework though. I just know that some of the things that were being talked about could not be the solution in an abolitionist world.

Did you hear similar conversations?

SYRUS: Yeah. I definitely—even just more recently when the police officer who killed Sammy Yatim was—his appeal was denied, and everybody was like, good. Wow! He should have got longer. And I was like, oh my God. Because that's not the answer, you know? This is not—yeah, the solution. This is not an example of the system working. That sort of then justifies us keeping the system because sometimes it works. No. That would be a terrible outcome. This young man lost his life because of rampant evilism and saneism and racism, and because of all those things and the way they came together, and gender, he was killed unnecessarily. He was killed out of fear. He was killed out of phobia, and the person who killed him . . . we know the criminal justice system is broken, so the idea of trying to seek justice through it is bananas to me. So, when this person's appeal was denied and everybody was like, yay! I was like, fuck! I don't know if this is the right conversation.

GISELLE: And then how do we have it? Knowing that there's no immediate solutions to these systems and the bigness of what we're building towards, how do we have conversations about the repercussions then?

SYRUS: Yeah. Knowing that there's going to be a time—it will take time to dismantle the PIC and ask that we don't have police. In the interim, what the fuck do we do? What do we do?

GISELLE: And some of the things neither of us would be comfortable putting in print, necessarily . . .

SYRUS: Yeah.

GISELLE: But I don't know. But, I don't want to talk about that publicly within this chapter . . . But it's something that complicates things terribly.

SYRUS: Yeah.

GISELLE: When we look at what happened to Tina Fontaine, I want to rage against everything. And I don't know what the possible immediate abolitionist solution could even be. I actually don't know how to talk about it at times.

SYRUS: Yeah. And I went to a lot of—I went to a lot of rallies for Tina Fontaine and for Colten Boushie, and I really understand. I could feel and sense the need for some sort of retribution. It's just reprehensible what has happened—Reprehensible? Irreprehensible?—what has happened, and so how do you sort of channel that into something, but I don't know what that could be. But I think, again, we have ideas for out of print. But, yeah, how do you channel that into something that ultimately produces a sense of healing?

GISELLE: Yeah. I know in some Indigenous communities there's such strength in using ceremony as part of that healing process. I've been able to experience this more recently that there is such healing in ceremony, but is this "enough" for me? It can't be and yet sometimes that's all I can do. I think about the use of spirituality to guiding, grounding, and informing my activist work so much more now.

Have you noticed the difference in that?

SYRUS: Oh, yeah. Definitely. Even just from within activist communities in Toronto, so many more people are bringing spirituality into their practice, into their lives. Even things like people reading tarot and being really into astrology and sort of alternative spiritualties, and I think it—creating senses of ritual, creating rituals together, I've seen a lot more of that, certainly in the last five years, than ever before. And that's really exciting to me because it does sort of bring people together in a totally different way, and it's powerful, I think.

GISELLE: Yeah. I think in Indigenous organizing, Spirit is almost always ingrained in Indigenous peoples' resistance, right? It's always part of it, but when I started doing cross-movement building, in some ways it doesn't hold in the entire group in the same way. So there are times where I notice that I bring in my own ceremonies and my own Spirit. I guess I am intentionally bringing that into spaces now. I notice how different resistance can be when I am just with Indigenous people.

When we talked last we talked about how the Freedom School was working in close solidarity with Indigenous people.

SYRUS: Yeah. The Freedom School, the BLM—TO runs is incredible, you know? It's, like, three weeks. It's like a training ground, really, for being an activist, and they learn about activist movements around the world. And they learn about across the African diaspora. And they learn a core principle of the camp is Black-Indigenous solidarity. So, that's—And disability justice. That's rooted in all of the teachings that they get throughout the whole camp. So, there is the entire first week where they're going to Six Nations and doing work with elders there and doing work with young people there and learning about the land. And then bringing that back to Toronto and how they sort of incorporate that into their daily lives, and it's really beautiful, you know? It's really exciting.

GISELLE: Yeah.

Is there ways that you could see strengthening more activism within Black and Indigenous communities?

SYRUS: Yeah. I think that there's so much potential. When I think about what happened with Tent City when BLM—TO took over [the Toronto] police headquarters in 2016, over the shooting of Andrew Loku. We had such incredible solidarity from Indigenous people—elders who kept medicines safe and onsite, who watched over us as we slept, who held the camp at times when we couldn't have solo. It was amazing. And then right after our action there was the INAC office shutdown and we offered support and ally-ship in return, helping to coordinate things on the ground outside the offices—goods donations and supplies, etc. It was beautiful.

GISELLE: I see strengthening connections between Black and Indigenous people through connection to the land and how we honour the land. I think it would be great to have really intentional conversations moving forward about how we want to work in solidarity. One of the teachings offered to me by an Anishinaabe elder, Banakonda Kennedy Kish (Bell) was about the "Ideal Wheel."[2] The reflection starts with our Spirit and asks: [we ask,] what are we reaching for? What are we longing for? [What do we value?] And then how does that inform our relationships to[/with] each other? Which then informs how/what we come to know, [how we think] and then how is this activated in our doing/behaving.[3]

I think this framework actually informs your work all the time. I think that's always governed your work naturally. I think that is who you are and I want to honour your gifts, Syrus. I think you are incredible for a million and one reasons, including your generosity of spirit, how you hold hope, how you think about the world, and how you hold hope for other people when they can't. I just think that you are one of the greatest examples of who we should all strive to be in the world.

SYRUS: Thank you, Giselle.

GISELLE: Yeah. I think the gifts that you bring into anti-PIC work and changing the world we live in, like, you live it every day as an everyday example. You're such a gift. I've loved working with you. When I think about organizing, I'm always like, "Organizing with Syrus was one of the best experiences, ever." You are just one of my favourite people to organize with because it was always big, and yeah, of course, we can do it. No questions asked.

SYRUS: Yeah. I do tend towards the anything is possible. Everything is possible.

GISELLE: Yeah. I think that was such a joy for me to get to have that experience with you.

And now as I am working in predominantly Indigenous communities, there is also something that's transformed for me. There is an intentional slowness in processes which I've really appreciated. When I'm working with Indigenous people at work, people are saying, "Slow down." "Have you gone out for a walk today? Have you eaten lunch?" I'm like, "People care about these things? What is this environment where we are not just driving our bodies into the ground? People are getting me to ask myself if I am in balance?" And there is the question of how do we strive towards balance. This was really a move away from activist cultures in the past, where it's like, be busy every single moment, and if you're not, the question becomes, am I doing enough? The question for me then became, am I enough? If I'm not tearing up the earth with my bare hands to ensure another prison not to be built, am I doing enough?

SYRUS: It's enough.

GISELLE: It's enough. We have to be in balance because that's how our centre fire burns. If we are not in balance then our centre fire is not gonna be as strong as it can be.

SYRUS: Yeah.

GISELLE: What does that mean in a world that's in crisis, where we kind of need to always be showing up *and* when we need to take care of ourselves so our centre fire burns?

SYRUS: Do you know, I've been doing these activist portraits. And when I interview people about their activism before I take their portraits, and every single person I've ever photographed has said that they weren't really doing enough and that they felt that they weren't really an activist because they really didn't do as much as everybody else. There was this mythical superactivist who was doing all the things all the time, and they were comparing themselves to them.

I just think that's so interesting because, of course, yeah, I think that there is a Western way that kind of drives activism, that it follows a capitalist process, where it's more accumulation, faster, better.

GISELLE: Productivity, productivity.

SYRUS: Yeah. I love the way you talk about indigenizing activism. That gives me so much hope.

GISELLE: Yeah, that slowing down was amazing for what it did for my mental health. Last year my Elder Banakonda Kennedy Kish (Bell) engaged me in a ceremony after a long and difficult time of doing prisoners' rights/abolition activism and organizing. We went down to the river, and I was putting tobacco down. I was looking up the river and the water was so rough and it was flowing so fast. It had represented how I had chosen to live my life up to that point, and I just remember thinking, "If I have to keep doing that for the rest of my life, I can't do it. It's impossible for me to do it." When I looked forward and I looked at a life of Spirit, ceremony and learning, it was smooth. The water was smooth and running slowly. I was like, "If I can do my next forty years like that, I am in." In that moment I chose a new way of being and a new way of living. Life is too hard in that other place.

SYRUS: Yes.

GISELLE: I have just spent time really honouring my spirit in a way that says, "Okay, I'm enough." I remember looking at a rock one day and just being like, "You're doing your part. The Creator created you and your spirit is doing exactly what it's meant to do." The Creator gave me gifts and I am created to live these gifts. I'm enough. It's enough.

When I was sitting in my four-day fast and contemplating taking my place in Creation I realized that the trees, birds, butterflies weren't asking if they we worthy. That is such a human question. In a moment, I realized that I'm worthy because the Creator has a purpose for me and I was created to be in relationship with all of these things.

SYRUS: Yeah.

GISELLE: Knowing these things meant that my activism wasn't driven in a way that I needed to produce. It allowed me to relax. It doesn't mean that I don't have panic moments of being like, "Whoa, that's not enough. I'm not doing enough. I should be doing this or that." But it did give me space to honour, in part, the contributions I have made and also look at what I can contribute into the future in a good way that maintains my mental health.

When I am manic, I'm busy. It fuels this productivity in a way that is such a colonial and capitalistic way of doing work. I had to be okay with myself by not doing it. It is a huge amount of personal work to just be okay with acknowledging that being in ceremony, for me, is a way of contributing to abolition. Being with the elders and learning my teachings is a way of contributing to abolition. Working on myself and burning my centre fire is a way of me contributing. Being in relationship to others in a good way is a way of contributing to abolition. And just having to change my framework on some of those things to make it okay that I can focus on me. Right?

SYRUS: That's amazing.

GISELLE: Yeah. It's such a gift because otherwise I couldn't go on the way I was living. Whenever I hear your hopefulness, I just want to hang on. I want to hang on to your hope because there's lots of times I don't feel that hopefulness.

SYRUS: Yeah.

GISELLE: I just feel tired. But somehow, when you speak, I can hang on and just be like, "Yes."

SYRUS: I feel that way too, though, the way you just described, being in ceremony as activism, the way that you described just living your gifts as being exactly what your spirit is supposed to be doing. When you talk about that, I feel very inspired. I feel very relieved. I feel very recentred when I hear you talk like that. It's wonderful.

GISELLE: And it's a balance. I heard a podcast that talked about our long, not game, but our long vision, that often we're responding to crisis in the moment, which, in many ways, we have to, but we don't plan for twenty or twenty-five years in our campaigns or in the way that we're working necessarily. What it would mean if we created a plan where it wasn't reacting but thinking, "What could we accomplish in twenty years?" If we moved towards that, what would it look like? It was just such an interesting thought for me, to be like, "Oh yeah."

SYRUS: And imagine if Black and Indigenous communities worked together on a process of dismantling the current state.

GISELLE: And I think having this conversation is part of that opportunity to open up doors to move towards that. Yeah, I feel excited about thinking how powerful we can be together.

SYRUS: Yeah, 100 percent. Well, that was my phone just saying five percent battery. But maybe this is a perfect place to end.

NOTES

1 Monture's exact quote is: "So why isn't there a more defined prisoner justice movement in the west as compared to the east, in a city like Toronto for example? I think part of the answer has to do with the poverty and social conditions that Aboriginal people are facing just to survive here.

When all of your energy is spent trying to get your family through the day safely, then where does the energy come from to develop a movement?" From "Prison Abolition in Canada," *Upping the Anti: A Journal of Theory and Action*, no. 4 (October 2009).

2 Wording changed with the elder's consent to better reflect the teaching.

3 Wording changed with the elder's consent to better reflect the teaching.

REFERENCES

Collins, Peter, Caitlin Hewitt-White, Kim Pate, Patricia Monture, and Julia Sudbury. "Prison Abolition in Canada." *Upping the Anti: A Journal of Theory and Action* (October 2009). https://uppingtheanti.org/journal/article/04-prison-abolition-in-canada.

4

BLACK LIVES MATTER BEYOND BORDERS: REFLECTIONS FROM BUILDING A GLOBAL MOVEMENT

RODNEY DIVERLUS IN CONVERSATION WITH PATRISSE KHAN-CULLORS AND JANAYA KHAN

The following is a conversation between three Black cultural producers, activists, and co-founders within the Black Lives Matter movement. They discuss what they view as the initial origins, impacts, and legacy of Black Lives Matter's work in Canada, the first iteration of Black Lives Matter outside of the United States.

Rodney Diverlus, a co-founder of Black Lives Matter—Toronto facilitates a roundtable dialogue between himself, Patrisse Khan-Cullors, the co-founder of the Black Lives Matter Global Network, and Janaya Khan, co-founder of Black Lives Matter—Toronto.

• • •

RODNEY: I want to focus this conversation on Black resistance in Canada today and how it's perceived, how it's taken up, how it exists in the broader global ecosystem, and, specifically, how it exists in relation to Black resistance in the United States. I'm hoping we reflect on the beginning of this movement in Canada in Toronto.

I'm specifically interested in your commentary on what it means to be building a global movement. I want to hear your brilliance, and because this is focused on Canada, I recognize that the perspective might be limited, but all the more important. I also want us to bring to this conversation our varying perspectives, as they relate to our personal relations to place, land, and home: Janaya as someone who used to live in Canada and currently lives in the United States, Rodney as someone who used to live in the United States and currently lives in Canada, and Patrisse as someone who has lived in the United States her entire life.

PATRISSE: Right.

JANAYA: Cool.

• • •

RODNEY: Let's start at the beginning. We'll outline our full origin story in a separate chapter for the readers, but there's some key details that are foggy for me. Patrisse, was it us that approached you or the other way around? Whatever the order was, I remember first meeting you through a teleconference with yourself and some of the early co-founders in Toronto to talk about the work starting to happen in Canada

PATRISSE: I approached . . . You know what happened? I approached some of the people who went to the Ferguson caravan a couple of months prior. There was a team of folks I was still connected with and they knew the folks who had begun to organize in Toronto.

JANAYA: Right.

PATRISSE: I had been watching y'all's work; it was brilliant. And then you all curated the online conversation: Black in Canada, or Black in Toronto, or . . .

RODNEY: It was #AliveWhileBlackTO

PATRISSE: Yes. I was watching that, reading the *Toronto Star*, and CBC interviews that were trying to make it seem like y'all were racist because you were asking Black people to be in the front; I was shocked.

JANAYA: Specifically segregationist. They called us segregationists.

PATRISSE: Yeah. I saw that and hit y'all up. I wanted y'all to become an official chapter of the network. In the call with the team, there was one tiny computer, but I remember it was Sandy, Janaya, Pascale, Yusra, Rodney, you were on the phone, and some others.

JANAYA: Mm-hmm. For me, like, I remember in 2013 when Zimmerman was not indicted there was this vigil happened in Toronto . . . organized by queer community folks, like Syrus, who later became a team member.

RODNEY: At a park.

JANAYA: Riverdale Park? The one with the . . .

RODNEY: Big hill, yep.

JANAYA: Yeah, I was there and I remember thinking this is important, but it just didn't feel like enough; and it was, I think, the first time I got a deeper sense of how something that happens stateside could translate in Canada. And at the time it was what people felt like they could do. They felt like they could get together for a vigil. But it didn't really address the fact that there's a lot of anger. Here's this man, this George Zimmerman, who had killed a child and is getting off scot-free. So I can light a candle, but I wanted more. I remember being really disturbed when I got home, like, really disturbed.

And then Eric Garner was killed. And then Mike Brown gets killed. I remember like five or six of us with two kids standing in front of the US embassy in August [of 2014] and we had signs and honest to God, there was literally like six to eight of us max. Just a bunch of Black, queer folks with our little signs and we were educating folks about what happened to Mike Brown.

And fast forward that, Sandy sending a Facebook message to a few of us folks, and then we just decide to throw on this first action. I don't think we were even calling it a rally; we called it a protest and we all had this huge debate about whether we should call it a peaceful protest because—because of how we would be received, and because of how the media would frame it.

RODNEY: I do remember that, going back and forth.

JANAYA: Yeah, we did, on whether or not we should use the word "peaceful."

RODNEY: I think it came down to safety, or really, perceived safety. We felt like if we say we are this thing, then we can use it to protect us as organizers of the event if things get out of hand. We were also clear to say that this action would be open to families, elders, and children in our community. We felt it was important to underscore a vigil tone, in hopes of attracting people who might not necessarily come to a protest. In the end, we reluctantly decided to use "peaceful" in the title of our action, the last time it appeared in BLM—TO.

JANAYA: So we spent the night planning this protest. We watch interest grow online; some of us know each other and some of us don't. In a night we put on this thing, a thing that had food, that had generators, that had lights, that had ASL interpretation, that had speakers, that had singers, you know? All by Black people. And it was freezing.

RODNEY: Yeah. Ugh!

JANAYA: It was so cold, so we thought we were going to get like fifty people. We put our little banner in the back and thousands of people came flooding in. It was just beautiful. It was one of the most beautiful things I had ever seen and it was the first time many of us saw power look differently in the city. Something significant happened between August, when a couple of us, with some signs, were first at the US consulate, and November, back at the consulate with thousands. And we were all freezing, we were all so cold that whole night. We couldn't feel our toes and this and that. We debriefed together and soon realized that we had to keep doing this; there was something there.

RODNEY: What a beautiful moment in our lives! I'm so glad I was there to share all of that with you. What else do you remember from the original days?

JANAYA: Likewise, homie. When we spoke with Patrisse, I remember at that time, we wanted to feel a sense of ownership over the work in our city. We felt that Americans, and Black Americans specifically, believed they had the blueprint for what success and freedom looked like, and it didn't translate in a Canadian context.

RODNEY: A lot of us had been in spaces where we had to inform people that, yes indeed, Black people were enslaved in Canada, that we too have a history of resistance.

JANAYA: Before we got on the call with Patrisse, we debated if we should stick with Black Lives Matter or if it made more sense to come up with our own thing. The worry was that just because there's BLM in the States doesn't mean it's going to necessarily translate here. A lot of Black Canadians identified with their other identities more, particularly at that time. Before you said you were Black, you'd call yourself Nigerian, you're Congolese, you're Haitian, you're Trinidadian, you're Jamaican. But generally you weren't so attached to Black as a political identity at the time.

RODNEY: The odd Black person called themselves African-Canadian. But most of us identified with the ethnicized markers.

JANAYA: We talked to Patrisse, and she was actually really cool. She wasn't like, "I'm going to take this over," and "This is how you should do things." The positive interaction gave us hope, and we kept the name, with the direct goal of building something that's uniquely ours.

RODNEY: I think we anticipated the worst but then got like, oh, yeah whatever, you can do your thing. We were used to everyone lumping our issues within the African American narrative. Everything from denying: "It's not that bad here," or "Why are you bringing an American issue to Canada?"

JANAYA: Yeah, so the first major fight that Patrisse and I had was around this actually. We were in the car with one of BLM—TO steering organizers; so you have someone who's from the Bahamas, very Caribbean, and you have me, who's Trinidadian and Jamaican, also very Caribbean. We both grew up in Canada. And then you have Patrisse, who's very much a Black American.

[As an aside] I think it actually would be accurate to argue that this iteration of the movement actually started in LA with Rodney King, and we saw that even in Toronto with the Black Action Defense Committee and the solidarity rally that happened right before, Lawrence—

RODNEY: In '92 right? Raymond Lawrence.

JANAYA: Yeah. Got shot in the chest.

PATRISSE: Let's back up and give context. In the conversation, y'all were talking about how Americans behave in the Caribbean.

JANAYA: Oh, that's correct.

PATRISSE: How awful we are.

JANAYA: How they behave in the Caribbean.

PATRISSE: And it was like just every stereotype about Black people and it was like infuriating to hear that from another Black person.

JANAYA: But I wouldn't just frame it as a bunch of stereotypes though. I think it definitely devolved into that, but that's not where it started.

PATRISSE: No, I think in retrospect, and now that I've had many years of conversations about this with other people, I think he was saying some real shit about bad behaviour from Black Americans.

JANAYA: The stories were centred on the fact that, yeah, Black Americans would treat staff really badly and treat local Black folks really badly, and they could be really loud and obnoxious and extremely entitled. And then they both had a back and forth. Patrisse was like, "These are pretty gross stereotypes that you're asserting; people say these things about black Americans all the time," which would be rebutted with acknowledging that Americans, in general, walk with a massive level of privilege.

And then, by that point I think it was like a healthy back and forth. Patrisse brought up, in an effort to explain these stereotypes, that America had a more violent experience of slavery. And then silence. It felt like the air in the car got thick. Because that's just simply not true.

What followed was a heated back and forth. We came out of it with an acknowledgement that *some* Black

Americans often don't know the stories of other Black people outside of their Black American context. In the Bahamas for example—

RODNEY: Why do you think that is?

JANAYA: I'll circle back to that question. In the Bahamas, for example, and throughout the Caribbean, the industry was sugarcane; here [the United States] it was cotton. Enslaved people in the Caribbean experienced a violent means of creating and collecting produce. Like, cane stalks can kill you; they can impale you; people lose limbs. Or you're mining salt. And the average body can't last very long mining salt in the oceans. The arthritic pain, bodies deteriorating, etc. And in the Bahamas, there was a particular history, because enslaved Africans who were plucked off from the motherland and brought to America were then plucked out of America and brought to the Bahamas.

And to your question: as Black people growing up in Canada, we were hyperaware of experiences of Black Americans because it was constantly presented over our own experiences.

And then, you know, there is a level of—and Sandy and I have been trying to sort of name it—chauvinism or narcissism, or actually as a result of being in America, an Americanism, that causes a deep focus on only what's happening here, right in front of you.

Early in our movement we had to have those hard conversations.

RODNEY: I think central to our work are the principles of pan-Africanism, that Black people will not be free anywhere unless we're free everywhere. And I know that our fights and contexts are different, but part of that is really understanding deeply what other Black people are experiencing elsewhere in the world and what those stories are.

JANAYA: I remember one of the first cross-border spaces that we were all at—with Americans. Sandy, Pascale, Rodney, and I represented Canada and spent a great deal of time debunking some myths about how racism isn't as bad in Canada and named some of the realities of Black life in Canada. We experienced pushback: "Well, you just don't understand our experience."

I can say now as a Black person who grew up in Canada, who's Caribbean, who now has lived in the States, I feel more empathetic, understanding, and compassionate about that sort of deep narcissism. Because I feel like an ambulance chaser in the States. I cannot keep up with the amount of Black death and mass incarceration here. I've seen how it's devastated Patrisse's family alone, first-hand. These aren't stories that I'm reading in a book, when it's the war on drugs, and it's, like, the crack epidemic, and the sheriff's department, there's a way that anti-Black violence feels more everyday here. And you know, we have our police brutality in Canada. We certainly have a huge amount of Black folks in Canadian federal prisons relative to the population. We too have all of the same kind of realities around removal from homes and foster care and poverty and these other things, particularly with Black Caribbean identities in Canada.

But because of the population difference, the numbers just aren't close. And so just the sheer magnitude of it. And in Canada, one Black person being killed by a cop is a multi-years-long campaign. So what do you do when it's happening every day, multiple times a day? In America, you're so inundated with Black death that you actually can sometimes find yourself confusing or forgetting names that you knew two months ago, because there's been so many more that's added to the list. So with that, I do feel like that's something I had not been exposed to before.

I understand them now as the same systems, but because of the population, how sophisticated this system is, how deeply entrenched it is, it [anti-Blackness] looks differently than it does in other places in the West that I've been.

And it's not to say that—and this is the problem, right, this zero-sum narrative: one has to be better; one has to be worse. It's like, no, they're actually both evil systems that are consistently bad. But how that evil manifests is based on the particular infrastructure that's set up around it. And the apparatus here around mass incarceration, around police brutality, and certainly under this current administration, it makes me more empathetic; though I still believe that Black nationalism is not the answer to Black liberation, or for Black liberation.

RODNEY: I think part of where we miss each other in this pan-African global struggle, and particularly when it's about the States, is that we, Canadians, come into the room feeling like we have to prove our oppression. And we have to prove that our particular experience of anti-Black racism is more impactful or as impactful. So we come up defensive with our backs up.

JANAYA: And then you have this thing that happens where we're also policing each other's Blackness in a really significant ways. You have Africa-born folks telling Black North Americans that they can't wear a kente cloth, or Black North Americans defining Black in opposition to Africanness. It's absurd. Why are we allowing colonial borders to define what is African and what is Black? As long as we come in with that energy and that idea, we're going to continue to butt heads and miss each other.

RODNEY: I do think Black people in the West have lots we need to work on. Specifically, I think Americans need to actively decentre their experiences as the default global story.

JANAYA: Yes! And I think Black people in the West, Canada, the UK, Australia, we need to stop coming up with our backs up, ready to go after Black Americans because we have a chip on our shoulder because no one ever believes us—

RODNEY: Yeah, no one believes us.

JANAYA: —when we tell it like it is.

RODNEY: It feels like we are forever dealing with issues that we haven't dealt with, of people not seeing our Blackness.

JANAYA: Yeah, and I think we really just have to own the fact that each of us are only experts in our experience of Blackness, and no other experiences of Blackness. We come in so ready to fight, ready to say that our oppression is separate and distinct from other forms of anti-Black racism. Black people globally don't have to trust each other 100 percent just because we're Black and African; 25 percent is a good place to start.

RODNEY: It's a great place to start. Globally, Black American continues to be synonymous for Black. There's a shared responsibility by African Americans and non-African Americans to dispel that. That conflation reduces the magic and complexity of Blackness. To reduce it to one ethnicized version of Black actually only limits our imagination, only limits our liberation, limits our ability to learn from other Black communities that are actively and have actively resisted.

And I think that's part of the reason that Black people, particularly [in] North America, here, Canada and the States, have been less unimaginative in the way that we've thought about our liberation. People in Haiti, Columbia, Brazil, in Ghana, in Panama, and all over the world have been so . . . their decolonial processes have been so creative. And we lack that imagination because we not only still buy that narrative, but we purport it.

JANAYA: We do.

RODNEY: There's a couple more things in that I want to tease out. I think the way that you approached us, Patrisse, was key to beginning a global relationship built on trust. For many of us who had connected with American organizers, there was something unique about the way we interacted. There was mutual respect, and more importantly, autonomy to build as we saw fit for our community. We anticipated the worst but then you were like, yeah whatever, you can do your thing. We were building this in a context where many continually lumped our issues within the African American narrative: "It's not that bad here," or "Why are you bringing an American issue to Canada?"

So I'm wondering if you can talk about the difference of what that approach, or what that mindset meant and when you've seen it be not like that. What was affirming about our first interaction was you recognizing these realities in Canada and the importance of doing this work. I'm wondering if we can tease out why does it not happen like that?

PATRISSE: Can you clarify that?

RODNEY: That sort of interaction, that sort of understanding, that sort of affirmation, that sort of, in a weird way, validation.

PATRISSE: Well, I'll say two things, one of which is: I was trained to be an internationalist. And most people in this country, born and raised in America, are not, whether they're Black or not. Literally, this is a isolating, insular country on purpose; it's how it's built its patriotism and it's how it has also survived: by ignoring the rest of the world.

I think the other piece for me is: Black American civil and human rights struggle has been a part of the liberation lexicon for a really long time. So if you go anywhere around the world where there's Black people, they don't quote Black people in their own country; they quote Black people in America.

RODNEY: Yes. I've seen that in other countries that I've travelled to; lots of that when you and I were in Australia.

PATRISSE: Exactly. Like, there's these key figures that have become Black global figures that are Black Americans: Martin Luther King, Marcus Garvey, etc. And that has a lot to do with a lot of things, American chauvinism being one. It's living in a really, really rich country that has a lot of resources, access, and has the ability to be present for itself and not everybody else. And I think it's why it's imperative that Black Americans learn about Black struggles across the rest of the world and also see themselves as part of a global Black diaspora.

And there's this other piece that I think is an important part of history. Historically Black Americans had been in relationship to other Black peoples across the world. And then there was a pivot, an intentional pivot, by the civil rights movement, groups like the NAACP [National Association for the Advancement of Colored People], like SCLC [Southern Christian Leadership Conference], you know, MLK's [Martin Luther King's] group, thought it would be better to position themselves within the context of a national civil rights struggle versus a global human rights struggle as a more effective strategy to get Black people free, here. Or I wouldn't even use the word free. Equal rights. Some sort of civil rights.

So that becomes appealing, obviously, to white people. I would argue that it also becomes appealing to people, like Zionists . . . we can't divorce different parts of history, right? So I think while—in the late '40s, early '50s, during the creation of the Zionist Israeli state, Jewish people were actually lobbying Black Americans for support, drawing connections between their respective struggles. There was a lot of civil rights activists like Harry Belafonte that supported the creation of the state of Israel, just on the perceived basis of it being the same struggle.

So I think Black Americans have to investigate the point in our history in which it became a strategy to distance ourselves from the global Black struggle. When Malcolm [X] came along, he was actually being like, "We are part of a pan-African diaspora, and this is a global resistance, and this is how it is." That's why he went to the continent, and that's why he went around the Caribbean. And so Black Lives Matter becomes for me a resurgence, and a differing from NAACP or National Action Network, and really situating a new conversation, that's an old conversation, but a resurrection around global Black struggle and how we are actually part of a diaspora.

And as for solutions, I think our movements have to train people. I'm proud of BLM for our relationship with Black people in Canada, the UK, Brazil, Australia. We have a long way to go, but I do think that we're in a much better place.

• • •

RODNEY: Switching gears a bit: what do you think is the most misunderstood thing regarding Black people in Canada?

PATRISSE: Yeah, I mean, let's be clear, I was very ignorant about Canada's history. I think that wasn't an accident. I think a lot of Americans, Black people particularly, see Canada as a haven for us. It's just, "Oh, we just need to go to Canada, and everything will be better." Which also means a couple things: one, the assumption was there is no Black people in Canada, and/or that Black people in Canada have better lives. I am even ashamed to say that I had no idea that there were Black people enslaved in the shores of Canada. Literally, I had no—I had never learned that until I met Janaya.

RODNEY: To be honest, a lot of Canadians don't know that either.

PATRISSE: That's wild.

RODNEY: I would go as far and to assert that most Canadians don't know that Black people were enslaved in Canada.

PATRISSE: But [Nova] Scotians know that, right?

RODNEY: Indeed. There is a long history of Black resistance in Nova Scotia. Black people were in Nova Scotia as far back as 1604.

PATRISSE: Scotians know their own history.

RODNEY: Absolutely.

PATRISSE: So that was embarrassing, though, you know? I know that there were enslaved Africans in Mexico, the Americas, the Caribbean, and the States. So how come I didn't know that was the case for Canada? That, in addition to recent Black migrants, y'all have Black Canadians who have lived in Canada that long. And I think the myth that y'all don't struggle, or that it's easier on y'all than it is on us. It's a general ignorance of Canadian laws, policy, process, all of it; just ignorance.

RODNEY: What's interesting [is] I feel like the erasure of Black Canadian histories is a mutual effort in both countries. I did most of my school in the States, but for the people that I know who did schooling in Canada, they learned way more about MLK and Malcolm X. In the same way that y'all look at Canada as a haven, I think many of us idolize the States. We are fascinated by the sheer size and influence of Black American culture.

Probably due to a lot of reasons, but I think isolation is a big one. In Canada, unless you are in one of the few big cities, Black folks exist in isolation. In many jurisdictions the numbers are just not there. There's something appealing about the Black American struggle because Black people in the States seem like hella vibrant, visible, therefore powerful.

I honestly think some people think that when Black Americans are free, there will be some sort of osmosis to us. Instead of betting on ourselves, it becomes more enticing to bet on America. People look at other issues like same-sex marriage, or legalization of cannabis, and see that what happens in one country trickles to the other, both ways.

I would also argue Black people in Canada have historically given more attention to the African American issue, which further adds to that Americanism mindset. And I do think a big shift has happened; migration really helped that. But I think that the surge of migration of other Black folks from the Caribbean, from the continent, from the '60s onwards has forced Canada to bet on itself.

PATRISSE: Yeah that makes sense, I feel like that's the case for a lot of places I have traveled to. When I went to Australia, so much was betting on us Black Americans to make it happen for Black people globally.

RODNEY: Totally agree. It was overwhelming actually.

PATRISSE: And part of that is, I think, is wanting to root for the underdog, in some ways. So many Black people freed themselves from their colonizers. Haiti liberated itself, Sierra Leone liberated itself, all these other places where Black people won their freedom. And here in the US, we've been engaged [in] a liberation struggle for centuries and it hasn't happened yet; so I think there is a looking to us as one of the last places with a significant amount of Black people. There's something about that I think is in our collective Black spirit—if Black Americans can do it then the rest of us can do it too.

RODNEY: Yeah, this has me thinking about how much of this [is] because of proximity to whiteness. If you're living in New Brunswick, for example, you're one of the x number of black families in town, you're more likely to support people who have the critical mass to push rather than doing the pushing yourself. To survive you have to do your best to assimilate into the white enclave around you. There is no "other side of the fence."

Additionally, while the conversation is usually relegated to Black or white in the States, in Canada Black folks are lumped into the broader racialization umbrella. We have comparable South Asian, East Asian, Latinx populations. We get lumped into the broader people-of-colour narrative.

Up until our last movement iteration, many refused to address anti-Blackness as its own phenomenon. I think it's more important now than ever to uplift the experiences of Black people globally. It's important to name anti-Black racism as a global phenomenon, and in North America we have to understand the ways that we are invested in such phenomenon.

PATRISSE: And we have to be invested in understanding how our countries invest in each other. For example, Canada has invested in [the] US money bail system. How does challenging these relationships together further a clarity about how do we get free? I think that's the thing that makes me excited about building, and it makes me frustrated when people don't make those connections.

I think the last four years since, [the] Toronto chapter has really developed its own identity and a particular clarity about what you are in relation to the Canadian state and the global community.

RODNEY: I think we really had to. I still remember doing interviews with *USA Today*, or *The New York Times*, or reporters from China, from Bolivia, from all corners of the world, and most of [the] time was spent explaining to them the bare-bones understanding of our community and our issues.

PATRISSE: I get frustrated that sometimes our folks are unable to see the use of being in real and deep partnership with Black resistance around the world. To me, our relationship between the US network and Canada has been an important experiment for our movement. Because of distance, we've been able to intentional[ly] build relationship together.

The Toronto chapter has also taken leadership in posing the right questions for our movement. I acknowledge that [all] of our US chapters aren't just led by Black Americans; we have migrants and Afro-Latinx and folks from the continent, but because the Toronto chapter is really made up of some immigrants and children of immigrants, there is a different context that you all bring around Blackness that is really useful for the rest of us.

RODNEY: Indeed. I think our movement as a whole has created a useful blueprint for future activists, groups, and organizers to learn from. I think it's fair to say that we have all messed up over time; there are many things that I would do differently if I did it again. But I think our commitments to shared struggle is, for me, the biggest lesson in this. We continually come back to each other when we agree, and especially when we disagree.

And with all of that, I want to thank you both for your time and diving in with me. I think these cross-border conversations are crucial to maintaining the global momentum gained by Black Lives Matter, but more generally, Black-led radical resistance.

Much love and appreciation to y'all.

5

TOWARDS BLACK AND INDIGENOUS FUTURES ON TURTLE ISLAND: A CONVERSATION

ROBYN MAYNARD AND LEANNE BETASAMOSAKE SIMPSON

These pages emerged from a conversation between Robyn Maynard and Leanne Betasamosake Simpson that took place in Tiohtià:ke (Montreal) on April 14, 2018, moderated by curator, art historian, and author Lindsay Nixon. We are both writers, academics, and activists who have engaged deeply with each other's works and are committed to thinking through the shared histories and realities faced by Black and Indigenous communities in this land now called Canada. Even more, we are both committed to thinking through what it means to engage in community-building across communities and toward building Black and Indigenous futures without relying on appeals to whiteness or to the state.

ON *POLICING BLACK LIVES* AND *AS WE HAVE ALWAYS DONE*

LEANNE: I'm so grateful to be in Kanien'kéha:ka territory, in Tiohtià:ke. In the summer of 1990, I watched Ellen Gabriel, on the CBC, as the spokesperson for the resistance at Kanehsatà:ke and Kahnawà:ke, this was perhaps the greatest political education of my life. I always think about that when I'm here. The strength of those Kanien'kéha:ka in the protection of their land and their Kanien'kéha:ka life, and I am so grateful for their example.

I am also so honoured to be here with Robyn. *Policing Black Lives* is the most important book of our time.[1] It is thorough, meticulous, uncompromising, and crucial for our understanding of state violence and the structure of anti-Blackness in Canada.

ROBYN: I just wanted to say—wanted to thank you for sharing this space and having this conversation with me. I'm so grateful for *As We Have Always Done*.[2] It is a paradigm-shifting book of political theory, one that allows us to rethink what it is to fight for racial justice right here, where we live.

Now, as I think about introducing my work and political commitments, I'm asking who, as a Black feminist, is my work accountable to, in a broad sense; any of us who do this writing are fighting for all of the Black lives that have been lost, and fighting, too, for the living. I think all activist–scholars use their writing to try to help not only expose injustice, but to use their words to help will transformative shifts, to will emancipation into existence. My work grows out of a long activist trajectory. I remember taking a week or so off writing after the police killing of Bony Jean-Pierre because of the kind of organizing that was necessary after that happened. I think my book was very much infused with that sense of urgency, with that sense that we're really fighting for our lives in many ways. Yet even in what Frank Wilderson III calls a "state of emergency,"[3] the present is always infused with the past. Just as it's urgent to address the present realities facing Black people's lives, we need to resuscitate our histories, particularly in a country like Canada that continues to downplay slavery's long legacy when looking at what's happening today across state institutions, including, but far beyond, the policing. With *Policing Black Lives* I was trying to do something that was place-based, to ground what it means to think through state violence and Black life in a place so committed to rendering that invisible. But despite being based in Canada, I'm explicitly not trying create some sort of Black Canadian nationalist text, rather I wanted to write the realities of Black folks in Canada into a larger, more global history and present of dispossession.

As an activist, and as a writer, I try to bring into view all the things that continuously endanger Black life, but I also try to work in a way that expresses my love for my communities and my appreciation for the brilliance of my ancestors and of freedom fighters today.

LINDSAY: Robyn, in your writing you worked hard to integrate issues of settler colonialism into your analysis of anti-Black racism within the Canadian context, and I think that's one of the first times that I've seen the integration of those two politics into one text by a Canadian scholar. Why is that so urgent and necessary, now, for us to be thinking about Black and Indigenous futures and relationships?

LEANNE: I can't think of a future for Indigenous peoples without listening very deeply to the visions of the future articulated by Black peoples—artists, scholars, activists, and visionaries. The kind of future I'm interested in is the kind of present I'm interested in: one that is based on Black and Indigenous freedom, self-determination, and one that continually generates Black and Indigenous life.

I had the privilege of writing a lot of *As We Have Always Done* during the beginnings of Black Lives Matter becoming visible to white Canada. My territory is the north shore of Lake Ontario. Our communities have experience being together for four centuries. Reading Robyn's book it became very clear to me that I cannot possibly fully understand the impact of colonialism on my people (and all of life, actually) without understanding the historic, contemporary, and global structure of slavery and anti-Blackness—on one hand, to work to not be complicit in it and to stand in solidarity with Black movements, but also because it is theoretically and politically imperative that I educate myself with this incredible body of work and action created by Black freedom fighters, writers, artists, and scholars so that I can fully understand how the forces of domination operate through white supremacy, heteropatriarchy, and capitalism.

Reading Robyn's book has led me and my thinking in a direction where I'm continually deepening this work for myself. When I write about Michi Saagiig nationhood, I'm not talking about any Indigenous desire to be a nation state. I'm talking about dismantling the nation state. I'm thinking about how I can share space and land in deeply reciprocal and relation ways with freedom fighters and diasporic communities in a way that supports each of our sovereignties and self-determinations, and I'm thinking about what relational solidarity might be like within Nishnaabeg thought.

I feel very, very grateful to the Black Lives Matter movement and also to Robyn's book and to the contemporary radical Black art and scholarship that's happening right now and over the past several decades, because it challenges me to articulate my visions for an Indigenous future and Indigenous nationhood that categorically and unapologetically refuse white supremacy and challenges anti-Blackness in all forms.

During Idle No More, I was involved in a lot of conversations about ally-ship and about what tactics we should and should not use, about what strategies we should and should not use. I heard a lot of, "we can't do that because we will lose the support of white people." Whiteness was so centred in our thinking towards solidarity. This moment that we're in right now offers brilliant alternatives to co-resistance without centring or bowing towards whiteness.

ROBYN: Your words are essential here, the refusal, to use your words, "to centre and bow towards whiteness," rings so beautifully in your work, it's really just a way of centring justice in a way that's not making an appeal to power but of creating a non-oppressive form of power, of building power within the communities that you're speaking of, and I think that's a great strength in your work. Thinking about anti-Blackness and settler colonialism and their often (but not always) overlapping logics and outcomes was incredibly important to me as I wrote the book, and there's a few reasons for that. I think one of them, first and foremost, is in my own personal life experience. I grew up in Winnipeg, which is an apartheid city. Of course I was experiencing anti-Black racism in my own personal life, but it was impossible not to be aware of the highly visible and constant articulations of settler-colonial violence faced by Indigenous communities in terms of policing, the way that the city is spaced, the distribution of housing, wealth and resources. It has always felt to me that to talk about racial injustice in Canada without speaking to the ongoing structure of settler colonialism is something that is neither ethical nor accurate. Leanne, your work, along with those of Audra Simpson, Patricia Monture-Angus, Sarah Hunt, Pamela Palmater, Chelsea Vowel, Arthur Manuel, and may others—along with centuries of Indigenous-led resistance from coast to coast—has meant that any study of this place now called "Canada" is beholden both to the historical violences enacted on the original inhabitants of these lands, as well as to the ongoing land-based struggles of our present.

Another way that helps me centre the interweaving realities faced by Black and Indigenous communities is by thinking about anti-Black racism through the prism of state violence with a historical lens. Slavery was one mechanism of racial control, but when it was abolished many of the ways of viewing and treating Black life were carried forward within the criminal justice system, the child welfare system, within schooling and more. These are all, as well, institutions that are foundational to settler-colonial violence. If schools are a site of racial violence, today, for Black youth, i.e. the school-to-prison pipeline, it's of course necessary to talk about those histories of state violence, for example, segregated schooling in many provinces. But we can't fully capture the racial violence institutionalized in the schooling system without also pointing to a long history of residential schools too. The same is true for policing and the broader criminal justice system and for child welfare. Histories of slavery and of settler colonialism and their present realities aren't identical, but they are foundational to this country that we live in. I'm thinking about the recent studies that just came out showing—no surprise here—that Black and Indigenous people are far more likely to be killed by the police,[4] that Indigenous women are ten times more likely than white folks to be street-checked by Edmonton police,[5] for example. The violences our communities face are intertwined even if they're coming out of fundamentally different logics in many ways. You addressed this beautifully, Leanne, in your essay "Indict the System: Indigenous and Black Connected Resistance."

Sylvia Wynter's work has really helped me think this through, in particular reading "1492: A New World View."[6] The work talks about the founding of the Americas, including the Caribbean, and has helped me really think about the racial logics of genocide and of slavery that were fundamental to the creation of what was called the New World. This laid the foundations for the kind of violence that impacts our communities today. These intertwined histories also help me to think, too, about Black and Indigenous futures. To quote NourbeSe Phillip: "make no mistake, if Black lives mattered or if Indigenous lives mattered, speaking to the two genocides at the heart of the unsettling of the Americas and the Caribbean, we would indeed be living in an altered universe."[7] If we're thinking of those freedoms for our communities then we're thinking about a world that is almost unrecognizable to the one we live in today. Nation states, as they have emerged in the so-called modern world, are inherently hostile to Black and Indigenous people's lives, and many of our freedom struggles are forced to attend to this fact in different ways. I think that that "altered universe," even if it's hard to conceive today, is what we need to be geared toward. Even if decolonization and abolition aren't necessarily identical projects, I like to think of them as interlocking justice projects that could actually turn this world that we live in today upside down in many ways. I think that's something that is actually far from being prohibitive but is actually very generative in terms of allowing different kinds of futures.

LEANNE: What she said! [laughs] NourbeSe Phillip's quote is so important: "speaking to the two genocides at the heart of the unsettling of the Americas and the Caribbean, we would indeed be living in an altered universe." It is not either/or, it is *and*. We need a layered and international understanding of the genocides our communities have faced and are facing. I think that, in my book, talking about generative refusal is exactly talking about this future that generates worlds out of Indigenous and Black brilliance in the present. As Robyn said, these are interlocking justice projects that will turn this world we live in upside down and give birth to spectacular futures.

Robyn's work, along with the work of Black Lives Matter—Toronto, people like Yusra Khogali, Rinaldo Walcott, Katherine McKittrick, Dionne Brand, Desmond Cole, Delice Mugabo, Hawa Mire, David Chariandy, Canisia Lubrin, Fred Moten, Cedric Robinson, Alexis Pauline Gumbs, Keisha Blain, Saidiya Hartman, Sylvia Winter, Angela Davis, Christina Sharpe, Ashon Crawley, Keeanga-Yamahtta Taylor, Patrisse Khan-Cullors, Ashley Farmer, and so many others are crucial in terms of thinking through the relationships between slavery, anti-Blackness, and settler colonialism and, to use Robyn's words, "their often (but not always) overlapping logics and outcomes." Activists and organizers in our communities are pointing to a series of issues that both our communities face and that are linked (although there are critical differences as well): state violence, the missing and murdered, the school-to-prison pipeline, the child welfare system, racist policing and the prison-industrial complex, abolition, anti-intellectualism in the academy, erasure in white Canadian society, and the relentless white denial of Canada's legacy of slavery, anti-Blackness, and colonialism.

Uncritical Indigenous participation in state reconciliation and recognition complicates this because it is currently affording certain Indigenous peoples more power, visibility, and access to the power structures of colonizers. I see a lot of co-option. I don't see structural changes that disrupt colonial worlds. Black and Indigenous activist communities are showing the rest of us that with ethical relationship-building based on consent and accountability from within both our communities, we can be effective co-resistors. Robyn's book is important to the Indigenous community because she affirmed our presence, our issues, and our scholarship, compelling the Indigenous academic and writing communities to do the same. It opens the door for conversations like the one we are having tonight. It opens the door for relationships beyond retweeting.

ROBYN: Co-resisters, as you term it, is a beautiful way to think about this; in some ways it's descriptive of the present moment, but it is also aspirational and can help us bring this into our future praxis.

LINDSAY: Something that stood out to me about both of your works is that your texts are feminist texts as well as political texts. Queer feminist. I think it's really special to look at your work and see that the future, our futures, are queer feminist ones.

ROBYN: Leanne, what you call in your book "the dispossession of the kwe" is a theoretically and politically brilliant way of looking at how institutionalized state violence is something that is always gendered. Of course, the dispossession of Indigenous women has a specificity that cannot be mapped onto Black women's lives, yet this framework nonetheless exposes the always-already-gendered nature of settler colonialism and state violence that is not an add-on but integral to its very functioning. That really impacts how we think about freedom struggles. I think that really allows us to recentre gender and sexuality in how we conceive of Black and Indigenous liberatory futures, reminding us that these will necessarily also be feminist futures and queer futures.

LEANNE: Sometimes, in the Indigenous community, we have a hierarchy around land and body that's very gendered. A lot of young, brilliant Indigenous two-spirit and queer youth have really taken this on and challenged the status quo in terms of saying, "Hey, our bodies are just as important as the land." They have taken on intimate violence and gendered violence as a core pillar of organizing. To me, dispossession is more than just removing bodies from the land. As an Nishnaabekwe, my experience of dispossession is expansive—I've been removed from my land and my body, my culture, my language, my spirituality, my present, and my future. For me, it is all part of colonialism. Land and bodies are both important. How we ethically and justly share space—our bodies and our land—is a much more generative discussion for me. Black and Indigenous futures of freedom are also feminist futures, and queer futures, and they are futures that to me categorically reject the scaffolding of white supremacy, heteropatriarchy, capitalism, and all of their forms and manifestations.

Reading Saidiya Hartman's theorization of the "afterlife of slavery" in *Lose Your Mother* has also become a book I read over and over because of how she talks about her relationship to land.[8] Land as both a physical and a relational concept is foundational to Indigenous thought and life—even if we are displaced, dispossessed, and even if the land is desecrated in the name of state interests, my interpretation of Nishnaabeg ethics means that I am also compelled to share land—and not just share, but respect the self-determination of plant nations, animals nations, and other nations in my territory in a way that promotes the sanctity of the earth for coming generations. The nation state has clearly demonstrated that it does not have the moral fortitude to engage on those terms because it cannot respect the jurisdiction or self-determination of Indigenous peoples, nor can it operate in a way that promotes the sanctity of life for the coming generations.

In terms of Black and Indigenous futures, though, I see some interesting places to engage, particularly those of us interested in building a future that refuses white supremacy, heteropatriarchy, and capitalism.

ROBYN: Discussions of land and place have been, in many ways, central to Black freedom and unfreedom: the formulation of nation states, which of course were also violently imposed onto pre-existing Indigenous communities, have always been hostile to Black life, so much of the history of drawing borders has always also been about containing Black people's freedom of movement, just as border regulation today continues to be about preventing Black migration—or enforcing the forced expulsions of Black peoples from nations the world over. Black life—for the African diaspora, in particular—has for so long been constituted by placelessness: this is so clear, for instance, when we think about the boatloads of displaced Africans dying en route to Europe, the thousands of deaths in the Mediterranean ocean, the over ten million dead, from centuries past, in the Atlantic ocean. So much Black life continues to be destroyed, so needlessly, today in what's being called the global refugee crisis in the so-called postcolonial world. But this does mean, then, that what we are up against is having no "rightful" place anywhere within the current global logics, living, as we largely do, in nation states premised on the expulsion of our humanity. And not just our humanity, but our entire being: as we are now seeing massive deportations of Black folks worldwide, including the Windrush generation in the U.K., for example, and the Haitians being deported from the US and

Canada. But solutions to "placelessness" aren't simple. I do not think our generation needs to bring back or overly glorify the problematic, if complex in its own history, "back to Africa" movement of the past. A big question of our time, that writers like Katherine McKittrick have helped to address, is how Black people continue to make our own forms of space regardless of carceral anti-Black logics—not if, but how. This is a particularly important question located, as we are here, on Indigenous territories that are being continuously encroached upon by the violent imposition of settler colonialism.

LINDSAY: Maybe that leads to discussing capitalism and the state, and about state violence and the criminalization of Black and Indigenous peoples. How does addressing these help toward thinking through the future that we want to create?

ROBYN: I feel like addressing capitalism explicitly is something that's maybe less "in" outside of relatively small social movements, if comparing the present to what was happening in the early or mid-twentieth century when I believe there was a more widespread belief that not only another world was possible but that it was *quite* possible—about "how," not "if." In this moment many within and outside of our communities have stepped away from very explicitly challenging capitalism and being vocally and unapologetically anti-capitalist. Yet as Cedric Robinson and W.E.B. Du Bois have so clearly articulated in many of their works, capitalism is an outgrowth of slavery.[9] It has always relied and continues to rely on ongoing racial and gendered classifications and hierarchies that also designate particular global regions in the Global South as particularly exploitable, as well relying on ongoing (and gendered) dispossession of Indigenous peoples and their territories.[10] The crisis in the Black Mediterranean, of so many Black people being displaced and attempting to be contained, that we need to look at both as an outgrowth of the racial hierarchies and logics that were set in place within the slave trade, colonization, and Indigenous genocide. Haiti is the poorest country in the Western Hemisphere; it's impossible to understand what's called the Haitian migration crisis, for example, at borders today without actually looking at how Haiti was forced to pay billions of dollars in reparations debt to France. Today's unequal economic histories have long and racialized legacies. If we look at the United States' and Canada's ongoing involvement in privatization in continental Africa and the Caribbean, it gives us a lot better understanding of why we have so many dispossessed Black people being forced to move from where they are into places that have always been predicated on whiteness by keeping free Black peoples out. I think that keeping a really strong understanding of racialized injustices by global capitalism, today, needs to be central for our movement work.

This necessary refocusing on capitalism—and the need to explicitly fight capitalism—is something that I loved about your work, Leanne. There have been really important critiques about how the way that we often talk about colonialism too often ignores the distinct reality of settler colonialism. Your work makes it impossible to do that, and it also makes central, in many ways, capitalism and the extraction of Indigenous resources. Because if we want to talk about what it would mean to fight about racial justice, and economic justice, we need to remember that global economic system organized such that Canada's wealth is from dispossessed people in sub-Saharan Africa, and communities in South Africa, and also from Indigenous communities here. That means that if we want to talk about equality it can't really be equality within that status quo. It really needs to be a fundamental transformation of what wealth is conceived as. Without fundamentally challenging that, we're unlikely to get any form of that economic justice without recreating so many of those harms that we see today.

LEANNE: I think that there is some reluctance within the Indigenous community to take on capitalism, even though many of us identify it as a huge problem. There are a lot of reasons for that. Many of our people and our communities are dealing with an intense imposed poverty, whether it's an urban or reserve situation, as a result of colonialism. The state also has this relentless narrative that it employs in Indigenous space that pits jobs versus the environment. The idea that we can have healthy, meaningful lives and a pristine environment, which is how my ancestors lived for thousands and thousands of years, is considered something unattainable from the past.

That's a mistake, and I wanted to think this through with my ancestors using Nishnaabeg thought, and explore what Nishnaabeg practices, ethics, and processes have to say about the capitalism. The more that I've thought about it, the more I realized that almost every kind of our thought and ethics, our practices, or our songs, are anti-capitalist. And so I began with these Nanabush stories, because there's such a large body of those stories in my nation, and they are well known. Nanabush gets into all kinds of trouble exploiting the labour of other humans, plants, and animals, stockpiling resources, being greedy, living out of balance, not tending to or listening to the relational aspects of creation. These stories (and many, many others) are told over and over again to reinforce collective, relational, anti-capitalist ethics. The idea that we need to think about what we can give up in order to promote the sanctity of the earth for the coming generations is the opposite of "sustainable development." I went back through the last twenty years of my life and started thinking about all the times I've been interacting with the land and with elders and hunting and fishing, and the kind of, the ethics that those folks were living in and practising on a daily basis and naming those practices as anti-capitalist.

I wanted to situate the conversation about capitalism from a different spot, so we've got people like Dene scholar Glen Coulthard, who has done a lot of work in Dene and Marxist contexts, but I really wanted to rethink that through an Nishnaabeg context. I think that was very valuable for me and I think that Robyn's right, we must be willing to take on this as a pillar and undo it, refigure out how to relate to each other in a non-capitalist or anti-capitalist way.

ROBYN: I think that also that there's an issue often of framing that often critiquing capitalism is seen as, like, a very white-social-justice-movement thing, but I think that some of the most valuable critiques of this really come from the Black radical tradition, or traditions, particularly those that were feminist. The Combahee River Collective, Toronto's Black Women's Collective, to name just a few important examples, were explicitly anti-capitalist, not to mention feminist, lesbian/queer: they articulated clearly that if we really want to understand the realities of Black women, we cannot ignore capitalism. We need to recentre those intellectual and political legacies as well and not whitewash them out.

LEANNE: Yeah, and I think that kind of Black radicalism is something that I remember reading in books like *Black Marxism* and more recently *The Future of Black Radicalism*, and thinking, "Where's the Indigenous radicalism? Where's our anti-capitalist thought? How do we map it?" Anti-capitalism isn't a white concept. Indigenous knowledge is often thought of as being very local, but a lot of our ethics and epistemology is internationalist in orientation. We are taught to make decisions and to think through the impact of those decisions through time and space, through seven generations, through the perspectives of the plant and animal nations and other nations with whom we are interconnected. This ethic of concern opens up an internationalism that I think is really important in terms of how we're mobilizing and how we're organizing and how we're kind of building this kind of world, this new world.

LINDSAY: Now let's move to our next discussion topic, which is "queering the revolution."

LEANNE: Well I think that comes from different places in my work, I think. One, I think there's this grand swelling of emerging Indigenous activists and scholars that are two-spirited/queer and are building upon the work of those that have come before us. I'm lucky to be learning from them.

One of the critiques of Indigenous resurgence, one of my critiques, is that issues around bodies and queerness and violence have not been part of the conversation. In my way of thinking, they have to be central. Diversity, consent, respect for individual self-determination, non-interference are all paramount. We have to take on transphobia and all the manifestations of heteropatriarchy in our work as a core project. I find dogmatic interpretations of tradition to be harmful and problematic, and I want to shine light on alternative ways of living and being. If the revolution isn't queer then I don't want to be a part of it.

ROBYN: Agreed. So very much agreed. So much violence has been geared toward controlling sexuality and gender roles; that has been a result of European colonialism around the world. We have Caribbean countries just now, for example Trinidad and Tobago, just getting rid of British laws that were put in place that are still restricting non-heterosexual activities. This is a colonial legacy that we as communities need to address and cast off.

Control over sexuality and gender norms has played such an important role in the advancement of white supremacist nation-building, and Black and Indigenous women have always been cast in the role of sexual deviant and threat in similar ways. Almost every time I've given a book talk over the course of this year, somebody would always say at the end: "State violence, sure, but 70 percent of Black families are led by a black mother. Don't you think that has something to do with it?" I think it's telling that somehow this idea that homes run by Black single mothers could be seen as so threatening that it is so widely believed to be *the cause* of police shootings, poverty, the school-to-prison pipeline, etc. This, to me, really goes to show how deep the demonization of Black women goes:

society is so threatened by the idea of a household led by a Black woman that it is something that doesn't fit into the patriarchal view that a household is supposed to look like. The rise of unpartnered middle-class white women having children isn't represented as the cause of "the unraveling of society" and nobody is blaming the rise of school shootings on that. It's about race, class, gender, and also sexuality. Sarah Haley, Hortense Spillers, and others have done such important work showing how Black women are, in some way, always queer, or queered subjects, because, in part, we have never been subjected to the protections of white womanhood. In Harvey Amani Whitfield's newest book, *North to Bondage*,[11] which is about the experiences of enslaved Blacks in the Maritime provinces, you can see that Black women were not protected from physical (or sexual) violence, even at the hands of the state. He talks about Sarah Ringwald, who was arrested for stealing condiments and was subjected to twenty-nine whippings at a public whipping post, and a Black woman named Diana, who was subjected to 250 lashes at a public whipping post one Saturday in Cape Breton and 150 whippings the next because of "petty theft." We can see this, again, with the self-reported treatment of pregnant Black women behind bars in the '90s in Ontario, who reported not receiving adequate milk and vitamins, and being forced to do very hard labour, even as incarcerated pregnant white women received these—what we shouldn't call "privileges" so much as basic dignities. I could go on listing examples of this: Black women have long been deemed to be threatening, possessing a non-normative sexuality, cast outside of "gender" norms, and punished accordingly.

That history also helps me think about "refusal," as you call it Leanne. If we embrace not the sort of degrading tropes that go along with that sort of perceived deviance, but if we actually embrace the way that, as well, Black women and queer and gender-non-conforming folks sometimes refuse, too, to fit into the idea of what "ideal" womanhood was supposed to be and what proper sexuality is supposed to be, if we embrace the threat that really does pose to white supremacy, I think that's something really valuable for us to reclaim this *refusal to fit into norms* in many ways. It's really exciting now to look at the visibly queer, gender-non-conforming, and trans leadership in the Black Lives Matter movement. Even though for preceding generations, too, Black communities have had queer women doing the work, today we are seeing a refusal to hide that fact. This is a major challenge to the status quo. Even though of course there's this pushback, this regressive pushback, that criticizes BLM for being "lesbians who are dividing the movement," which is silliness, straight up.

LINDSAY: Tracy Lindberg says, "we can't get together to talk about who came before us and who comes after us," so in that vein, let's talk about activism from a whole new generation, and what are the voices that you're excited about and who inspired you?

ROBYN: There is an incredible renewal of Black activism in Canada and around the world. One of the things I get really excited about is that so many young folks are pushing for broader and more transformative justice, beyond reform. I'm thinking about how the many calls that we're starting to see that very explicitly say what if we defunded the police and actually used that money to build up our communities, our community's health, our community safety? I think that also the fact that we're starting to have more conversations about Black–Indigenous solidarity—even though we're not yet at a place where we have all the answers of what that can and will look like. It seems in some way we're just at the beginning, and so many members of communities are in many ways just trying to survive. But it's an important moment, one that involves sometimes difficult conversations, but necessary ones.

LEANNE: I think that I've been inspired by a lot of what Robyn spoke of, I think that Black Lives Matter is a very inspiring force—their Freedom School in Toronto, their relentless work against police violence and to make Pride accountable, the way they have materially supported Indigenous struggle, most recently during our vigils for Colten Boushie and Tina Fontaine. I'm grateful for that. It is propelling me to think through some of the ways that the Indigenous community is embodying solidarity and to think through how we are mobilizing and strategizing. It is deepening my understanding of building across communities and movements.

I am also inspired by the Indigenous arts community. The arts is a site of Indigenous struggle and generative refusal. Artists are offering critique, building other worlds, and producing Indigenous joy and care and vision, and sort of compelling us to want to get up again the next morning and dedicate ourselves to not just our struggle, but those who are also striving for freedom.

A few weeks ago, my band was playing at Megaphono, a music festival in Ottawa. My sister and I had been on Parliament Hill for a vigil in support of Colten Boushie. That was an important gathering. Over the course of the weekend every Indigenous and Black artist I saw, from rap to folk singers, spoke out against the acquittal of the white farmer that murdered Boushie. The crowds were mostly white. It was a powerful moment to see the arts community engaging politically in a space that was not necessarily a political space. There was some interesting energy there in those rooms—and we were not at a protest, or in a classroom, or at a teach-in. We were in a bar with the expectation to be entertained. Sydanie, Silla + Rise, and Lido Pimienta lovingly and fiercely called out the injustice around the murder of Boushie. Lido called all the Black and Indigenous, people of colour, queer and trans audience members to the front. I felt a little glimpse of what freedom might feel like for two seconds, and I think that was valuable. I think that's an important space that artists open up for us.

NOTES

1 Robyn Maynard, *Policing Black Lives: State Violence in Canada from Slavery to the Present* (Black Point, NS: Fernwood Publishing, 2017).

2 Leanne Betasomosake Simpson, *As We Have Always Done: Indigenous Freedom through Radical Resistance* (Minneapolis: University of Minnesota Press, 2017).

3 Frank B. Wilderson III, *Red, White & Black: Cinema and the Structure of U.S. Antagonisms* (Durham, NC: Duke University Press, 2010), 34.

4 Jacques Marcoux and Katie Nicholson, "Deadly Force: Fatal Encounters with Police in Canada: 2000–2017," CBC News, April 5, 2018, https://newsinteractives.cbc.ca/longform-custom/deadly-force.

5 Andrea Huncar, "Indigenous Women Nearly 10 times More Likely to be Street Checked by Edmonton Police, New Data Shows," CBC News, June 27, 2018, https://www.cbc.ca/news/canada/edmonton/street-checks-edmonton-police-aboriginal-black-carding-1.4178843.

6 Sylvia Wynter, "1492: A New World View," in *Race, Discourse, and the Origin of the Americas: A New World View*, eVera Lawrence Hyatt and Rex Nettleford, eds. (Washington: Smithsonian Institution Press, 1995), 5–58.

7 Marlene NourbeSe Philip, "Jammin' Still," in *Bla_K: Essays and Interviews* (Toronto: BookThug, 2017), 18.

8 Saidiya Hartman, *Lose Your Mother: A Journey along the Atlantic Slave Route* (New York: Farrar, Straus & Giroux, 2008).

9 Cedric J. Robinson, *Black Marxism: The Making of the Black Radical Tradition* (Chapel Hill, NC: University of North Carolina Press, 2000).

10 Glen Sean Coulthard, *Red Skin, White Masks: Rejecting the Colonial Politics of Recognition* (Minneapolis: University of Minnesota Press, 2014); Audra Simpson, "The State is a Man: Theresa Spence, Loretta Saunders and the Gender of Settler Sovereignty." *Theory & Event* 19, no. 4 (2016), https://muse.jhu.edu/.

11 Harvey Amani Whitfield, *North to Bondage: Loyalist Slavery in the Maritimes* (Vancouver: University of British Columbia Press, 2016).

REFERENCES

Coulthard, Glen Sean. *Red Skin, White Masks: Rejecting the Colonial Politics of Recognition*. Minneapolis: University of Minnesota Press, 2014.

Hartman, Saidiya. *Lose Your Mother: A Journey along the Atlantic Slave Route*. New York: Farrar, Straus & Giroux, 2008.

Maynard, Robyn. *Policing Black Lives: State Violence in Canada from Slavery to the Present*. Black Point, NS: Fernwood Publishing, 2017.

Philip, Marlene NourbeSe. "Jammin' Still." In *Bla_K: Essays and Interviews*, 13–37. Toronto: BookThug, 2017.

Robinson, Cedric J. *Black Marxism: The Making of the Black Radical Tradition*. Chapel Hill, NC: University of North Carolina Press, 2000.

Simpson, Audra. "The State Is a Man: Theresa Spence, Loretta Saunders and the Gender of Settler Sovereignty." *Theory & Event* 19, no. 4 (2016). https://muse.jhu.edu/article/633280.

Simpson, Leanne Betasamosake. *As We Have Always Done: Indigenous Freedom through Radical Resistance*. Minneapolis: University of Minnesota Press, 2017.

Wilderson III, Frank B. *Red, White & Black: Cinema and the Structure of U.S. Antagonisms*. Durham, NC: Duke University Press, 2010.

Whitfield, Harvey Amani. *North to Bondage: Loyalist Slavery in the Maritimes*. Vancouver: University of British Columbia Press, 2016.

Wynter, Sylvia. "1492: A New World View." In *Race, Discourse, and the Origin of the Americas: A New World View*, edited by Vera Lawrence Hyatt and Rex Nettleford, 5–58. Washington: Smithsonian Institution Press, 1995.

6

UNBORDERABLE BLACKNESS: HOW DIASPORIC BLACK IDENTITIES POSE A THREAT TO IMPERIALISM AND COLONIALISM EVERYWHERE

SANDY HUDSON

When we started the Black Lives Matter—Toronto project, I knew from its inception that we needed to challenge the world's conception of anti-Black racism in the Americas as a problem exclusive to the United States. Beyond even that instinctual responsibility, I felt intellectually and ideologically that my own social location, and the space and place that I inhabit, meant that I had a duty to disrupt the Canadian narrative. In that story, anti-Blackness—and more broadly, Blackness—simply does not exist. I felt very strongly that our experience needed to be connected to the experiences of our Black kinfolk south of the forty-ninth parallel.

We could not orient ourselves to resist a singularly "Canadian" anti-Blackness; our "terrain of struggle" had to be much broader.[1] Though I did not understand it as such at the time, this was a demand for a radical, geographic shift in our understandings of Blackness in the Americas.

Our first demonstration captured the frustrations of a community that was as upset about Michael Brown's murder by Ferguson police officer Darren Wilson[2] as they were about Jermaine Carby's murder by Peel Regional police officer Ryan Reid.[3] At the time, Canadian news media was eager to tell the story of how Wilson had shot Michael Brown to death and left his body lying in the street for hours in the majority-Black city of Ferguson, Missouri.[4] They saturated the airwaves with the story, airing footage of his covered body lying in the street, questioning Wilson's actions, and airing footage of the anti-racist resistance actions that had erupted across the United States.

That same Canadian media was much less inclined to tell the very similar, and far more local, story of Jermaine Carby. Jermaine Carby was a passenger in a car who police shot in a suburb of Toronto. He was not being pursued by police and was not a suspect in any crime. A police officer had simply decided to card[5] Jermaine Carby, decided he was a threat, and as with so many other cases of Black interaction with police, shot him to death. Even the notoriously toothless Special Investigations Unit (SIU), a body meant to provide a measure of accountability to police interactions with the public, declared that there were irregularities in the way the police had handled their interaction with Jermaine Carby.[6] Yet the SIU decided not to lay charges against the officer, and media barely reported on the story.

Such was the context behind the first demonstration held by Black Lives Matter—Toronto. And in every facet of that first action we made sure to name the similarities between the two heinous ruptures of Black life and ensure Jermaine Carby's story was told. In flyers for the demonstration, in the literature we distributed, in every media interview, and when speakers addressed the demonstration we elevated Jermaine Carby's story alongside Michael Brown's.

Beyond a simple act of solidarity or desire to hear our stories told, this insistence on elevating the local context of anti-Blackness and relating it to an experience elsewhere represents a radical concept. Try as it might, white supremacist imperialism cannot border Blackness. The strength and very existence of the African diaspora is a threat to the bordered containment of Blackness throughout the globe. As Katherine McKittrick puts it, "black geographies demonstrate both the limitations and possibilities of traditional spatial arrangements through the ways the Black subject is produced by, and is producing, geographic knowledges."[7] By naming Canadian anti-Blackness alongside American anti-Blackness we were eviscerating the mythological strength of the border, a colonizing force, in containing anti-Blackness south of the forty-ninth parallel.

More than just a conceptual truism, our global framework is a radical commitment. We must rigorously refuse white supremacy's attempts to illogically separate our struggles through all-too-convenient borders, false histories, and warped geographies. Black kinship across white supremacist borders is not simply imagined; the Black diaspora's connection to each other throughout the globe is a central tenet of Blackness, and this shared experience and connection represents a threat to the rigidity of borders in society as a whole.

But it is important to also understand the local particularities of Black struggles. Our experiences are necessarily localized and fundamentally shaped by local events, local manifestations of white supremacy, and local governments. Nonetheless, our experiences across borders are so connected as to obliterate the rigidity of borders for our people. We therefore cannot only consider the level of the state in our organizing, any more than we can allow ourselves to be restricted by the level of the body, community, or region. The colonial state is not the most relevant nor is it the preeminent level of analysis when it comes to Blackness, and the more we realize this, the more we can put the resulting possibilities for resistance into action.

What happens when we make connections between the resistances we create locally and resistances we could insist upon creating on a global scale? What possibilities and knowledges can be derived from unravelling "what is beneath and beyond existing geopolitical landscapes"?[8] This is an orientation that I am terming Afroglobal.

HAITI, A CASE STUDY IN AFROGLOBAL ORIENTATION

As I write this, the Government of Canada is conducting an operation that is likely the largest mass arrest of Black people in its history. Haitian asylum seekers are attempting to escape deportation authorities in Trump's America by crossing the border en masse. RCMP officers meet and arrest them. According to the media's abbreviated narrative, Haitian asylum seekers are fleeing the Trump administration's repeal of a law meant to shelter them after the 2010 earthquake in Haiti.

But a rigorous commitment to Afroglobalism, a palimpsestic approach, and a refusal to understand this event through the convenience of white supremacist colonial borders reveals a much more complicated and nuanced narrative of Blackness. Haitian history includes forcible removal from lands, families, communities, languages, religions, and customs between 1669 and 1864.[9]

Throughout that time, these African people who ultimately were brought to Haiti were traded across the Americas between colonies and jurisdictions. In landing on the island the Spanish named Hispaniola, they are likely to have been under the ownership of Spanish or French human traffickers and traders. In the case of the French, the ships carrying cargo that included Black slaves moved from as far south as the France Antarctique (located in what is now Brazil) to as far north as New France (contemporary Québec) and as far east as the New Hebrides (contemporary Vanuatu). The relations and kinship between the contemporary Black communities in each of these places, and everywhere in between, are *real*, although white supremacist global colonization obscures our ability to trace them.

The ancestors of those under French control on the island of Hispaniola fought and defeated their captors, creating the first free Black republic, Haiti—named in honour of the people indigenous to the land on which they reside. The French (still in control of various jurisdictions in the Americas, from St. Martin to New Orleans to Quebec) threatened to declare war and overtake the island unless the Haitians paid France for the loss of capitalist gain. France demanded a bounty of the equivalent of $21 billion as compensation for lost slave labour, lost raw materials, etc.[10] The Haitians agreed to pay the debt to avoid more loss of life among their people.

For decades into the twentieth century, the Haitian state was made to buttress France financially. France used its spoils to finance projects that benefit global capitalism to this very day, including the Panama Canal: built by Black labour (largely imported from across the Caribbean), using money generated through enslavement. This context explains how the world's first free Black republic was prevented from developing a prosperous state. With so much money owed to extortionist France each year, how could Haiti develop a sustainable infrastructure capable of protecting its inhabitants from the natural disasters to come?

In 2004, sensing a threat to Western capitalism, France, the United States, Canada, and Brazil joined forces to oust democratically elected Haitian president Jean-Bertrand Aristide, who could very well have changed the trajectory of Haiti from an exploited state to a thriving one. This affront to Black sovereignty sparked a refugee crisis across the Americas with Haitians seeking refuge in the very states that were colonies of France dozens of years earlier. But now, states like Canada and the United States, parts of which were previously French colonies, have relatively new borders conveniently drawn to erase the culpability and responsibility of these former French jurisdictions in the crisis.

To recapitulate this complex, Afroglobal, anti-colonial reframing of history: Haiti's infrastructure problem was caused in part by the trafficking and exploitation of Black people and Black sovereignty by France, the United Kingdom, and Spain. Haitian people enriched the world by helping to finance the Panama Canal, responsible for six percent of the world's total maritime trade, through the bounty paid to France.[11] Later manifestations of these same colonies of the United Kingdom, Portugal, and France (Canada, Brazil, and the United States, respectively) interfered in Haitian sovereignty, sparking a refugee crisis.

The infrastructure problem became a more acute crisis with the devastating earthquake of 2010, which resulted in the death of over 300,000 people,[12] and a renewed refugee crisis, with tens of thousands of people seeking refuge in the jurisdictions they had financed and built: the United States and Canada. And now, years later, a white supremacist narrative explains to us how both the Canadian government and the American government have revoked their seemingly generous commitment of providing refuge to the Haitian people seeking asylum from a long-past earthquake (long-past according to contemporary conceptions of political relevance). Canadian and American policy makers intend to deport what they see as empty, history-less, "unsuffering"[13] Black Haitians who conspire to "overstay their welcome" and "take advantage" of Canadian and American lands illegally—an anti-Black narrative that clearly does not withstand a critical Afroglobal, palimpsestic view.

This palimpsestic, spatial scale-crossing narrative of Haiti is just one history, laying bare how the African diaspora's very existence reveals borders to be fraught with inconsistency. Black people's histories are the proof that borders exist on a logic of thinly veiled, white-supremacist, colonial terror and are respected only when convenient. The Afroglobal point of view contains innumerable histories and geographies.[14] In order to reveal these Afroglobal narratives, we must understand the processes that allow white supremacy to present Blackness in such an ahistorical, ungeographic way.

BLACK GEOGRAPHIES

White supremacist logics mark Blackness and Black people as ungeographic, regardless of what borders we reside within.[15] As they demarcated African people, and we *became* Black, we were "anchored to a new world grid that is economically, racially, and sexually normative, or, seemingly nonblack; this grid suppresses the possibility of black geographies by invalidating the subject's cartographic needs, expressions, and knowledges."[16] The white supremacist demarcation of the world into nation states has created a landscape that is an assumed "transparent" geography. Such geography, as McKittrick describes, assumes the guise of being both naturally true and innocent; the construction of the land, and the geographic makeup of space and place, are supposedly apolitical and objective.

An Afroglobal paradigm shift would consistently and systematically contest the assumed transparent white supremacist geography that McKittrick describes. It would actively refuse to simply accept the demarcation of the globe as it is currently presented to us. This global terrain of political struggle can—and should—create new strategies for radical resistance struggles. An anti-racist, Black, feminist interrogation of this geography reveals to us that white transparent space is contestable.[17]

I began to think concretely about these concepts when the Black Lives Matter Global Network held its second "national" convening. There is a certain seduction in assuming that "space 'just is,' and that space and place are merely containers for human complexities and social relations."[18] Of course, as described above, space and how it is defined in and of itself is an incredibly political process and cannot simply "just be." I came face-to-face with the "seduction" that McKittrick describes during this convening.

Black Lives Matter is a largely United States-based movement. It makes sense for much of its focus to be contextualized in a United States context. But at this national convening, two Black Lives Matter chapters outside of the United States were present: Black Lives Matter—Toronto and Black Lives Matter—United

Kingdom. Our presence elicited tensions between those solely committed to organizing on a nation-state-wide scale and those who insisted that anti-Blackness must be confronted on a global level. Those of us from Black Lives Matter—Toronto and Black Lives Matter—United Kingdom quickly made connections with folks who had an Afroglobal frame but were having difficulty establishing an Afroglobal paradigm shift within their local chapters. We forced the conversation about global organizing at the convening.

The lack of an Afroglobal perspective, and the concealing function of transparent space, was negatively affecting our collective ability to create anti-imperial, cross-border resistance strategies. It became clear that an unquestioned framework of white supremacist borders clearly affected many attendees' understanding of history, of Black settlement, and of responsibility to Black people worldwide.

At one point during the convening (which occurred prior to Donald Trump being elected the forty-fifth President of the United States), some attendees suggested that, should Trump be elected, the movement should consider a present-day Underground Railroad of Black people from anti-Black America to Canada. Those proposing the idea assumed that Black people would escape many of the injustices that Black populations face in America.

When those of us from Canada challenged this notion, we were met with resistance and confusion from some attendees. Canada did not have the same history with slavery, some attendees insisted. The Black people of Canada were privileged because we had all had the means to emigrate from other places in the world. Canada was peaceful and simply accepting of difference, and it would be welcoming to Black people seeking refuge.

I was also personally challenged by some attendees on my ability to fully appreciate anti-Black racism as a person of Jamaican heritage. One attendee argued with me that Jamaicans did not have the same experiences with slavery as Black Americans, and that is why many Jamaicans are privileged enough to travel to other locations to live. I was disturbed at the power of a border to so effectively shape our understanding of our own kinship and shared histories.

White supremacist borders had seemingly obfuscated the pan-African organizing that our elders and ancestors had engaged in across lands. I was disturbed that these myths had *any* cachet, and I was horrified at how widespread they were. The idea that the forty-ninth parallel—an imaginary line drawn to benefit the colonizing relationships of the United States, the United Kingdom, and France—could not only erase hundreds of years of history of enslavement, human trafficking, and anti-Black racism, but could also provide a smokescreen to the continuing injustices that Black people in Canada face today was powerfully troublesome.

Those of us at the convening who reside outside the United States' borders became acutely aware of how white supremacy boxed us into borders through myths that hid our collective experience from one another. Possibilities from our perspective were not immediately obvious to those who did not have an Afroglobal orientation.

I was especially concerned about what that would mean for our organizing strategies. Would those of us residing in the centre of global white supremacist imperialist power understand that we would be implicated in the destruction of Black life elsewhere if we were simply content to struggle for Black life within the borders where our centuries-long struggle had landed us?

These discussions came to play a significant role in the proceedings of the convening as we collectively decided that it was necessary for our movement to reject white supremacist geographies and struggle for global resistance to anti-Blackness. We declared that we could not be a movement fighting for Black liberation while ignoring the white supremacist and global anti-Black functions of the American empire.

I tell these stories without critiquing the American movement or painting it with broad strokes. These are just a few of the conversations that catalyzed my own thinking on the subject of Black geographies and Afroglobalism. These assumptions and erasures can be found throughout the diaspora whenever a critical engagement with geography and history is lacking.

McKittrick addresses this when she says, "what you cannot see, and cannot remember, is part of a broader geographic project that thrives on forgetting and displacing Blackness."[19] This is reminiscent of the call for a different sight produced through the methods of Lethabo King, Alexander, Sharpe, and Brand.[20] Ultimately we did force a confrontation, encouraging attendees to reorient themselves to see what white supremacy was rendering invisible—and for the better. Our common struggles and debates at this second Black Lives

Matter convening shifted the movement toward a commitment to global resistance organizing.

THE WHITE SUPREMACIST CONVENIENCE OF BORDERS

The abbreviated narratives I detail above have a convenient white supremacist, anti-Black geopolitical function. Such narratives in the Americas are conveniently spun to suggest that the "bad," racist people exist south of the forty-ninth parallel, and the "good" people exist north of the border. After all, the mythology will suggest, issues of anti-Blackness (like police violence) can be traced back to an enslavement project that did not occur north of the border.

Yet, if we palimpsestically examine our geo-histories, the logic disintegrates. The issue of police violence in the Americas existed before the borders separating our various jurisdictions were concretized. At the time, there was simply a landmass invaded by white settlers who committed various types of genocide, brutalization, and theft to acquire their wealth. They then set up various institutions in an attempt to control and protect what they deemed their "property," including Black people, through slave patrols and police. Across the landmass, local settlements learned from each other and replicated the strategies that worked. The Toronto Police Service is older than the Los Angeles Police Department,[21] and both services predate the forty-ninth parallel's concretization.

Though white folks in their various European and "New World" allegiances could and would settle wherever they wished on the landmass and respect the borders they declared for each other's convenience or out of respect for the spoils of war, Black folks had no such luxuries. We were asylum seekers everywhere on the landmass, bordered or not. Our history is full of examples of our people ignoring such borders, whether by air, land, or sea, in order to survive. Consequently, slave patrols, police officers, and contemporary governments were and are content to obliterate the supposed strictness of the borders in order to control our bodies and secure white supremacist, capitalist wealth, and such activity continues to this day.

A critical examination of the convenience that a white supremacist colonial border provides to a specific brand of Canadian anti-Black racism is important to interrogate here. Around the world the dominant Western society understands Black people as landless and ungeographic. Our lineage is typically unconsidered, as are all our cultural and spiritual relationships with land.[22] It is part of our construction as subhuman.[23] In Canada, we are not only landless, Canadian mythology strips us of any historical existence on this land.

Because of the convenient ways that the contemporary borders have been drawn, white supremacist society can falsely claim that anti-Black racism is not an issue here above the forty-ninth parallel: there were too few Black people here and the scale of enslavement was minor, or so the myth goes. These borders create an effective framework that neglects to interrogate the fact that anti-Black enslavement and trafficking occurred before Canada was considered Canada. Black geographies of the Americas are and always have been connected across the landmasses.

On a Black terrain of struggle that is Afroglobal we resist the reification of the forty-ninth parallel—contesting Canada's erasure of our existence. "Black Canada is not invisible, nor is it . . . simply *in* Canada; rather, black Canada exhibits stories, places, and spaces that are materially detectable in the local landscape and through and beyond the nation-state."[24]

White folks as settlers and enslavers used the trans-Atlantic trade to traffic in Black people and goods, and enslaved Black people were trafficked multiple times for multiple reasons across jurisdictions. The reasons Black people were trafficked "were attached to local, community, familial and personal interests. Increasing home or field labor, bankruptcy, sex and rape, reproducing the slave population, selling 'unruly' resistant slaves, breaking apart slave allegiances . . . ."[25] Regardless of the reasons, the forced movements benefitted white supremacy and colonization.

Only when Black people moved ourselves were these movements on the terrain of struggle, for such movement itself was for the purpose of resisting our conditions. This remains true today. So many of the reasons that Black people have come to be in Canada begin in other lands. Black geographies above the forty-ninth parallel extend from Maroon communities of Jamaica to Nova Scotia, from Somalia to the greater Toronto area, and everywhere in-between. Black Canada is global, as indeed, is the entirety of the Black Americas.

It follows that we must contest colonial borders when we consider Blackness "because they do not sufficiently speak to the ways in which black geographies in Canada are made and upheld."[26] Our diasporic identities drive how we got to this landmass—whether within or beyond the framework of "Canada"—and how we exist on this land. Anti-Blackness was a large-scale economic, political, and cultural strategy of the United Kingdom, France, Spain, what would become the United States, and other European states. It remains this way. The entire strategy of enslavement and settlement is the foundation of the modern economy and fully informed whether or not those economies would become their own nation states or not.

Why would we consider Black experiences as fundamentally different because some colonizers and slave owners had an allegiance to the United Kingdom over here, others to France over there, and others to a "new world" over there? Anti-Blackness demands that we forget the imprints that history has had on our geographies and how we are constructed as perpetually in a place of unbelonging. Blackness exists beyond white supremacist constructions of place, both geographically and temporally.

As a final note on a critical geographic history: the Afroglobal framework, charting a Black terrain of resistance, has a scope that by its very nature is unavailable to us in its entirety. Some of our geographic knowledge is lost.[27] So much of our ancestors' survival as trafficked people was dependent upon our particular understandings of geographic knowledge being clandestine. Indeed, writing our geographic history and knowledges in the Americas could mean death or capture, whether we consider the Underground Railroad, maroon communities, Assata Shakur's escape from prison to Cuba, or undocumented migrants. Though these geographies are unwritten, uncovering them reveals to us the importance of considering the possibility for Black resistance and liberation beyond the borders that white supremacy draws and concretizes on top of us.

Consider the kinship relationship between Black peoples across the world born out of a similarity of experience, regardless of our geography. The shared experiences are the reasons why the murders of young Trayvon Martin or Michael Brown—stories elevated worldwide by the powerful media of the United States—can spark Black Lives Matter movements in the United Kingdom, Brazil, Canada, the Caribbean, and elsewhere. Black struggles are similar and related, regardless of a white supremacist geographic construction that conveniently suggests that they should not be.

RESISTANCE ACROSS BORDERS

These linked experiences of anti-Blackness, struggle, presumed landlessness, presumed subhumanness, and oppression create a terrain of resistance that can look similar across vast geographies and histories. Our lived experiences and the systems under which we reside have very unique local contexts, and yet they are consistent across geographies because our *bodies* have become mapped onto the white supremacist landscape. Where white supremacy *permits* us to be is geographically consistent with respect to political power, economic power, surveillance, pollution, health outcomes, and educational opportunities—the list goes on.

It only makes sense that we should resist our oppressions locally, globally, and in every jurisdictional level in-between. We have historically and contemporarily continued to do incredibly resilient work: naming, denouncing, and resisting these processes on a local, statewide, and sometimes national level. So far we do not use that kinship to challenge colonial border policies, or to organize on a global scale, in this current iteration of the Black liberation struggle.

But we must. Our experiences are linked and have been throughout the period of the white supremacist economic organization of our globe. For example, the way the evening news throughout the world often depicts Black people is a contemporary representation of how anti-Blackness spatially positions and assesses Black people. When media discuss our deaths, when we are sought after for arrest, or when we are arrested, they choose particular representations of Black people.

These depictions consistently describe us as delinquent and relegate us to particular spaces—whether those spaces are prisons, police cars, rundown public housing, refugee camps, ships, or other such insecure, oppressive spaces. This is how we are objectively marked as landless, delinquent, and dangerous. There is a certain carceral, worldwide geography that an anti-Black system reserves for Black people alone across the globe.

Wynter clearly articulates the consistencies of these geographies: "the criminalized majority of Black and dark-skinned Latino inner-city males now made to man the rapidly expanding prison-industrial complex, together with their female peers—the kicked-about welfare moms . . . that [are] internal to (and interned within) the prison system [are part of a geography, a] global archipelago . . . of the so-called 'underdeveloped' areas of the world—most totally of all by the peoples of the continent of Africa (now stricken with AIDS, drought, and ongoing civil wars, and whose bottommost place as the most impoverished of all the world's continents is directly paralleled by its Black Diaspora, with Haiti being produced and reproduced as the most impoverished nation of the Americas)."[28]

The stark truths of these observations have particular contemporary meaning. In over ten years of the International Criminal Court's existence, only Africans have been brought to trial.[29] The United Nations Special Rapporteur on extreme poverty and human rights recently visited an area of Los Angeles densely populated by homeless Black people and released statements about the crisis of homelessness. The resultant press conference highlighted a concern that the area's inhabitants' political and economic rights are potentially being violated on a systemic scale.[30] American lawmakers suggested that United Nations troops be sent into majority-Black areas of Chicago on peacekeeping duties to curb gun violence.[31]

SETTLEMENTS OF REFUGE

The way Black people across the landmass of North America have been treated upon creating "settlements of refuge" is also a good example of how Black people resist borders to sustain Black life. I use the term to distinguish between the reasons that Black people settle in a space—for refuge—and the reasons for white supremacist, colonizing forms of settlement. Black people's systemic movement patterns across the globe are typically in search of refuge: whether due to escaping enslavement, environmental disaster, economic instability in exploited states, war, etc.

Across North America, Black settlements of refuge were razed and destroyed across official state jurisdictions. From Africville and Hogan's Alley to Greenwood and Oakland, settler-masters have consistently made Black settlements of refuge inhospitable for Black folks. Even in contemporary times, the processes of gentrification, environmental racism, and economic collapse are destroying Black settlements of refuge and actively attacking our ability to create thriving Black-majority communities.

Communities like the Bloor and Bathurst area in Toronto and cities like Detroit are examples of areas where the processes of gentrification, environmental racism, and economic collapse push Black inhabitants out. We can expand these conclusions about Black settlements of refuge to majority-Black settlements in the Caribbean and South America. I have already discussed the case of Haiti. Consistently, forces of white supremacy and colonization exploit the places we inhabit.

Whether colonialism strategically entangles with enslavement or contemporary neoliberal structural adjustment programs of international organizations claiming to work for the betterment of exploited states, it impoverishes and creates destitution wherever Black people live. Even the not-for-profit-industrial complex, a system of largely white institutions ostensibly created to provide relief from disaster and poverty-related problems, destabilizes and recolonizes economically exploited states of non-white people (particularly in Africa). Anti-Black systems are implemented wherever we settle, constantly forcing us to seek refuge, no matter where we are.

Certainly, local realities are particular. The jurisdictions of Canada and the United States, for example, use different strategies with which to attack Black settlements of refuge. In Canada, as I discussed above, the white supremacist myth-making projects of the "nation of Canada" has falsely mapped Canada as white, non-Black space that was empty prior to the arrival of white colonists. Canada's contemporaneous reconciliation projects are revising its mythology to accept that terrible things occurred in its past to Indigenous people. Canada's mythmaking constructs itself as regretful of the colonial processes that require reconciling. It also presents such colonial processes as a distant past, despite its ongoing investment in a colonial project.

In Canada quiet concealment and erasure of history is the government strategy on state, provincial, and municipal scales. McKittrick describes several examples of Canada's careful elimination strategy as follows:

> Concealment is accomplished at least in part by carefully landscaping blackness out of the nation: specifically, the demolition of Africville in Nova Scotia and Hogan's Alley in Vancouver; threatening and administering black diaspora deportation; the renaming of Negro Creek Road to Moggie Road in Holland Township, Ontario; the silence

> around and concealment of Canada's largest unvisible slave burial ground, Nigger Rock, in the eastern townships of Quebec; racist immigration policies; the ploughing over of the black Durham Road Cemetery in southwestern Ontario; the relocation, and recent renaming, of Caribana; and the commonly held belief that black Canada is only recent and urban. When considered alongside other practices of discrimination, economic injustices, and racial-sexual oppressions, landscaping blackness out of the nation coincides with intentions to put blackness out of sight.
>
> Unseen black communities and spaces thus privilege a transparent Canada/nation by rendering the landscape a "truthful" visual purveyor of past and present social patterns. Consequently, "truthful" visual knowledge regulates and normalizes how Canada is seen—as white, not Blackless, not Black, not non-white, not native Canadian, but white. "Other" geographic evidence is buried, ploughed over, forgotten, renamed, and relocated; this illustrates how the practices of race and racism coalesce with racial and racist geographic demands.[32]

In contrast, the United States' mythology with respect to Black communities is similar to the mythology Canada is newly creating with Indigenous populations: terrible things happened in the past for which the United States is sorry, but those occurrences are over, goes the myth. Such different historical myths with respect to Black people have resulted in different strategies for targeting and eliminating Black settlements of refuge.

In the United States forceful destruction has been the strategy. Multiple examples exist of white civilians and either the federal or state government becoming involved in razing Black communities, presumably as ways of containing and constraining Black communities.

It is no accident that Greenwood, one of the cities in Black American history that a white riot razed, was once deemed the "Black Wall Street" of Tulsa, Oklahoma. Free Black towns were a threat to white supremacy. White people distributed photos and memorabilia of the terror inflicted upon Black people when the town was razed as if to say "Negroes beware."[33]

The examples above have the effect of keeping Black life within a Third World space across the globe. Even the ways in which the prison is marked a space meant for the Black person to inhabit under anti-Black colonialisms is a reconstruction of a Third World place through incarceration.[34] Whereas businesses and products cross borders freely under neoliberal policy, humans are allowed movement based on their capitalist utility. Neoliberalism has exponentiated what has been a historical commodification of immigrant labourers. When the economy has changed and certain occupations have fewer vacancies, Canada has returned to more restrictive immigration and temporary work permit policies. Refusing to grant citizenship or status to unauthorized immigrant workers guarantees the material benefits of cheap labour while avoiding many of the costs associated with recognition of worker rights.[35]

The construction of Black people as landless and without place continues throughout time: across the border, within the border, and by the states that police the border. We continue to provide non-Black society, and white society in particular, an anti-human against which to define themselves.[36]

CONCLUSION

We resist the existence of borders through our continued existence, and through our migration, as "landless" people with no legitimate claims to space anywhere to move and seek new settlements of refuge. "These historical practices, of vanishing, classifying, objectifying, relocating, and exterminating subaltern communities, and desiring, rationally mapping, and exploiting the land and resources, are ongoing, firmly interlocked with a contemporary colonial agenda."[37]

The strategies are different, so when resisting these issues on a local scale the strategies should naturally be particular to each space. But we should be aware that the outcomes are similar. This similarity of outcome, regardless of the strategy of the anti-Black state force, could be a serious threat to white supremacist borders.

Our resilience across our terrain of struggle belies the fragility of colonial state borders. Should our resistance frameworks become Afroglobal, we could develop cross-border de/anti-colonial methods to protect our communities from white supremacist destruction and to create sustainable Black shelter and sustainable, healthy Black communities.

The United Kingdom's imperial colonization project created multiple contemporary states. These states continue to work closely with the United Kingdom and similarly to replicate their control of Black bodies across the landmass. Does it make sense to respect their separation through borders, helping to prop up a mythology of Canada's innocence? Does it make sense to respect these borders in our analysis of the data surrounding violence against Black lives across the Americas? What does this mean for theorizing Blackness beyond physical borders? It makes far more sense to consider the experience of Black folks in spite of the border.

For example, why would we limit ourselves to examining data regarding police violence at a federal level? The local data is necessary and important for the various strategic measures we may use to fight anti-Blackness. But we should be collecting continent-wide, hemisphere-wide, and global information to inform us as to the full scope of anti-Black racism's hold on our existences. Stunting our data collection and analysis, simply because of imaginary lines drawn across the land between disputing European settler colonists, plays into white supremacy.

Similarly, conceptual borders between different Black and African people through the divide-and-conquer strategies of colonialism must be interrogated. Such conceptual border reproductions conveniently serve the settler-master. The theorizations of Blackness, as separate from Africanness, as separate from Caribbean Blackness, as separate from Indigeneity, are in and of themselves anti-Black. Should we accept these settler-master conceptual categories, using logics of white supremacy and anti-Blackness, we again play into white supremacy.

And what of the struggle for reparations? If we continue to engage in a reparations project as an incremental step toward abolition, does it make sense to leave European colonizer states off the hook and focus our demands for reparations only on a statewide scale? To do so would be a serious strategic and conceptual error.

Our subjugation is not bordered, and we should not be fooled by white supremacist geographies into limiting our terrain of struggle to the terrain of our subjugation. Those who came before us in the pan-African movement knew this. Paul Gilroy has said that "the realm of freedom is conceptualized by those who have never been free."[38]

White supremacy, anti-Blackness, and colonialism have created a geography that continually reproduces white freedom and Black captivity. In our struggle to conceptualize our liberation we must understand the various tools that white supremacy has used to manufacture our subjugation. Developing our own tools of resistance will require envisioning possibilities beyond those parameters. We must understand our history in a palimpsestic way and resist the temptation to understand the world through white supremacist notions of linear time and distance.

"Black and African peoples [like other Indigenous peoples] have always recognized multiple readings of our world. We also recognize contestations, contradictions and complexities of culture, the past history. But we resist amputations of our past, histories and cultures not because we want these to imprison us. It is because they offer important lessons that can contribute to new imaginaries and new futurities for us. Our present is very much inclusive of the past and the future ahead of us."[39]

NOTES

1 Katherine McKittrick, *Demonic Grounds: Black Women and the Cartographies of Struggle* (Minneapolis: University of Minnesota Press, 2006).

2 Jake Halpern, "The Cop," *The New Yorker*, August 3, 2015, https://www.newyorker.com/magazine/2015/08/10/the-cop.

3 Oliver Sachgau, "Officer who shot Jermaine Carby says he wouldn't do anything differently," *Toronto Star*, https://www.thestar.com/news/gta/2016/05/13/officer-who-shot-jermaine-carby-says-he-wouldnt-do-anything-differently.html.

4 2010 Census Quickfacts, United States Census, accessed August 10, 2019, https://www.census.gov/quickfacts/fact/table/fergusoncitymissouri/RHI225218#RHI225218.

5 Carding is a practice of street-checking employed by police officers in the city of Toronto and the province of Ontario more broadly. The practice permits police officers to arbitrarily stop people on the street to demand identifying information. The information is then put into a police database, which can affect job prospects and other opportunities in the future. Various studies by the *Toronto Star* have shown that the police stop

Black people more than non-Black people. For reference, see Jim Rankin and Patty Winsa, "Known to police: Toronto police stop and document black and brown people far more than whites," *Toronto Star*, March 9, 2012, https://www.thestar.com/news/insight/2012/03/09/known_to_police_toronto_police_stop_and_document_black_and_brown_people_far_more_than_whites.html.

6 "SIU Concludes Shooting Death Investigation in Brampton," News Release, Special Investigations Unit, July 21, 2015, https://www.siu.on.ca/en/news_template.php?nrid=2343.

7 McKittrick, *Demonic Grounds*, 6.

8 McKittrick, *Demonic Grounds*, 100.

9 David Patrick Geggus, ed., *The Impact of the Haitian Revolution in the Atlantic World* (Columbia, SC: University of South Carolina Press, 2001).

10 Jeffrey Sommers, *Race, Reality, and Realpolitik: U.S.-Haiti Relations in the Lead Up to the 1915 Occupation* (Lanham, MD: Lexington Books, 2015), 124.

11 Peter Vanham, "What the new Panama Canal tells us about globalization," World Economic Forum, July 11, 2016, https://www.weforum.org/agenda/2016/07/what-the-new-panama-canal-tells-us-about-globalization/.

12 Allyn Gaestel and Tom Brown, "Haitians recall 2010 quake 'hell' as death toll raised," Reuters, January 12, 2011, https://www.reuters.com/article/us-haiti-quake-anniversary/haitians-recall-2010-quake-hell-as-death-toll-raised-idUSTRE7094L420110112.

13 McKittrick, *Demonic Grounds*, 70.

14 Tiffany Lethabo King, "In the Clearing: Black Female Bodies, Space and Settler Colonial Landscapes" (PhD dissertation, University of Maryland, 2013).

15 McKittrick, *Demonic Grounds*; Wilderson, *Red, White & Black*.

16 McKittrick, *Demonic Grounds*, 3.

17 McKittrick, *Demonic Grounds*.

18 Ibid.

19 Ibid., 33.

20 King, "In the Clearing"; Jacqui Alexander, *Pedagogies of Crossing: Meditations on Feminism, Sexual Politics, Memory and the Sacred* (Durham: Duke University Press, 2005), cited in King, "In the Clearing," 134; Christina Sharpe, *In the Wake: On Blackness and Being* (Durham, NC: Duke University Press, 2016); and Dionne Brand, *A Map to the Door of No Return: Notes to Belonging* (Toronto: Vintage Canada, 2001).

21 Anthony Morgan, *The Blackening Margins of Multiculturalism: The African Canadian Experience of Exclusion from the Economic, Social and Cultural Promise and Prosperity of Canada: A Report on the Canadian Government's Compliance with the* International Covenant on Economic, Social and Cultural Rights *for the 57th Session of the Committee for Economic, Social and Cultural Rights* (Toronto: African Canadian Legal Clinic, 2016).

22 George J. Sefa Dei, "Spiritual Knowing and Transformative Learning," NALL Working Paper no. 59, New Approaches to Lifelong Learning, 2002, https://nall.oise.utoronto.ca/res/59GeorgeDei.pdf.

23 Wilderson, *Red, White & Black.*

24 McKittrick, *Demonic Grounds*, 102–3.

25 Ibid., 71.

26 Ibid., 103.

27 Wilderson, *Red, White & Black*; King, "In the Clearing."

28 Sylvia Wynter, "Unsettling the Coloniality of Being/Power/Truth/Freedom: Towards the Human, After Man, Its Overrepresentation—An Argument,"*The New Centennial Review* 3, no. 3 (Fall 2003), quoted in McKittrick, *Demonic Grounds*, 132.

29 See Alexandra Zavis and Robyn Dixon, "Q&A:: Only Africans have been tried at the court for the worst crimes on Earth," *Los Angeles Times*, October 23, 2016, http://www.latimes.com/world/africa/la-fg-icc-africa-snap-story.html.

30 See, Gale Holland, "U.N. Monitor on Extreme Poverty Tours Skid Row in L.A.," Los Angeles Times, December 11, 2017, http://www.latimes.com/local/lanow/la-me-ln-un-skid-row-20171211-story.html.

31 Ibid.

32 McKittrick, *Demonic Grounds*, 96–7.

33 Archer, Seth Archer, "Reading the Riot Acts," *Southwest Review* 91, no. 4 (2006): 500-516, http://www.jstor.org/stable/43472750.

34 McKittrick, *Demonic Grounds.*

35 George J. Sefa Dei, *Reframing Blackness and Black Solidarities through Anti-colonial and Decolonial Prisms* (Dordrecht: Springer, 2017).

36 Dei, *Reframing Blackness*; Wilderson, *Red, White & Black*; Frantz Fanon, *Peau noire, masques blancs* (Paris: Editions du Seuil, 1952).

37 McKittrick, *Demonic Grounds.*

38 Paul Gilroy, *The Black Atlantic: Modernity and Double Consciousness* (Harvard: Harvard University Press, 1994), 68.

39 Dei, *Reframing Blackness.*

REFERENCES

Alexander, Jacqui. *Pedagogies of Crossing: Meditations on Feminism, Sexual Politics, Memory and the Sacred.* Durham: Duke University Press, 2005.

Archer, Seth. "Reading the Riot Acts." *Southwest Review* 91, no. 4 (2006): 500–516. http://www.jstor.org/stable/43472750.

Brand, Dionne. *A Map to the Door of No Return: Notes to Belonging.* Toronto: Vintage Canada, 2001.

Dei, George J. Sefa. "Spiritual Knowing and Transformative Learning." NALL Working Paper no. 59. New Approaches to Lifelong Learning, 2002. https://nall.oise.utoronto.ca/res/59GeorgeDei.pdf.

Dei, George J. Sefa. *Reframing Blackness and Black Solidarities through Anti-colonial and Decolonial Prisms* (Dordrecht: Springer, 2017).

Fanon, Frantz. *Peau noire, masques blancs* (Paris: Editions du Seuil, 1952).

Geggus, David Patrick, ed. *The Impact of the Haitian Revolution in the Atlantic World.* Columbia, SC: University of South Carolina Press, 2001.

Gilroy, Paul. *The Black Atlantic: Modernity and Double Consciousness.* Harvard: Harvard University Press, 1994.

King, Tiffany Lethabo. "In the Clearing: Black Female Bodies, Space and Settler Colonial Landscapes." PhD diss., University of Maryland, 2013.

McKittrick, Katherine. *Demonic Grounds: Black Women and the Cartographies of Struggle.* Minneapolis: University of Minnesota Press, 2006.

McKittrick, Katherine. "Demonic Grounds: Sylvia Wynter." In *Demonic Grounds: Black Women and the Cartographies of Struggle,* 121–142. Minneapolis: University of Minnesota Press, 2006.

Morgan, Anthony. *The Blackening Margins of Multiculturalism: The African Canadian Experience of Exclusion from the Economic, Social and Cultural Promise and Prosperity of Canada: A Report on the Canadian Government's Compliance with the* International Covenant on Economic, Social and Cultural Rights *for the 57th Session of the Committee for Economic, Social and Cultural Rights.* Toronto: African Canadian Legal Clinic, 2016.

Sharpe, Christina. *In the Wake: On Blackness and Being.* Durham, NC: Duke University Press, 2016.

Sommers, Jeffrey. *Race, Reality, and Realpolitik: U.S.-Haiti Relations in the Lead Up to the 1915 Occupation.* Lanham, MD: Lexington Books, 2015.

Wilderson III, Frank B. *Red, White & Black: Cinema and the Structure of U.S. Antagonisms.* Durham, NC: Duke University Press, 2010.

7

ORGANIZING DIRECT ACTION IN THE DIGITAL AGE

JANAYA KHAN

When someone asks me how I came to be an organizer, I am unable to articulate precisely the moment that something fell off the shelf for me. It could have been being called a nigger on the 63 Ossington bus on my way home one day. It could have been the daily indignities of growing up in public housing. Or having immigrant parents who struggled to make sense of the constant precariousness of our lives. Or going through the system of group homes, women's shelters, and foster care throughout Toronto. It could have been the increase of police interactions I experienced as a disenfranchised Black youth. Or an educational system that failed me in many ways, that connected me to both terrible teachers and amazing educators who gave me a glimpse into what learning and life could really be about. It could have been one, all, or none of these things that led me on a path to protest, but that I am deep in the throes of it and will be for the rest of my life, I have no doubt.

I certainly did not see myself becoming an organizer. Partly because I had no idea that it existed before my early twenties, and partly because if you had told me that fighting for change was something one could do, I wouldn't have thought I was special enough to do it. I think there are some people who believe themselves to be special, or are believed to be special because they are remarkably smart, or beautiful, or tall, or tenacious, or whatever else we look up to in society. I had just enough to get by, minus the height (which, through Prince, I am at peace with), but would never had thought myself special enough to fight for something massive like changing societies and the conditions within them.

The thing is, for myself and many of us, organizing begins less as a choice and more as a compulsion—a compulsion informed by injustice, or grief, or rage, or indignity, or most importantly, love. The need to do something, anything, because doing nothing is not an option is what everyone doing social justice work has in common. The work to focus and hone that grief, or hurt, or rage, or love into action starts a journey that can lead to becoming an organizer. When I decided to continue the work beyond the compulsion, it became a choice. And while it can be one of the most difficult life paths, to fight for changes to a system you may not live to see, it is one of the most rewarding.

Since choosing activism ten years ago, organizing has evolved with the digital age. I went from being resistant to joining Facebook in 2007 to creating notifications on my phone that help to lower my screen time per week (because staying informed too often means staying online). The revolution of communication through the Internet and social media has changed how we approach organizing, how we access each other, and how we share information. I still remember VHS, reader. Cassettes! CD Walkmans and iPods that were the size of your palm. Now in North America smartphones are the norm and behemoth monopolies like Facebook, Apple, and Google shape what we know and how we know it. But movements have refused to be left behind and have harnessed the power of social media to support real action on the ground.

Witnessing and participating in direct action* movements like the Tamil shutdown of the Gardiner Expressway and Idle No More led to my becoming a leader in Black Lives Matter—Toronto and the Movement for Black Lives. Even over the five years or so of experience that I draw from in this chapter, technology advanced and became more deeply entrenched in our day-to-day activities.

The digitization of information and concretizing of instant-access culture has meant that organizers in the digital age must grapple with the reality of infinite content versus finite attention. The digital age has streamlined the process of mass mobilization: the coming together of hundreds or thousands of people demanding or calling for justice, a form of direct action I discuss throughout this chapter. And while coming together is in of itself a powerful act, the examples below illustrate just how much is required to make the moment count and to connect that moment into a movement for the people.

We are the first generation to have the tools that we do, and in many ways we are building the plane as we are flying it. Still, there is something pretty remarkable in being tasked with bringing our twentieth-century models of organizing, activism, and direct action into the twenty-first century, of creating the blueprint for winning in the digital age.

*WHAT IS DIRECT ACTION?

Just in case more needed to be said on the matter, direct action is an effort to leverage, seize, or demonstrate power against oppressive systems and institutional forces. As mentioned above, we tend to understand direct action as a mass mobilization of hundreds or thousands of people, but direct action can also involve only a small number of people coming together to create a leverage point. Shutting down a highway, occupying a building, blocking railways and pipelines, taking down an offensive flag, or using their bodies to stop bulldozers, etc. are all examples of direct action. Direct actions, by nature, are not state sanctioned and we tend to use them when negotiations or opportunities for those in power to do the right thing go unacknowledged or fail.

One of the best things about having access to each other through social media is the ability to potentially reach hundreds and thousands of people when staging a protest, rally, or some other call to action. But mobilization in of itself means nothing if it's not rooted in a larger organizing strategy to win a specific goal that shifts power structures. An effective direct action has a clear demand (or demands) that is meant to create leverage to meet the goals outlined by movement leaders.

Direct action is all about forcing people with decision-making power to respond to our demands instead of ignoring them. If we could trust that people in power, from police officers to mayors to corporations, would do the right thing, movements wouldn't need to exist. But we do. And we are responsible for curating a spectacle that will live beyond the moment through deliberate considerations of location, imagery, clothing, marshals, routes, legal support, medical support, banners, participants, symbols, colours, props, etc. The other significant piece is around arrest. Arrest is always a possibility with direct action; inherent in civil disobedience is the breaking of unjust laws. Spontaneous arrest, strategic arrest, and planned arrest are all possibilities, and despite how great a plan may be, law enforcement can be violent and unpredictable.

Every time that we stand outside of what is socially acceptable to present a solution or meet a demand, we win. Direct action is, at the heart of it, about disrupting power rather than appealing to it (permitted marches, petitions, etc.). In most cases, though not all, people who use direct action recognize that every effort to reach a solution has been tried and failed, as in the case of police brutality. It is an escalation and tactical response to a system that only offers outcomes that maintain the status quo.

TAMIL SHUTDOWN OF THE GARDINER EXPRESSWAY

In 2009, two years after I joined Facebook because my best friend literally made my profile for me, my Facebook (FB) newsfeed was flooded with powerful images of Tamils in Toronto shutting down the east and west side of the Gardiner Expressway in Toronto. Two thousand people, largely from the Tamil community, had completely halted traffic to demand that the Canadian government use economic and diplomatic sanctions in response to the civil war and genocide in Sri Lanka against the Tamil population.

This was one of my earliest experiences of witnessing what I now understand to be a direct action that utilized online platforms as an integral intervention and education point to amplify the Tamil struggle in Toronto. I had met some of the organizers on my university campus and through mutual friends. And while I was just beginning to learn some social justice themes, I hadn't seen anything like this before in Toronto. Because of their posts on FB, I learned about the oppressive conditions imposed on the people of Tamil Eelam. I learned about international foreign policy that exacerbated the political upheaval existing in the country. I learned about the conditions of Tamils living locally in the city. I understood that, even though the Tamils in Toronto lived thousands of miles away from their home, they could still influence action to support their people.

I also witnessed police repression of Tamil action, consistent and yet distinct from the ways that police had terrorized Black communities in Toronto throughout my youth. Elected officials were not moved to action around the crisis in Sri Lanka despite the growing concerns of Tamils in the city, and several smaller actions had taken place leading up to the Gardiner blockade in an effort to prompt elected officials to act. Elected officials refused to move on it. The Tamil community's use of disruption and civil disobedience created a platform for them that they otherwise had been denied to force a response from the Canadian government.

Both the mayor and premier at the time articulated concern for the conditions in Sri Lanka, yet simultaneously condemned the action of shutting down the Gardiner, then Mayor David Miller saying that "occupying roads like the Gardiner isn't acceptable, and the police will prevent you from doing it and will remove you when you do."[1]

The photographs shared online showed intergenerational groups, from elders to toddlers, grieving and determined and engaging in peaceful protest, linking arms and sitting-in as they blocked the Expressway, opening up a path for justice. Yet police, who kept growing in number throughout the day, were deployed against the peaceful assembly.[2] On the same day at the same time, Tamils were staging a die-in at Queen's Park, the home of Ontario's legislative assembly. Over a dozen Tamils were arrested at this time, despite Canadian mainstream media coverage that underplayed the severity of police repression.[3]

Posts, photographs, and live updates from Facebook friends and shared posts alike described in detail police using white, unmarked vans to "disappear" protestors in an effort to create fear and force people to leave. Police also used stadium-style lights to blind protestors intermittently after the sun went down, adding an element of disorientation to the fear they sought to create. This directly contradicts former Toronto Police Chief Bill Blair's "concern" over a possible "stampede" down the Expressway ramp that could injure protestors.

The discord between the reporting of the protest and the live reporting from protestors brought home the importance of a platform like Facebook for organizers to tell the truth that mainstream media cannot be trusted to tell. When it came right down to it, Tamil organizers won the day. Former Leader of the Liberal Party of Canada Michael Ignatieff responded to their demand for acknowledgement and government intervention.

The Tamil community turned their presence—one that was easily discounted as just too immigrant, too dark-skinned, too foreign to listen to—into a powerful force not to be denied. When they set up the blockade and national media flocked to report the story, they forced millions of Canadians to confront the devastation that they were experiencing, the pain of listening to the known names of the dead in Sri Lanka over a Tamil station broadcasting in Canada, hoping that they wouldn't hear the name of a loved one. They pushed for Western accountability, had several intergenerational actions, and united as a people to send a message to the Canadian government. And most importantly, they sent a lifeline to their people back home, letting them know that they were tremendously loved.

This moment anchored in me an immense sense of possibility. Truly, much of direct action stems from a moment of inspiration, but as author Octavia Butler said, habit will not fail you. The objective for a fledgling activist or organizer is to grow from a place where you aren't just moved to action by external forces, but are instead the one moving others closer to justice. The same organizers in the Tamil protest became some of our strongest supporters and comrades during the rise of Black Lives Matter—Toronto, acting as both consultants and conspirators around some of our more intense direct action moments.

IDLE NO MORE

Participating in Idle No More all those years ago remains an incredibly formative experience in my earlier years of activism. This Indigenous liberation movement, founded by three Indigenous women in December 2012, was born in reaction to legislative abuses of Indigenous treaty rights by then Prime Minister Stephen Harper and the Conservative federal government, and especially as a push back against omnibus bill C-45. C-45 removed protections for forests and waterways across Turtle Island, drastically compromising Indigenous peoples' sovereignty over their land. The country now called Canada remains a main architect of abuse and genocide against the Indigenous population above the forty-ninth parallel and around the world, perpetrating abuse, land theft, and genocide through isolating and disenfranchising reserves, overpriced and limited resources, systemic racism, police brutality, the disappearance of Indigenous women, and the continuing legacy of the theft of Indigenous children through child welfare services. It is these circumstances, and innumerable others, that led up to the moments where a movement like Idle No More was conceived.

Every time I recall some of the most beautiful and transformative direct actions, I also think of the terrible conditions that inform their necessity. The historical and socio-economic political conditions that lead to mass mobilization inform what pressure points and interventions are needed, but direct action never just happens by some twist of fate. It is a spark lit by hundreds of people tired of the indignities, of the daily humiliations, of continually having to push back against a system that is not failing but rather operating by design to continue to oppress marginalized people.

When the organizers of Idle No More put out a press release explaining who they were and why they came to be, outlining their values and their commitment to grassroots organizing, they were ensuring that no one political organization could speak for the many. Much like the Tamil shutdown a couple years earlier, this set a precedent for digital mobilization as the statement was shared widely across social media and not dependent on traditional media to cover the story. Their clear, decentralized stance made sure that they were not owned by funders or political agendas bound to corporate interests. Idle No More's commitment to Indigenous practice and a grassroots model of organizing ensured a diversity of tactics required to meet the attack on both the environment and the abuse of treaties.

Idle No More used traditional round dances done through flash mobs in shopping malls as a consistent tactic during the pre- and post-holiday shopping season in 2012. These direct actions took place in dozens of cities across Turtle Island and led to solidarity actions across the border in the Mall of America in Minneapolis, Minnesota.

And while flash-mob round dances were a consistent tactic, more direct forms of action were executed through blocking highways and congregating around statues and war memorials that celebrated the country now called Canada's violent past.

On December 30, 2012, as part of a day of nationwide actions, a group connected to Idle No More blocked the Canadian National main railway line between the country's two largest cities of Toronto and Montreal near Belleville, Ontario, for hours. Every time an action took place, it elevated the message of defending the land and respecting the sovereign rights of Indigenous people. In fact Idle No More played a pivotal role in normalizing the language "Indigenous sovereignty" across leftist and movement cultures, academia, and non-Indigenous communities.

Sharing stories on social media played a pivotal role in amplifying Idle No More's message. Too often the media does not report on Indigenous people and their experiences, and when it does it is inaccurate or inauthentic. This is especially true outside of main cities. The hashtag #IdleNoMore was frequently used as a challenge to everyone to do better and be better for humanity and the planet's sake.

I understood then that, for Black people, there was not another population of people more closely linked to us through the hideous process of colonization than Indigenous peoples in Canada. I followed Idle No More and their actions and tactics and celebrated their wins.

I learned about a call to action in Toronto both from friends and online via Twitter and Facebook. We made a massive circle around the fountain of the Eaton Centre in Toronto and began our round dance led by the Indigenous women in the group. I looked up and saw that the same thing was happening on the two levels above us. It was beautiful. I am always humbled and amazed when we come together, despite having every reason not to, because we believe in a better world where the strength of a people is not determined by how much suffering they endure. Similar to the Tamil protest, Indigenous communities, some of whom were a part of Idle No More, became some of the most active warriors and allies in the Black Lives Matter movement in Canada, especially during Black Lives Matter—Toronto's encampment at Toronto Police Service Headquarters. This moment directly connects to my push for the Black Lives Matter Global Network to go to Standing Rock in 2016.

BLACK LIVES MATTER—TORONTO ORIGIN STORY

Black Lives Matter—Toronto, the first chapter of the Black Lives Matter Global Network outside of the United States, became my first real movement home. Sandy Hudson put out a message thread on Facebook in 2014 to organize an action around the murder of eighteen-year-old Mike Brown and the subsequent non-indictment of then police officer Darren Wilson in Ferguson, Missouri. This was the first time I was in a room full of Black millennials for the sole purpose of organizing our own protest.

Though the group of us didn't know each other very well, we all understood that we had to steer the momentum of Black Lives Matter in the United States and the outrage over Mike Brown and connect it to local issues. Carding, the legal practice of police racially profiling random people whose names would then be entered into a database, was devastating Black communities across Ontario. Carding was directly connected to the recent murder of thirty-three-year-old Jermaine Carby, a Black man who was killed by police in a suburb of Toronto only minutes after leaving his home. Neither the media nor the general public seemed to understand the connection between police brutality in the land now called Canada and police brutality in the United States. Anti-Black racism in the country now called Canada's coding is more sophisticated than in the United States, but the colossal apparatus of mass incarceration in the United States is often used to overshadow police brutality and racism this side of the border, despite the fact that these experiences are a reflection of population and not severity.

We had twenty-four hours to put together our rally for Mike Brown, Jermaine Carby, and a call to end the practice of carding. We weren't thinking about the numbers on our Facebook event page as we laboured over collecting data to put on pamphlets on carding we would hand out, or when we contacted Jermaine Carby's family to speak, secured singers, a generator and sound system, and an ASL interpreter. We wanted to ensure that we didn't miss a single thing because it felt like so much was at stake, and it was, because Black folks aren't allowed mistakes. Suddenly one of our folks in the room mentioned that the online numbers were swelling and thousands were saying they were going to attend. Canadian media began contacting us for info, asking us if we were going to be "violent" and called us segregationist for using Black Lives Matter in the event name.

The night of the action about twelve of us were working as leadership to put it on. By the time folks started to show up we already couldn't feel our toes, the November day was so cold. Over three thousand stood with us for hours in front of the United States consulate demanding justice. We knew that we had to keep going and spoke with the leadership of Black Lives Matter in the United States. We became an official chapter shortly thereafter.

#BLMTOTENTCITY/#BLMTOBLACKCITY

By 2016 we had evolved into a full-fledged movement. We had our core team established, an ally team, volunteer and membership platform, and several targets with rolling direct action tactics. Here is the reality: while many people see the posts and hashtags when a person is killed by police and think that is the work, and while that is certainly a part of it, the necessary unseen work is a years-long effort that requires sophisticated strategy and consistent effort for the visible campaign to succeed. Gathering the name(s) of the officers involved, securing any and all video footage associated with the event, fundraising for the family, pushing back against law enforcement, putting pressure on both media and elected officials, and targeting the Special Investigations Unit are all part of long- and short-term strategies that we know to utilize when police kill our people. The more we organized against the brutality throughout the city, the more antagonistic law enforcement officials became towards us,

In 2015 we shut down both sides of the Allen Road, a highway in Toronto, over the murder of Andrew Loku, a forty-five-year-old man from South Sudan. Police killed him in his own home over a noise complaint. In 2016, the Special Investigations Unit (SIU) was in the process of ruling on whether or not police had acted within policy to kill a man in a matter of seconds, while he was in crisis, over a noise complaint. The SIU is meant to be a watchdog body that holds police accountable, but instead is little more than a group of mostly ex-cops with a non-existent indictment rate of police who kill citizens. We knew that as the date for the ruling neared, we would have to create pressure on the SIU to do the right thing since they could not be trusted to do so on their own.

Our pitching of tents in front of the Toronto Police Service headquarters was not meant to be a weeks-long action that extended from

March to April, but being adaptive is required in direct action strategies. I remember clearly pitching the idea to the team and us going back and forth on pieces we would need to make it meaningful. A strong team takes an idea and elevates it to the next level. Our sometimes fiery debates on strategy led to curatorial brilliance in actions. When the tents were pitched and small, contained fires were lit to keep the freezing weather at bay, Toronto police used an extreme amount of force against the people present. They arrived wielding batons, with some wearing hazmat suits as they threw chemicals on the fire and kicked, punched, and dragged organizers, elders, women, and children off the premises. The violence that Toronto police demonstrated that night was disgusting and unjust. And we used it as a moment to amplify our urgent call to action for Andrew Loku.

Social and independent media were used to capture the police brutality that night, and we called for more people to join us in front of the Toronto Police Service Headquarters. In the following weeks, the police cut the power from their external outlets so we could no longer access power from their buildings. They also used force anytime tents were pitched or fires were lit. Yet despite their efforts, we stayed for twenty-one days. We turned our protest into an occupation and created rapid response infrastructure to make it sustainable. A legal team, harm reductionists, clothing donations to keep people warm, a food team that made five hot meals a day, a fundraising team, a programming team that focused on entertainment and spirituals, and a healing justice area were just some of the amazing organizational structures that came together over the course of those three weeks. We also created more direct action opportunities while there, from turning our occupation into an art gallery to marching to City Hall to confront a mayor too intimidated to show up.

One of the most impactful moments for me and for us as a team was the collaboration between us and our Indigenous relatives. They literally never left our side the entire action and had their own leadership and sovereign zone within our occupation. We had hard moments and soft ones, and the trust that we built throughout the occupation led us to take up an active role in the #OccupyINAC national action that was called only a few weeks later.[4] We closed Tent City in a march to Queen's Park, where we confronted former Ontario premier Kathleen Wynne.

By this time we were under constant surveillance by police, from being followed home after actions to monitoring our social media activity. It was a given that if we were organizing a protest, rally, or event, police would be stationed in unmarked vans and on horseback in the surrounding area in full-on riot gear. The level of state violence and surveillance increased as our power in the city increased. This was brought home to us following our Pride action, when Black Lives Matter—Toronto expanded what was possible, not just in our city, but throughout North America and globally.

PRIDE 2016

After our Tent City action, despite the increasing animosity law enforcement felt towards us, most people under the age of fifty felt that we were doing right by activating citizens to action against injustice.[5] I bring this up because in the days following our stoppage of the Pride parade, all bets were off for a little while. When Pride Toronto reached out to us to be the Honoured Group to lead the Pride march in 2016, we sought out Black folks already active within Pride Toronto to assess whether or not we could make this meaningful in a more transformative way that was bigger than just us. After discussions with Black Queer Youth and Blackness Yes!/Blockorama, both groups operating under the umbrella of Pride as the only spaces where queer and trans Black people felt welcome, we learned of budget cuts, ignored requests, and deprioritization of Black space despite its growing popularity. We decided to accept the invitation to help in pushing Pride Toronto to be more inclusive.

I also want to be clear about something. I am Black. I am queer. I am non-binary. So, while I write as if we were all separate entities, I want to highlight that many of us in Black Lives Matter—Toronto are also part of the queer and trans community. Too often organizers are required to pick a certain identity and fight for it alone, despite the fact that all of our experiences are intersectional. Pride, and the police presence in it, had directly impacted many of us personally. Myself included.

Over a dozen different police floats were in the march in 2016, a fact that not only jeopardized the safety of any Black people who wanted to celebrate Pride, it directly contradicted the beginnings of Pride, in Toronto as with the Stonewall in New York, as a protest against police brutality. We knew that in order to be responsible, we had to use our platform to elevate the voices of our community members who had been doing the front-line work. These groups had tried over the course of several years to air their grievances with Pride Toronto, from slashed budgets to restricted stage position, all to no avail.

With our new comrades, we crafted a list of demands, ranging from restoring budgets and stage space to the removal of police floats and recruitment booths from the Pride parade, that we would present to the executive director of Pride Toronto.

We were at the very front of the parade, the largest in North America, with Prime Minister Justin Trudeau's float behind us. We initiated our direct action as a sit-in, effectively immobilizing the entire parade until the executive director signed our demands and committed to incorporating the necessary changes. Costumes, coordinated hairstyles, Pride-themed smoke bombs to provide cover until we got into place, mini coffins we marched with to represent our beloved ancestors, and a float entirely designed by Black artists are just a few out of many props we had in place. It was magnificent.

Our hashtag, #NoPrideInPolicing, was amplified by a designated social media team and iconic images were captured and shared to inspire similar actions coast to coast. Community supporters went "live" to report and show their solidarity. The following years saw #NoJusticeNoPride spring up in cities across the United States, a clear nod to our action in Toronto.

That year we had to create a strong narrative strategy as long-term strategy of our direct action as the media turned on us. We were attacked on every level, and police used this moment to try and discredit us by using gay police officers who co-opted our language around marginalization. We created our own media, from videos to art installations, accepted interviews where we redirected the hostility being thrown at us, we wrote articles and op-eds and we galvanized the larger queer and trans community into action. It is because of community that the board of Pride Toronto was flipped on its head; once overwhelmingly white, the membership changed to reflect more people of colour from different walks of life. The membership voted in a new board and this new board voted in all of our demands, most significantly the removal of police from Pride.

The death threats, harassment and attacks from police, the swinging pendulum of public opinion, and the level of surveillance we endured took on a new level of intensity. Reporters, police, and police sympathizers began cyberstalking some of our team members, doxxing us and sleuthing our online profiles in an effort to weaponize posts we made days or even years ago. Our security culture changed dramatically following this action. We stayed firm, held the line, and rallied people behind us. Before long we began to receive more support for our unapologetically Black action as our narrative strategy took effect. Because our action began rooted in organizing with and for community, we were not alone. Together, we won.

CONCLUSION

Direct action without organizing can only have temporary impact; it requires long-term strategy and community buy-in to be impactful. As organizers we are meant to facilitate dialogue, create campaigns, and move resources towards a strategic goal determined by a larger vision and mandate of freedom. An organizer is not just about creating momentum but seizing it and redirecting it towards that vision. Direct action is instrumental for organizers to build containers around momentum. The best direct action strategies don't just involve organizing people, they help to organize people's political thoughts.

The job of the organizer is to bring mobilization and direct action to a place where it translates to tangible wins/shifts for Black people, Indigenous people, Muslims, migrants, the LGBTQ community, etc. If I have learned anything about direct action in the digital age it is that mass mobilization can be powerful, but critical mass is hollow without critical community connections, which are necessary to win.

The direct action moments I shared in this chapter have been pivotal in shaping my approach to this work. In Black Lives Matter one of the most consistent ways we were criticized was for our lack of civility, as if we should ask for our dignity quietly and die politely. Civil disobedience is a duty, civility a choice. There was something particularly offensive to the white imagination about Black people demanding better, demanding more, and demanding accountability. Five years into Black Lives Matter and the movement has become global. What started out as a Facebook post to reach out to other Black people who were grieving turned into a vision and a movement actualized around it.

Direct action does not appeal to power, it disrupts it and redirects that power to communities that have been exploited, erased, and disenfranchised by the imperialist white supremacist state. The work of redirecting power can take you out if you aren't careful. Having a team is one of the most important aspects of sustainable organizing and effective direct action strategies since so much of it requires trust. The Tamil shutdown of the Gardiner, Idle No More, and Black Lives Matter laid a foundation for me that has translated to every place in the world I have been since. Freedom fighting is a universal language, and I am humbled by the ferocity of my team and of those that influenced and continue to influence us.

Thank you to all the revolutionaries out there who have put their lives on the line, on- and offline, because they believe enough in freedom to fight like hell for it.

NOTES

1 Nicole Baute and Kenyon Wallace, "Mayor warns defiant Tamils," *Toronto Star*, May 12, 2009, https://www.thestar.com/news/gta/2009/05/12/mayor_warns_defiant_tamils.html.

2 Iain Marlow, Henry Stancu, and Nicole Baute, "Tamil protest moves off Gardiner to Queen's Park," *Toronto Star*, May 10, 2009, https://www.thestar.com/news/gta/2009/05/10/tamil_protest_moves_off_gardiner_to_queens_park.html.

3 "Police make 15 arrests at Tamil protest downtown," CTV News Toronto, April 29, 2009, https://toronto.ctvnews.ca/police-make-15-arrests-at-tamil-protest-downtown-1.394164.

4 Victor Ferreira, "Aboriginal protesters occupy federal offices across Canada, demanding Trudeau visit Attawapiskat," *National Post*, April 14, 2016, https://nationalpost.com/news/toronto/idle-no-more-protesters-occupy-federal-office-building-in-toronto-to-demand-action-for-attawapiskat.

5 Sarah-Joyce Battersby, "Majority of Torontonians support Black Lives Matter: poll," *Toronto Star*, April 14, 2016, https://www.thestar.com/news/gta/2016/04/14/majority-of-torontonians-support-black-lives-matter-poll.html.

PART III

CREATIVE ACTIVISMS: ARTS IN THE MOVEMENT

8

BLACK ARTS AND THE MOVEMENT: A CONVERSATION

RAVYN WNGZ AND SYRUS MARCUS WARE

The following is a conversation between two Black trans activists who are actively involved in contemporary arts practice in Canada. They discuss the role of the arts in the movement for Black lives and the activism fuelling the burgeoning Black cultural renaissance that surrounds the movement. Activist, dancer, and choreographer Ravyn Wngz, and activist, visual artist, and performer Syrus Marcus Ware explore art, social change-making practices, and the need for more space to showcase the work of Black artists.

SYRUS: You are such a brilliant artist and activist. Can you talk about how you are involved in the movement?

RAVYN: How I am involved in the movement? Well, I'm thirty-three. I'm a new "involvee" in the movement, new to doing direct action, actually. A lot of my work has been based in creating powerful nuanced representations of Black, Indigenous people of colour, LGBTQ folks in media and performance on stages. I'm a dancer, and so a lot of my work is about how we show up in public, how we're allowed to show up in public, the stories that are hidden, and the stories that we want people to know about us or even share within our own community. And so, a lot of my work has been based in that. That was originally what I was doing, before I officially joined the fight for Black lives. Right now, I'm a steering committee member of Black Lives Matter—Toronto, focusing on eradicating anti-Black racism and creating a condition where Black people can see their futures and have success and healing.

SYRUS: I'm happy to be in this fight alongside you. I'm forty-one. I am also a steering team member for Black Lives Matter—Toronto and I have dedicated myself to this movement for Black lives. And in a lot of ways, I joined this movement long before there was a Black Lives Matter.

In the '90s I was really involved in organizing around, or trying to get freedom for, Black political prisoners from the MOVE family—the MOVE 9[1]—trying to get them free from prison during the late '90s and then working to support the campaigns for Mumia Abu-Jamal's[2] freedom. So again, just looking at Black political prisoners and to fight for their life and self-determination.

And then I got involved in a lot of organizing around Black queer and trans communities in Toronto through Blackness Yes![3] and really trying to figure out how to support and create the conditions that would allow for a flourishing Black queer and trans community in Toronto, which I really think we do have now in a lot of ways. And then, now, most recently being involved in Black Lives Matter and really being interested in how the art that is being made out on the streets and in the galleries is connected to our movement and to the movement for Black Lives.

RAVYN: Yeah. 100 percent. What is your artistic art practice? How would you describe it?

SYRUS: My artistic practice is rooted in Black activist culture, exploring Black activist culture. And I'm an interdisciplinary artist, so I do a lot of work in super-large-scale drawing—really, really large-scale drawing—but I also do performance art and mixed media. Sometimes I do painting, I used to be a really active painter. I'm also a DJ. I like making art in lots of different formats. My work is focused on exploring activists' lives and exploring the experiences of Blackness on Turtle Island. Sustainability of activist lives is a primary goal. I use humour a lot in my work—especially in my performance work. My work is really huge in terms of size and scale, and concentrates on love and sustainability and survival and hope. All of that permeates through all of my work.

How would you define your artistic practice?

RAVYN: I recently heard this title and I thought, "this is perfect for me." I'm a multi-hyphenate individual. Which means that I do multiple things. I'm a movement storyteller. I have danced in companies and collectives and have created my own company and collectives. In Toronto, I'm a writer, vocalist, an actor, choreographer. I direct theatre and dance and have been a part of supporting others to do the same thing. So I have really invested in myself over the past fourteen years in the growth of the artistic conversation around who we are, living here right now on Turtle Island and how we are connected, and then also, the ways that we're not connected.

A lot of my work has been through a multi-racial dance company.[4] With that company, we discussed all of our differences and how unique they were, from growing up in Bermuda, to Vancouver, to Toronto, and how that really affected the way that we saw the world, affected the way that we engaged in our own activism, our language around activism. And, I find, an art practice is a beautiful way of connecting people.

I find that whenever I witness dance or some performative art practice, I am transported into this other realm of possibility and excitement. It helps me to deal with the everyday or moving through life as a Black trans person and how difficult that can be, to exist: to exist within your own mind. The art that I create and the people around me expand my ideas of survival and success and health.

SYRUS: It's so interesting because there's this heightened sense of connection amongst activists and community in the movement. I find myself in social situations more often—situations wherein I have more interaction with other Black people than I have ever had before, just because I meet so many people now, through this work.

RAVYN: Yes. Me too.

SYRUS: But also, we are in the middle of some sort of magical Black cultural renaissance, wherein the arts are flourishing and there's this overflow of creative practice. There is also greater interest in showcasing, promoting and highlighting this Black creative practice. This flourishing of new work is not just happening in a vacuum. And I wonder—what do you think of this cultural renaissance that is flourishing through this movement for Black lives, this renaissance that seems to chant that Black artists matter too?

RAVYN: I think we are finally getting back to a space where the art that is being produced is reflective of what is happening out in the streets—on the ground. You see, there was a time when Nina Simone and similar folks were talking about what was happening right there and then to people in their communities. They were documenting everything that was happening, like a live commentary and play-by-play. And then musicians, we shifted to a space where we were trying to move away from only talking about the political climate.

We did so to distance ourselves from the pain—which makes sense to me. We began to filter what we wrote about. And as a result, we got detached from politics. We got detached from each other and, of course, from Black narratives. And it's been cyclical: in and out of this process and way of working.

For example, in the '90s there were all these Black television shows. There were Black women on television, in their fullness, you could see it in the way that they looked. Their looks were all different and unique. Then in the 2000s all of that kind of dwindled.

Right now, it feels like Black Lives Matter has incited a space where everyone wants to get involved in the movement in some way. Everyone wants to create new work about our lived experiences. Everyone wants to be part of making art about the movement. Even in Shondaland—there was an image included in one of her shows of a protest by Black Lives Matter—Toronto.

In terms of reflecting what is happening, people are moved to write songs about the movement, to create art about it, because what else can we do other than talk about our lives and express our experiences? It feels exciting to be part of a time where Black voices are being recognized and celebrated. It's amazing to be an artist during a time when Black artists are being recognized.

You have all of these great directors creating art that is allowing folks to see themselves in a new way. What is interesting about directors starting to document our realities, I think, is that queer and trans people have had to do that forever to create images of our realities for ourselves. It's an interesting thing to see it happening in a mainstream media type of way. I find it exciting and I feel like it's encouraging. It keeps me going.

SYRUS: I went to this conference about art and activism in the Netherlands in December of 2017. The scholar Susan Cahan was there lecturing from *Mounting Frustration: The Art Museum in the Age of Black Power* and she talked about how, for a lot of mainstream art galleries and museums, theatre houses, performance venues, etc., they really only are interested in showcasing or highlighting the work of Black artists during times of really big social upheaval, around social movements about anti-Blackness.[5] So during the civil rights movement, during the Black Power movement, and now, during this movement for Black lives and this movement of Black Lives Matter, you see a sudden uptake where they're suddenly interested in showcasing our work. But it's a cyclical thing because, of course, it doesn't seem to be translating into actually collecting our work, acquisitioning into the actual collection of the museum, their permanent collection. I just think it's so interesting, her research and what it tells us. I too, I'm so excited about being a part of this movement at this—at this time. I feel like Faith Ringgold or one of the artists during the Harlem Renaissance—Billie Holiday, Zora Neal Hurston, or whomever—part of this magical time.

RAVYN: Yeah. 100 percent. I do, too.

SYRUS: There's just so many artists and so much crossover and interplay and exchange and conversation and dialogue and forum, and it's just so thrilling, it's just so, so exciting. I was part of this Black Futures Month[6] initiative that Black Lives Matter and this network in the States did in February, and they partnered us up with two artists who worked in very different mediums, together, to create a collaborative work. And so I was partnered up with an artist named Funmilola Fagbamila, and she's a rapper and a spoken-word artist. I did a whole bunch of large-scale drawings and she made a video of her rapping. We just collaborated across this distance. That's such an exciting thing to be able to do because there's just so much beautiful amazing Black art that's happening right now. That's really exciting.

RAVYN: I agree! Right now in theatre, there's a wave of really powerful Black female directors and writers being showcased across this city. And that's due to a lot of the work that some folks are doing to find these lesser-known folks, which is awesome. I find the conversations in theatre to be more focused; lots of folks are asking questions about what it means to be a Black artist, what it means to be an artist who is Black. And if those are two different experiences, how are they different? And if they are, what is the difference? I find it fascinating that a lot of people are questioning where they're situated in the movement. The movement of feminism and all that kind of stuff, I feel like it's making theatrical works really, really political in a way that people used to try to avoid. A few years ago people were trying to do things that are more abstract, trying to create more of the dance or fantasy, so to speak. Now we are seeing much more direct, political works: more political, more personal work, things that are thought-provoking and aren't just "nice." They aren't just laid out for the viewer in this pretty presentation, like a Disney movie. Now the work has changed. People are very raw about what they're talking about, like shows about the death penalty or about all the things that Black women have to go through. So it's kind of exciting to see these different perspectives and different voices being expressed. Right now, in Toronto specifically, that's what's happening in theatre. So it feels a time where most—well, more—folks have the space to be recognized, too, which is awesome.

SYRUS: It's amazing. I mean, I guess, how the movement . . . How does the movement use art to mobilize and engage people? Because when I was doing this residency in November in the West Coast, I had the chance to meet Emory Douglas, and he was the revolutionary artist for the Black Panther Party. And that was his official title. He recreated this work, used the art, his art, so intentionally in that movement, to engage communities, particularly poor and working-class communities, to get involved in the fight and to get involved in organizing and to get involved in supporting things in their community. Then he used his art practice to promote the programming of the Panthers: the free clinics, the breakfast programs, the free food programs. By using art and design, he created a branding and an identity for the Panthers that was hard to ignore, right? And I think we're seeing that a lot with the Black Lives Matter movement as well, where there's these movement colours of black and gold and there's just a particular aesthetic, a certain kind of Black activist aesthetic right now.

RAVYN: Yeah. Yeah.

SYRUS: That is very identifiable, I think, in the movement and that can kind of connect arts practices across a huge distance. Like Beyoncé's Formation and the aesthetic that she used in that, and how that references and relates to some more emerging artists up here in the north part of Turtle Island and how their work is speaking to each other, because it's using a similar aesthetic.

RAVYN: Yes. I agree, I agree. Yeah, 100 percent.

Interesting in mentioning Beyoncé and folks. Like I was saying, how doing what we're doing to bring the conversation of Black lives to the forefront in a way that it hasn't been in a long time—or not in display—it's forcing people—even Beyoncé has to change the way that she expresses herself. Even she has infused with something different, in terms of imagery. And all her imagery has been very, very pro-Black-movement. And so I just feel that's the way that we have engaged outside of the direct action movement.

For me, I feel like the way that the movement has engaged me was basically how I joined. I joined through creating a flash mob for one of the rallies that we had for the Take Back the Night collaborations. I had never done any direct action before. I had been to maybe a handful of rallies before in my life. And this was the first time I had involved myself in it, and I was like, I'm just going to do it through the dance avenue, creating this flash mob right in the middle of the street. And then I did it. It was the first time I realized how powerful dance was in this space and how it could lift people, how it could infuse people. So then we had Black—Tent City, art city. It was so powerful an experience. It was so intensely traumatic and violent in so very many ways I felt like I had to go in that space and dance and create a space for people to stretch and for people to move and for people to move the violence out of their bodies and out of their personal space.

And so that was the way that I engaged my talent with the movement in a real way. Not that they're all not real ways, but in a way that I actually saw the shift in people. And so now, when we march down the street, we dance and we chant. We create rhythms that allow us to keep moving and keep excitement and keep people engaged in a way that makes them feel powerful. When you're marching down the street with those, you feel powerful. It's so many things, right? It's scary. But it's also exciting because you're part of something so much larger than yourself while utilizing something that is your art practice. I think it's one of those really powerful gifts, where you understand why you have the gifts you have.

SYRUS: Amazing.

One of the things that I have done a lot of reading about is about art during the Black Power movement and in particular the visual arts, and I often wonder, when historians are looking back at a movement like that, do they get it right? It's really hard to record the actual experience of being there. And so I wonder, two or three generations down the road, thinking back to this moment and the kind of art that's being created in the Black Lives Matter movement right now, what would you want people to know.

What's happening now that you just think is really exciting or really key for our movement right now?

RAVYN: Oh. Wow.

What I want people to know about right now? That's so interesting. 'Cause you're right, it is really particular. I mean, there is really something special about being right in the centre of it. I've never thought about . . . 'cause for me, it feels . . . it's a feeling.

I'm a mover, so articulation is not really as easy. But that's a fascinating question. I don't know. I'm always wanting people to understand who is in the room, everyone who's in the room, from mothers and the fathers and the parents and the kids. And we have generations of folks who are marching with us. Maybe that was always the case, but I don't know if I always knew that. I don't know if I always knew who else, other than who was at the front was there, who else was around, what were the other things that were happening. Like Freedom School, for example, and things like that.

I feel like, right now, that's what I want people to know: that we are fighting for Black lives in this one aspect of what we do. And then we are also creating a space where kids can reimagine their futures and understand Black history and grow into who they are as full beings.

SYRUS: Totally.

RAVYN: That's what I'm excited about. I'm excited about the healing. I don't know if people think of us that way, but I guess that's what it is. If I was to create more art that was specifically dealing with the BLM movement, I want to show more of the healing aspect of what we do: the communities that we've brought together to fight this massive beast of institutional everything, the healing spaces, friendship. The friendship that we have is something that is so unique and beautiful to me. I love each and every one of you and I'm inspired by each of you. Even in this conversation when you were talking about your art, I was like, wow, I just could watch you talk all day. And I could do that with everyone on our team and I'm really excited about that. I'm really excited about people that I work with. I don't even know if we've all reached the potential of what we can do yet. And we've already done so much together.

SYRUS: It's so true. And I wonder so much—you don't know what what's going to happen with the movement, you don't know which direction it's going to take. But I hope that, no matter what happens, that one of the things that gets to remain with it, that people remember about it, is that it was a lot of fun. You know, activism is such a beautiful and life-giving thing, but I think we often think about it as being something that is quite hard and stressful. And it is really hard and it is really stressful, but it is also wonderful. It is also life-giving. Like you just described, right? The ways that you can feel so empowered, walking down the street, in the middle of a demo, just really enlivened by the power of the people. Ain't no power like the power of the people 'cause the power of the people won't stop. That whole thing is really true, right?

RAVYN: It is, it is.

SYRUS: I hope that that's something that people, when they look back . . . Again, thinking about the Black Panthers, so much of what we know about their fight is that there was such an armed struggle. And when you think about the amount of gun fire that plays in the middle of their battles, that's terrifying and it's hard to imagine the fun. But I bet you that their movement was also fun, otherwise why would people . . . ? It was also life giving and joyous and all of that. I just think it's really a beautiful thing, that part of our movement.

RAVYN: Yeah, it is. Part of it is because we're actually seeing the best of humanity within each other. Being able to look over at someone, who was also afraid, who was also trying to protect themselves and their family, but they get up in front of this interviewer and they say what needs to be said.

SYRUS: Yeah.

RAVYN: Really, they step up to the plate, in this really powerful, unique way that makes them almost seem invincible, but because you're part of a team, you see how much work it took for them to get up there and do it. I feel like that's also something that people don't get to witness; people don't get to see what it takes to step into these spaces. I saw pictures of myself during the Pride parade, right?

Out in front, marching down Yonge Street. And I'm still baffled by those photos, because part of it is like, is that me? Would I have ever thought that I would do something quite like that?

SYRUS: Yes. Yes.

RAVYN: It forces you to meet yourself at the scariest of moments, and I think that that is hard and frustrating that it still has to be a thing, but it's so beautiful to me that I get to see you in these really powerful ways. And I'm like, wow, this is also what people are. Because if I was just watching the media, if I was just involved in some messy dynamics in community, then I'd be like, oh well, there's no faith in people. But if I also get this experience of watching all of you and seeing us work together and strategize, and thinking about these creative ways that we make something happen. You creating the cheese and stuff for the action, that was just brilliant to me. I was like, yes, we should be using humour. We should be using these things that we have at our disposal, to illustrate the buffoonery of people.

SYRUS: Yes. It makes me think of this line in that LAL song, in "Brown Eyed Warrior," where she says, "it's not all we've got but they still can't figure that shit out." We actually have so many tools at our disposal to expose the buffoonery of the system. And they can barely figure out half of what we've even shown them. And we've only shown them 1 percent of what we're capable of, and I think that's the magic and beautiful thing you learn through activism: how much the people are capable of.

RAVYN: Yeah, and you see how afraid power is of what we're able to create. Their minds can't even imagine how we'd come up with some of the things that we have. We are many, many steps ahead, which is why they do the hyper-over-surveillance, right? It's such an interesting, powerful space to be in. I say this all the time but I'm just so grateful to be a part of this movement in the direct action kind of way. It's really a unique perspective to have.

I mean, we talked about a bunch of things. I mean, I've always been curious about this, because you have had a longer period of time doing this work, right? We were standing in front of Angela Davis and something went through my mind like, how do you feel? What did it feel like before and what does it feel like now? Is it the same? Has it shifted? What keeps you motivated to continue in the way that you do, because you're able to do it with humour, still having hopes, still having all the things necessary to make something happen. How do you keep that fire brewing? 'Cause I find, even in myself sometimes, I can get a little bit pessimistic. How have you done it for this amount of time and still manage to have an optimism?

SYRUS: Well, I think part of the longevity of being an artist and an activist for as long as I have been is that I have had both outlets to explore these issues. I don't have to rely on just one thing; I can kind of do both. And so both of those are very life-giving practices for me. Being able to have an arts practice that was really political and being able to have an activist life that was very, very creative. It allowed me to have the ability to stay involved in organizing as long as I have, right? And I think when I look back at some of our early days of organizing, I started organizing in the mid-'90s and a lot of the organizing that I was doing was around Black freedom fighters in the States and organizing around prison abolition. We were doing banner drops and we were having large-scale concerts, with so many different artists donating their time to raise money for legal funds for Mumia. We were marching around in circles every Saturday at the US consulate in support of Mumia, so much so that they ended up building up the front of the consulate so that nobody can march in front of it anymore, actually. I remember, before they did that we used to be able to march right in front of the door. I think, at the time, activism really was a very fringe thing. It didn't feel as mainstream as it is now. I think it's much more accepted, and in fact admirable, to be an activist now.

RAVYN: Yeah. Yeah.

SYRUS: And I think it should have always been that way, perhaps. But it wasn't. There was a sense that we were really, really, really on the left, really, really, really seeing the world in a different way than the majority of people. And the majority of people would have thought that any type of direct action was "taking things too far." And, so that feels very different to now where—

RAVYN: Wow.

SYRUS: —there's a lot of mainstream uptake—in fact perhaps, in a way that we should be cautious of—of direction action techniques. That can be co-opting of our message as well, too. But there's just much more of an integration of activism as a good thing, a sensibility within our society, which is really interesting. I mean, unfortunately there are activists, of course, on the right as well. There are right-wing activists.

RAVYN: Yeah.

SYRUS: They are also being very supported, right now, in doing their right-wing activism.

RAVYN: Yeah. 100 percent.

SYRUS: I mean, I think that's a huge difference. It's just the amount of support that there is now. When I say I'm an activist proudly, most people are like, wow, that's really great. Whereas before people would be like, oh . . . .They weren't totally sure about it, right? I think we've learned a lot. We've learned a lot over the years. I mean, I've been organizing for about twenty-five years, and we used to fight for and work so hard to make sure that we avoided arrest as much as possible. We really worked on that and then our politics started to shift as we started to realize that, in fact, being arrested was actually part of this movement—

RAVYN: Right. Yeah. Yeah.

SYRUS: Prisons are political sites: sites where we need activism to be happening. And so why would we be afraid of going into those environments? It's interesting to see how politics have shifted and become more and more progressive. Politics and understanding of gender and trans stuff I think has really shifted. And the way that disability is integrated into so much of our direct action right now is just so exciting. For me, those are big changes.

RAVYN: Okay. Wow, cool. Thanks for sharing that. I have always been so curious about that. Because even the word activist or the title of activist I find myself these days in, is interesting. People ask, hey, you're an activist, right? And I'm like, well y-yes. Yes, yes, I am. It takes me a while to recognize this is what I'm doing, and I think that's because of the way that I've lived my life, right? As a dancer, it's always about the pathways, always about finding the best way to move through a situation. And so I find that's kind of how I live my life.

So I didn't fall into this, but in terms of creating my dance company, for example, that was just based on wanting to have fun. Being in a relationship where we were like, yeah, let's just explore this fun thing called drag. And that became a movement that fought for inclusive dance and accessible dance and dance that reflected people of colour and that would . . . I had no idea that that would lead me all the way to marching with Black Lives Matter in Toronto. That is just a huge . . . yeah.

I never could have imagined that this is where my art practice would lead me. And I'm still doing my art practice. But it's just so interesting that it's completely infused now, whereas before, I was inspired by it. But I find that a lot of what I was inspired by was American activism. You want to be deep, so you create a piece to Nina Simone, that's just what you do.

As opposed to thinking about and finding the artists here in Toronto and Canada. We're also doing really powerful work. And I feel like that's what's also exciting about right now, this beautiful Black renaissance. It's also happening right here in Toronto, in a really tangible way. Where I don't have to look across a border, even though the borders are not all that real.

But I don't have to look everywhere else for inspiration or for challenging opinions or whatever. I'm excited about the environment that's being created right now, here in Toronto, that allows all of this different art to be happening.

SYRUS: Totally. What else do you want to say about art in the movement?

RAVYN: What else do I want to say about art in the movement? I mean, people say art is a reflection of the time, and I feel like a lot of our work does that. But in relationship to Afrofuturism or what we are leading to, are you having thoughts around what you see, what you see this renaissance opening us towards?

SYRUS: Yeah. I think that the beautiful thing about artists' practice is that artists help us to kind of imagine futures that we might not be able to otherwise see, right?

RAVYN: Right.

SYRUS: And so, if we're in the middle of this renaissance where artists are creating all of this work, there is also this renaissance within Black speculative fiction, right? So disciples of Octavia Butler are writing stories that tell us and kind of help us to plan for the next thirty years. We have visual artists who are creating beautiful reflections of both the contemporary moment, and also this

Afrofuturistic possibility. We have scholars and thinkers who are helping us to consider Afrofuturism and Afropessimism and really trying to think through what's coming for Black people and what are our next moments. We have dancers moving and creating pieces that really engage us with this question of futurity.

So I think it's a really exciting time to be alive, it's a really exciting time to be an artist, and it's a really exciting time to be an activist.

RAVYN: Yeah. I agree. I agree. I agree. I'm hoping that it will, I don't know, I feel like there are always waves of things and I hope that what it helps to do—this particular renaissance of Black art—I hope that it helps to establish us as the staples in art. Do you know what I mean?

So we don't necessary go out of style and so that all of what we create isn't co-opted into these white spaces for them to springboard off of what we create. I hope that we, as Black artists, just like you talked about, some folks who are now the children of Octavia Butler's work.

And just like how the next springboards will be Black children and Black youth, who are springboarding off of the work that we create to lift it and to shift it and to change the narratives or whatever it needs to be at that time.

NOTES

1 The MOVE family is a Black revolutionary community dedicated to Black justice, environmental justice, and self-determination of all peoples. Members take the last name Africa, and they follow the teachings of MOVE founder John Africa.

2 Mumia Abu Jamal is a political prisoner who has served more than twenty-five years in prison for the shooting of as police officer, a crime that he did not commit and that someone else confessed to. He was on death row for much of the 1990s and drew large-scale public attention to his case, inspiring countless art projects, campaigns, and international solidarity efforts.

3 Formed in 1998, Blackness Yes! is a community collective that programs Blockorama, the Black queer and trans stage at the Toronto Pride

Festival. They also program Blockobana and other Black queer celebrations throughout the year.

4 Ill Nana Diverse City Dance Company, created by Rayvn Wngz and Sze Yang Lam.

5 Susan Cahan, "Passing the Torch: Genealogies of Arts Activism," lecture presented at the Arts & Activism: Resilience Techniques in Times of Crisis conference, Leiden University and National Museum of Ethnology, The Netherlands, December 15–17, 2017.

6 Black Futures Month is an annual celebration of Black queer and trans artists celebrated by the Black Lives Matter national United States network. Artwork is showcased throughout the month of February through online platforms and social media.

9

RELENTLESS

DR. NAILA KELETA-MAE

this blackness
this realness
this queerness

this rising
        bridge-building
        lying
        tongue-holding

this doing
        making
        spending
        breaking

this loving
        sharing
        releasing
        feeling

this working
    marching
    dreaming
    grieving

this being
    jaw-clenching
    questioning
    truth-telling

this life
this erasure
this hope

so much
demands
so much

and so,
we summon stillness
    enter silence
    hear quiet
    and know freedom.

10

THE AFRONAUTIC RESEARCH LAB

CAMILLE TURNER

Ten thousand years ago our Dogon[1] *ancestors left their beloved home and set off on a journey through the galaxy. Each generation passed on the knowledge that Earth is our mother. From light years away, we heard the desperate cries of those we left behind. We have now returned home on a mission to love and to heal. We stand as a beacon to humanity to recover and reckon with the past in order to gain the strength and wisdom needed to create the future.*

The Afronautic Research Lab is a performance/installation created by Camille Turner in 2016. Citizen researchers are invited into the Afronautic Research Lab to consult archival documents that provide evidence of a past that has been erased. The documents include eighteenth-century Canadian newspapers that advertise enslaved people for sale, amongst other goods and services, blackface minstrel shows in places such as Georgetown, and photos of Ku Klux Klan activities in Calgary, Toronto, and Oakville!

Advertisement by Canadian slave owner offering reward for recapturing person they claimed as property. *Quebec Herald*, December 14, 1789. SOURCE: Library and Archives Canada/OCLC.

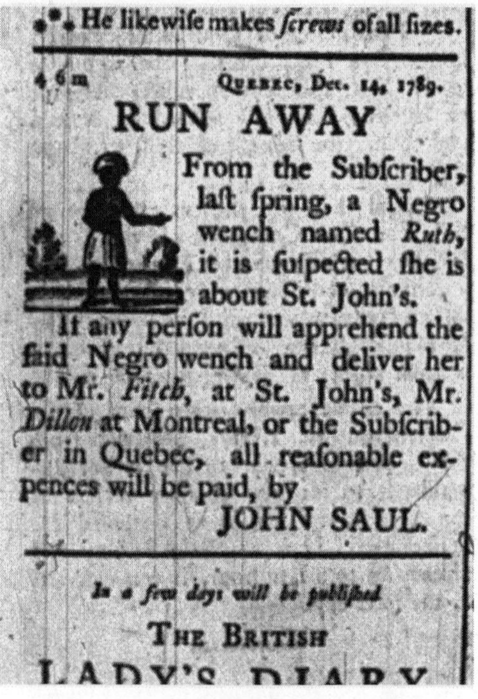

*** He likewiſe makes *ſcrews* of all ſizes.

4 6m QUEBEC, Dec. 14, 1789.

RUN AWAY

From the Subſcriber, laſt ſpring, a Negro wench named *Ruth*, it is ſuſpected ſhe is about St. John's.

If any perſon will apprehend the ſaid Negro wench and deliver her to Mr. *Fitch*, at St. John's, Mr. *Dillon* at Montreal, or the Subſcriber in Quebec, all reaſonable expences will be paid, by

JOHN SAUL.

In a few days will be publiſhed

THE BRITISH

LADY'S DIARY

FIVE DOLLARS REWARD.

RAN away from the Subſcriber on Wedneſday the 25th. of June laſt, a NEGRO MAN ſervant named JOHN, who ever will take up the ſaid negro man and return him to his Maſter ſhall receive the above reward and all neceſſary charges. THOMAS BUTLER.

N. B. All Perſons are forbid harbouring the ſaid Negro man at their peril.—NIAGARA, 3d July, 1793.

Advertisement by Canadian slave owner offering reward for recapturing person they claimed as property. *Upper Canada Gazette*, July 3, 1793. SOURCE: Public domain.

HERALD, Miſcellany & Advertiſer:

NUM. 50.] THURSDAY NOVEMBER 4, 1790. [VOL. I.

50 *Quebec*, Monday *Nov.* 1, 1790.

Concert.

THE unexpected delays which have attended the ſubſcription, and the time required for the preparations in the rooms, render it neceſſary to poſtpone the firſt *Concert* until *Monday* the 15th inſtant.

The ſubſcribers are requeſted to meet at *Free-Maſon's-Hall*, on *Wedneſday* next, the 3d inſtant, at one o'Clock, to chuſe a *Treaſurer* and *Committee* agreeable to the *Rules*.

50 MONTREAL, 20th *Oct.* 1790.

RUN AWAY

From the Subſcriber,

A Negro Man  named Richard,

About five foot ſeven inches high, twenty ſeven years of age, and has a caſt in one eye; had on when he went away, a dark brown jacket and long trowſers; whoever will apprehend and return him to the ſubſcriber ſhall receive two guineas reward and all reaſonable expences paid.

Roſſeter Hoyle.

49 50 QUEBEC, *Oct.* 25, 1790.

FOR SALE,
By WM. CLEIGHORN,
At the *River de Loup*,
A FEW
HEIFERS,
Of the true ENGLISH *Breed*,
AND SOME
YOUNG BULLS,
Of the SAME *breed*.

QUEBEC, *Nov.* 4, 1790.

CASH,
Wanted for

SUBSISTENCE BILLS on ALEX. ADAIR, Eſq. Paymaſter to the Royal Regiment of Artillery, from 3 to 4 thouſand pounds, at thirty days ſight. Propoſals of Exchange to be addreſſed to Major Brady, Captains Marlow, Edwards and Schalch of the Royal Artillery.

50 *Quebec*, Nov. 1, 1790.

Evening School.

THE ſubſcriber propoſes to open his *Evening School*, in the *Biſhop's Palace*, on *Monday* next the 8th inſtant, for the enſuing ſix months, at ſuch hours as will be moſt convenient for thoſe young Gentlemen who wiſh to attend. The Theory and Practice of the *French* and *Engliſh* Languages will be the main object for this winter, as he intends dedicating the next to Mathematical Lectures.

N. B. Nothing but French will be ſpoken by the Gentlemen who are ſtudying that Language and vice verſa.

James Tanſwell.

42t 50m MONTREAL, *Sept* 6, 1790.

FOR SALE BY
James Caldwell,
MADEIRA, *in pipes & Qr. caſks*,
PORT, do.
VIDONIA, do.
FYAL, do.
SIEGES WINE, do.
MADEIRA, *in caſes of* 3 *doz. each*,
PORT, *in* do.
CLARET, *in* do.
LISBON, *in* do.
BOTTLED PORTER,
FRENCH BRANDY,
SHRUB,
BURTON ALE, *pr. doz.&c. &c.*

General Intelligence.

London, *Auguſt* 14 *to September* 2.

PARIS, *Auguſt* 1.

THE FAMILY COMPACT.

Extracted from the Debates of the National Aſſembly of France on Monday laſt.

THE Preſident read a letter from M. Montmorin to the following purport:

" The King commanded me laſt May to lay before the Aſſembly the reaſons which made it neceſſary to order an equipment of 14 ſail of the line, which meaſure the Aſſembly approved. I muſt now lay before them the reaſons which ſeem to make it neceſſary to encreaſe this armament, which is in perfect readineſs,—It is prudent that we ſhould have an equal force with Great Britain, who is haſtening her's with all poſſible activity. The King of Spain has claimed the execution of the Treaty with Great Britain, and his Ambaſſador here claims that of the *Family Compact*. The King therefore has thought proper to bring this demand of the Spaniſh Ambaſſador before the Aſſembly for its deliberation.

" The Aſſembly will have two points to deliberate upon. 1ſt. The augmentation of the armament neceſſary to be made: and 2d. The anſwer given to the Court of Madrid."

Beſides the above letters from M. Montmorin, another from the Count Fernanda Nunez, the Spaniſh Ambaſſador at Paris, to M. de Montmorin, was likewiſe read. It is dated the 7th of June, and after mentioning the negociation going on with England, concludes thus:

" The ſpeedy and exact execution of the Treaty, ſigned at Paris 15th Auguſt 1761, under the title of the Family Compact, becomes now an indiſpenſible preliminary, in order to be able to treat with ſucceſs; and it is on account of the abſolute neceſſity of having recourſe to the aſſiſtance of France, that the King, my

Advertisement by Canadian slave owner offering reward for recapturing person they claimed as property. *Quebec Herald, Miscellany & Advertiser*, November 4, 1790. SOURCE: Library and Archives Canada/OCLC 20177850/ Cover page.

36 Toronto Street—Building where the KKK was first set up in Canada; headquarters for Ontario activities. SOURCE: Alvin Luong.

SECOND SECTION **THE TORONTO DAILY STAR**

TORONTO, FRIDAY, OCTOBER 16, 1925. TWO CENTS

...CE ACCORDED ...SING WELCOME ...ARRIVAL TO-DAY

Family and Thousands Citizens Greet Him at Victoria

...EETS BEDECKED

LARGE BULL RUNS AMOK DEFIES CAPTORS' EFFORTS

PUP CHARGES HUGE BULL ATTACKING MASTER

Knocks Stock Yards Employe Into Air—Charges Golf Club Official—Almost Knocks Automobile Off Road in Ferocious Attack—Dog Sinks Teeth in His Hind Legs

POLICE, WITH RIFLES, GO ON THE WARPATH

MASSEY DECLARES HIGH PROTECTION STRAIGHT-JACKET

Would Delay Recovery of the Dominion Were It to Be Enforced

NOT A FREE TRADER

Received Rousing Reception at Garden Hill—Sentiment Swinging His Way

KU KLUX KLAN OF KANADA HOLDS RALLY NEAR LONDON, ONT. FOR INITIATIONS

HOME SECRE... REMARKS M... CALLED CON...

Asks Audience to Re... Notorious Comm... Are Arrested

MAY MAKE TR...

WOMEN'S COURT

CAME BACK TO CITY DESPITE COURT ORDER

One Year for Helen Gray—Court Order No Joke Says Magistrate

HUSBAND LOSES CASE

Charged Mother-in-Law With Theft, Following Difference With Wife

NOT GUILTY OF MURDER EAGAN FAINTS IN COURT

Justice Meredith Discharged Man With Warning That New Charge Is Possible

HITCH A RUDE SHOCK TO GERMAN PEOPLE

Awake to Find Negotiations Back at Beginning on Important Points

NAME OF ESIOFF ENIGMA EVEN TO MR. PATENAUDE

Is Most Uncommon Cognomen But Has Been in Family for Years

LOW-FLYING AIRPLANES DEMORALIZING CHICKENS AND STOP EGG-LAYING

BISHOP ISSUES WA...

ISN'T IT THE TR...

TEACHER AT HUMBERSIDE LEAVES $26,227 ESTATE

FOUND DEAD IN BED

SUBMARINE SIDESWIPED

KKK in London, Ontario. *The Toronto Daily Star*, October 16, 1925. SOURCE: Torstar Syndication Services.

J. J. MALONEY
IMPERIAL WIZARD

J. E. McINNES
IMPERIAL KLABEE

HAROLD WRIGHT
IMPERIAL KLIGRAPP AND KLEAGLE

503

P. O. Box 152
EDMONTON, ALBERTA.

July 16, 1932.

Mayor and Commissioners,
City of Edmonton.

Gentlemen:

The Ku Klux Klan will hold a convention in the City of Edmonton, August 6 - 8 inclusive, and as part of proceedings will hold a demonstration on August 8, at which among other features of the program, an open air initiation will be held, during the course of which a fiery cross will be burned.

As admission fee is to be charged, it has occured to us that the Exhibition grounds, on account of being fully enclosed, would be a desirable place to hold this demonstration. As we understand the grounds are not being used for other purposes on this date we would be glad to know if we could arrange to hold the demonstration there.

An immediate reply would be greatly appreciated.

Yours very truly,

Harold Wright

HAROLD WRIGHT.
Imperial Kligrapp and Kleagle.

HW/GH

Knights of the Ku Klux Klan, Alberta Convention, Notice to City of Edmonton Mayor and Commissioners, July 16, 1932. SOURCE: City of Edmonton Archives, RG-11 7-2 76, Box 6, File 76.

503

COPY FOR THE INFORMATION OF:-

CITY ENGINEER HADDOW.

FIRE CHIEF DUTTON.

CHIEF OF POLICE SHUTE.

JULY 26th, 1932.

Harold Wright, Esq.,
P.O. Box 152,
EDMONTON.

Dear Sir:-

This will certify that the Commissioners have granted the Ku Klux Klan the use of the Grandstand and Race Track enclosure at the Exhibition Grounds on August 8th for demonstration purposes. This permit is granted on the understanding that no smoking will be allowed on the Grandstand also that Fire Marshals will be allowed to be present to safeguard the property and that the grounds will be cleaned up after you are through with them at your expense or that the City be remunerated for the expense of doing so. It is understood that if the fiery cross is burned, it will be in the centre enclosure at sufficient distance from the buildings that they will not be endangered by fire.

Hoping that this is satisfactory to you, I am,

Yours truly,

DANIEL K. KNOTT.
..........MAYOR.

Letter from City of Edmonton Mayor to Knights of the Ku Klux Klan, July 16, 1932. Source: City of Edmonton Archives, RG-11 7-2 76, Box 6, File 76.

THE GEORGETOWN HERALD
Thursday, May 23, 1963
PAGE 9

MINSTREL SHOW FRIDAY

—Peter Jones Photo

PIPING UP SOME INTEREST

GEORGETOWN GIRLS' PIPE BAND piper Marilyn Mackenzie serves as a pretty "attention compeller" for one of the posters plugging the Minstrel Show.

Slight Tax Rise In Chinguacousy

LEGION NOTES

by Don. N. Platt

A New Member

Cribbage

Victoria Day

No Boom, But Industry Eyeing Georgetown Lately

Though it's hardly in the Brampton category as far as industrial growth is concerned, Georgetown is at least being looked at by potential industry.

William Henry Mitchell Native of New Zealand

Manitoulin Lady Leaves Two Grandchildren Here

Arnold Rathbun
Representative
Sun Life of Canada
GEORGETOWN
13 Gower Court

MILTON KINSMEN – LEGION
BINGO
Starts May 29th and continues every Wednesday evening at 8 p.m. sharp, at
MILTON ARENA
$1,000 IN PRIZES EACH WEEK
26 GAMES - - - 3 at $100 — 5 at $50 — 18 at $25
$3 Admission includes 13 cards covering all games
FREE BUSSES will be available, details next week

WATCH FOR –
WAIT FOR –
GRAND OPENING
– OF –
CONGDON'S
SHOE STORE
WITH A COMPLETE
LINE OF
FAMILY SHOES
SOON!
21 MAIN STREET SOUTH

CONCRETE GRAVEL
BUILDING SAND
ROAD GRAVEL
FILL and TOP SOIL
STONE WORK
TOM HAINES
Glen Williams - TR. 7-3323

YOUR
GARDEN
HEADQUARTERS
LARGE SELECTION OF
EVERGREENS — at $2.00 to $5.00
SOIL CONDITIONERS AND FERTILIZERS
GOOD STOCK OF EXCELLENT QUALITY
PETUNIAS – ZINNIAS – ASTERS
SNAPDRAGONS
SWEET SCENTED STOCKS
SPECIAL!
POTTED ROSES
$1.19
PRICED TO CLEAR!
Lawn Chairs $4.98
Chaise Lounge 6 ONLY $9.98
WYNFIELD
GARDEN CENTRE
160 Guelph St. at the IGA Store 877-4663

WE NEED
USED CARS
NOW YOU CAN PURCHASE
A NEW 1963 RAMBLER
FOR AS LOW AS
$2295
YOUR CAR IS NOW WORTH
DOLLARS MORE ON A
NEW 1963 RAMBLER
H.E. "CHIC" SIMPSON MOTORS LTD.
310 QUEEN ST. E.
277-9597 451-2490

RIGHT: Advertisement for minstrel show. *Georgetown Herald*, May 23, 1963.
SOURCE: Indexed from Halton Hills Public Library.

As visitors enter the lab they are handed a magnifying glass and flashlight to examine the evidence in the darkened room as a looped computer voice recounts stories of the past that resonate in the present. Pencils and notepads are provided for those who wish to leave messages for the Afronauts.

Afronautic Research Lab: Arts Against PostRacialism performance at Agnes Etherington Art Centre, October 25, 2017. PHOTO: Garrett Elliott.

Afronautic Research Lab: Arts Against PostRacialism performance at Agnes Etherington Art Centre, October 25, 2017. PHOTO: Garrett Elliott.

Afronautic Research Lab: Arts Against PostRacialism performance at Agnes Etherington Art Centre, October 25, 2017. PHOTO: Garrett Elliot.

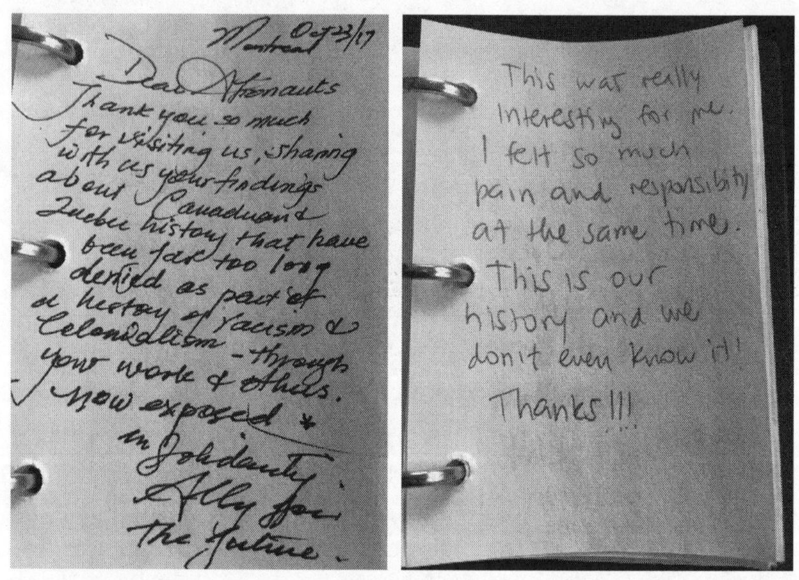

Montreal Oct 23/17
Dear Afronauts
Thank you so much
for visiting us, sharing
with us your findings
about Canadian &
Quebec history that have
been far too long
denied as part of
a history of racism &
Colonialism - through
your work & others.
Now exposed *
in Solidarity,
Ally for
The Future.

This was really
interesting for me.
I felt so much
pain and responsibility
at the same time.
This is our
history and we
don't even know it!
Thanks!!!

Notes left for the Afronauts. PHOTOS: Camille Turner

These photographs document a performance of the Afronautic Research Lab that was part of a Social Science and Humanities Research Council–funded project entitled Arts Against PostRacialism (AAPR) led by Dr. Philip Howard of McGill University. AAPR sought to challenge contemporary Canadian blackface and the ways in which it fosters a climate of anti-Blackness, particularly on Canadian university campuses. The Afronautic Research Lab at AAPR featured the obscured history of blackface minstrelsy in Canada, its relationship to Canadian slavery, and its afterlife in contemporary blackface incidents in Canada. AAPR included an exhibition of the works of artists Anique Jordan, Esmaa Mahamoud, Nadine Valcin, Quentin Vercetty, and myself, as well as a keynote lecture by Dr. Howard.

NOTES

1 The Dogon people of Northern Mali are heirs to knowledge of star systems that predate Western science. Their stories reference Sirius B, a companion star to Sirius that cannot be seen with the naked eye and was not observable by Western scientists until 1862. According to Dogon stories the Nommos people of Sirius came to Earth to give them this knowledge. Since the Nommos could travel through space and the Dogon have inherited their knowledge, I was inspired to think about the Dogon as space travelers. In my story they left the Earth 10,000 years ago and have traveled through the galaxy acquiring great knowledge. Each generation is born knowing that Earth is their sacred home. They have returned in order to heal the Earth.

11

CHOREOGRAPHIC DESIGN AND PERFORMING BLACK ACTIVISM

RODNEY DIVERLUS

Parts of this chapter are reprinted with permission from University of Toronto Press (https://utpjournals.press), and its original publication in the Canadian Theatre Review, *DOI: 10.3138/ctr.176.011.*

25 November 2014: the night is frigid and brisk. The air is moistened by bouts of snow and freezing rain—and, for a brief moment, hail. Within hours, the full spectrum of Canada's hostile climate is felt. Huddled in a courtyard across from the United States consulate, 3,000 Black Torontonians and their allies repeat, in choral-like unison, again and again: "Black Lives Matter," a provocation uttered en masse for the first time in Toronto. This is the beginning of a renaissance of radical Black activism in Canada, the beginning of Black Lives Matter—Toronto, which became, among many things, an artivist collective who collaborate on the creation, curation, and development of large-scale public performative direct actions and installations.

In that inceptive moment, Black Torontonians were full of rage. The night prior, a grand jury delivered a no-indictment decision for Darren Wilson, a police officer in Ferguson, Missouri, who shot and killed eighteen-year-old Mike Brown. Although Brown was unarmed, he was shot twelve times—while his hands were in the air, a universally understood gesture of surrender. Around the same time a Brampton, Ontario, man named Jermaine Carby was killed by a Peel Regional Police officer during a routine traffic stop. His death, resulting from a series of escalations, began with carding, the widely rebuked and racist police practice of random searches, interrogations, and data collection. As with Brown, Carby's family were left with no answers and a system more invested in establishing the cause of his death resulting from his own actions, rather than systemic anti-Black racism.

Stemming from these injustices, our collective rage brought us together—into the street. Voices hoarse, our bodies quiver. The crowd is at times roaring and at times hushed, transfixed by the speakers rotating to the microphone. Thousands shuffle into new formations, confined by the borders of the courtyard, our performance space for the evening. At the end of each speech, a new round of chanting begins: "*Black lives matter,*" "*No justice, no peace,*" and "*Let us live*" in rotation. One voice starts, then hundreds join. When one chant peters out, another set of voices begins a new provocation. The crowd is so large that multiple chants can be uttered simultaneously. The microphone amplifies an impassioned plea for solidarity, and with little prompting, fists raise into the air. Infectiously one fist turns to thousands, raised tall in reference to the Black Power salute. As these hands go down, other pairs spring up—above heads, palms exposed—while protestors scream "Hands up! Don't shoot!" a visual memory of Mike Brown's final moments. The crowd alternates between the two arm gestures, sporadically but persistently—sometimes in unison, but often in canon.

This dance of bodies loops itself throughout the evening. This people-driven performance is not meant for concert, nor for an audience's gaze. It is not meant for consumption, nor entertainment. This show of resistance is an act of political choreography fundamental to the Black communities relegated to surviving in a settler-colonial and deeply anti-Black society. Its choreographers were an ad hoc group of Black organizers who would go on to co-form Black Lives Matter—Toronto (BLM—TO), the first iteration of the Black Lives Matter movement external to the United States. The evening's emcee functioned as dance captain. The performers were the thousands of people whose desperate quest for justice engaged them in hours of ensemble improvisation, of follow and repeat. This action was a living piece of political choreography, deliberately curated to awaken a battered community and to confront the pervasive anti-Blackness in Canadian society.

In five years, BLM—TO has mobilized tens of thousands of Black people and allies in cities across Canada. Each event is carefully planned, with room for set actions and improvisation. Blockades, occupations, marches, die-ins, and surprise actions are choreographic tactics in our arsenal. These performative protests employ disruption and interrogation as strategy. For us, business cannot continue as usual as long as anti-Blackness is allowed to thrive.

Grounded in the historical and ancestral significance of Black-led politicization, our work recognizes all that is at stake when Black people converge. We recognize physical interventions as vital to Black-led resistance and that our work builds on a lineage of successful and powerful choreographies of Black political assembly. Dance scholar Anusha Kedhar speaks to its importance: "Movement matters. Bodies matter—particularly when people are protesting the black body's disposability at the hands of the state. Choreography, movement and gesture are not peripheral but central to the politics of protest."[1]

From the Haitian slave revolts to the Underground Railroad, from the diner sit-ins in Greensboro, North Carolina, to the schoolyards of Soweto, South Africa, Black communities have repeatedly enacted well-coordinated mass convergence as a tactic for resisting the state apparatus. We recognize that any power we now hold was not gifted to us; instead, said power was fought for tirelessly and unapologetically—by pushing our communities to reimagine the collective presence of Black bodies as powerful, and by using that power to deliberately disrupt otherwise white spaces.

In this chapter I will interrogate the racial politics of assembly and public performance as it relates to Black liberation struggles historically and in a post-Trayvon Martin present.[2] Using Black Lives Matter—Toronto as a case study, I will assess the impacts of the recent global rebirth of radical Black-led mobilizations and the choreographic and performative elements that contributed to our success. Finally, I will contextualize Black-centric and Black-led community organizing's vital role in efforts to eradicate and dismantle colonialism.

BLACK OCCUPATION OF SPACE, HISTORICALLY

Black communities are continually asked to reimagine how our bodies occupy space and how we relate to and within space. Systemic anti-Black racism does not allow us an alternative, for anti-Blackness relies on the control, ownership, and manipulation of Black people, our relation to land, and the spaces in which we exist.

I use "Black" as an evolving sociopolitical umbrella to describe people and communities of African descent. This term is inclusive of present-day Africans born on the continent itself; descendants of enslaved Africans peppered throughout the diaspora; and, as a result of five centuries of anti-Black colonial projects, Black migrants who have cultivated communities in jurisdictions across the globe—including those who continue to risk their lives crossing the Caribbean and Mediterranean Seas and other vast waters in search of freedom. Within this narrative of Blackness is a shared political identity: a political home that acknowledges our shared history and struggle and one that supersedes real or perceived ethnic differences. This particular analysis excludes communities who are not of African ancestry but identify with Blackness: for example, Aboriginal, Torres Strait Islander, and South Sea Islander peoples in Australia, and the Semang and Bateks peoples in Malaysia. The exclusion of these peoples is not an act of erasure, but rather a deliberate omission that recognizes the distinct experiences and realities from which these communities organize and the differing contexts from which we draw our histories and contemporary issues.

In Canada, Black bodies have had to define the ways in which we occupied space, out of necessity. As early as the seventeenth century, enslaved Africans were traded throughout the Americas, including the northern half of Turtle Island, or present-day Canada. As forced settlers to this land, Black individuals were subjected to centuries of violence and dehumanization. Following the era of enslavement, descendants of these captives converged to create various communities across this vast geography—consider Africville (Nova Scotia), Wilberforce Colony (Ontario), and Amber Valley (Alberta).

More than a century of overtly racist anti-Black Canadian immigration policies followed the emergence of these communities.[3] These draconian practices heavily restricted—and for the most part prevented—the movement and migration of Black people from the United States, the Caribbean, and Africa into Canada. At the time, these laws contributed to the construction of a Canadian identity devoid of Blackness. In reference to 1898 government correspondence from Ottawa, policy analyst Rachel Décoste notes the attempts of immigration officials to restrict Black migration: "In US cities where there were no Canadian immigration agents present to discriminate openly, civil servants would write to the local (presumably white) American postmaster and ask whether the applicant was Black. Those few Blacks in Canada had apparently got to here either by persistence or through accident."[4] In addition, in 1911 an order-in-council was approved by Prime Minister Sir Wilfrid Laurier's cabinet that prohibited the migration of "any immigrant belonging to the Negro race, which race is deemed unsuitable to the climate and requirements of Canada."[5] The newly formed state of Canada was clear that Black people were not welcomed and that there would be an active suppression of Black presence in these lands.

These were deliberate attempts by the state to keep Black folk from converging en masse. It was not until 1962 that the federal government introduced immigration reforms.[6] Black migrants, most of whom were descendants of the North Atlantic slave trade, were now permitted to join the already existing—but sporadic—pockets of Black communities in Canada. The regulatory changes brought subsequent waves of Black migration into Canada: in the 1960s Jamaican women labourers were sought through the West Indian Domestic Scheme; in the 1970s Haitian political refugees arrived, escaping the Duvalier regime; and in the late 1980s and 1990s, Somali families displaced by civil war arrived. This racist and anti-Black history lays the foundation from which our present-day institutions, norms, practices, and policies emerge. However, Black people in Canada continue to have a relatively small population and an even smaller claim to the country's resources and wealth.

For generations, the state's control of our bodies dictated where we lived, how we moved, and where we went. Therefore, we became accustomed to moving en masse. Whether we were shackled in formation at the bottom of slave ships or huddled together as "boat people" crossing tumultuous seas, working collectively has been an integral strategy for survival. The communities we have built are concentrated and close. We see this in the concentrations of Black populations today. Of the 1,200,000 Black people in Canada, more than half (630,000) live in one province: Ontario;[7] and of those, two thirds (400,000) live in the Greater Toronto Area.[8] Black folks have historically lacked the resources, economic freedom, or desire to scatter. It has always been in our shared interest to move in tandem with each other. Left with little, our communities have always drawn power from a shared interdependence—from sharing power.

Our resistance against those who hold power amassed from our subjugation relies on the assembly of our bodies. From the multi-kilometre-long civil rights marches to staged sit-ins, our response to systemic and state-sanctioned oppression has always been to gather our communities and show collective force, a lineage embraced by BLM—TO.

BLACK-CENTRIC POLITICHOREOGRAPHY

Where there are Black people, there is Black resistance.

Faced with the choice of living with the abhorrent anti-Black conditions or fighting for freedom, Black communities have consistently chosen the latter. A central tenet of our resistance is physical intervention. Political scientist Gene Sharp identifies twelve forms of physical intervention essential to protest culture, including sit-ins, walk-ins, pray-ins, and occupations.[9] These tactics were commonly used in past Black liberation movements and they continue to be important to present-day Black Lives Matter movements.[10] Black resistance leverages the power of mass movement; consider the collective displays of brute force that characterized the Haitian revolution, or the collective marching up and down streets, alleyways, and thoroughfares in the Ferguson uprisings.[11]

Black-centric direct action is deliberate about its use of space and intentional about the movement of Black people in that space. In co-creating BLM—TO I believed it was crucial to follow the legacy of Black resistance; for our work to follow a pulse, a rhythm. In our work, music, poetry, rapping, and spoken word are supported by unison gestures: a waving of limbs, stomping to a beat, marching in sync. These actions are artistic and choreographic, but they are also more than that. I identify these as acts of *politichoreography*. Stomping, marching, raising fists: these movement vocabularies are carefully selected, curated even, to agitate and harness the protestor's rage. These choreographed movement elements, like a raised fist, are crucial in determining the tone of the protest itself. Similar to much choreography for the stage, politichoreography strikes a balance between the planned and the improvised.

Black-centric politichoreography is a show of Black power. Dance scholar Susan Foster attends to the physical dimension of protest:

> The process of creating political interference calls forth a perceptive and responsive physicality that, everywhere along the way, deciphers the social and then choreographs an imagined alternative. As they fathom injustice, organize to protest, craft a tactics, and engage in action, these bodies read what is happening and articulate their imaginative rebuttal.[12]

Moreover, Black-centric politichoreography uses expertly curated movements as tactics. Consider the Black Panther Party, a militant group of Black freedom fighters who shook the world with their tightly controlled show of collective force. A mass movement that pushed toward a new politics of Black power, the Black Panthers were deliberate and meticulous with their use of uniformity. Bobby Seale, co-founder of the party, observes that "strategy, in many ways, defined the Black Panther Party, as did discipline."[13] They choreographed their look, vibe, and pace, marching to a pulse in unison and en masse with exacting precision. Today, when Black protestors form a shoulder-to-shoulder barricade opposite riot cops, it is both a physical tactic to maintain control of the space and avoid separation or police kettling, and also a symbolic reclamation of power and a mimicry of police protocol. This power is exuded by the resulting image that the formations create: images that depict Black people standing together with dignity—Black people manifesting their power.

MOVEMENT VOCABULARY

From these displays of Black power emerge distinct sets of Black protest movement vocabularies. These are collectively determined movements that have become visual markers of Black-led resistance—the fist in the air comes to mind as a prime example. BLM—TO uses a broad range of these gestures of resistance and choreographic tactics to strengthen our rallies. These recognizable physical acts expose the conflicting nature of politichoreography: these gestures function both as narrative symbols and as rallying points for an impassioned crowd. For example, our die-in at Yonge and Dundas, Canada's busiest intersection, was a metaphor for those who have been killed by anti-Black violence, but also represented the forced submission of living Black people. The prone bodies remind us of the ways state-sanctioned violence keeps us down. And yet, the die-in also functions as resistance, as strength.

In response to the murder of Mike Brown, who was killed with his hands in the air, BLM protestors used a physical expression of "Hands up! Don't shoot!" as the core movement vocabulary at the Ferguson uprisings. This simple gesture became the unifier for the hundreds of BLM solidarity events that took place globally. Analyzing the protests, Anusha Kedhar insists, "the gesture reminds us that Michael Brown was shot while he was kneeling, with his head down and his arms up. It reminds us that the police violated the code not to shoot when a person's hands are up. It reminds us that the black body is never presumed innocent moving in white spaces. That space itself is white."[14] This gesture exposes the injustice of police violence against Black bodies: we are killed even in acts of surrender. Further, the gesture refigures surrender as resistance: "The bodily act of the hands-up-don't-shoot protest takes those same bodies that are surveilled, disciplined, controlled, and killed and infuses them with power and a voice. It resurrects those dead bodies left lying in the street, and asks us, *compels* us to confront the aliveness of the black body as a force of power and resistance."[15] These movement vocabularies—embodied acts of resistance—connect protestors as an ensemble akin to that of a company of dancers. The chant leader signals the count-in—"five-six-seven-eight" replaced with "what-do-we-want?"

BLACK LIVES MATTER—TORONTO

BLM—TO's core organizers recognize that at the centre of Black liberation movements is a leveraging of politichoreography and a Black reoccupation of public space. Our most notable actions used ancestral tactics to reshape public discourse on Blackness and Black resistance. Our 2016 Pride parade blockade was meticulously choreographed, with the organizers acting as co-choreographers, chant leaders as dance captains, seventy-five Black queer and trans community members as performers, and the 200,000-person crowd as audience. Our 2017 Pride action took a different tone: here, we staged a silent piece, with solemn mourners weaving in and out of formation, and unison gestural movements. Both installations integrated sound, movement, smoke, and design. BLM–TO Tent City, a two-week occupation in front of Toronto Police Service Headquarters, was a durational combination of actions, speeches, and twenty-four-hour programming. When we shut down the Allen Road expressway, it was through the creation of three units of people moving as one: roadblockers, navigators, and protestors, each with their own sets of movements and tasks.

We choreograph our actions in response to the meticulous organization of our opposition. Our work recognizes that a direct threat to Black-centric politichoreography is what dance scholar André Lepecki calls "choreopolicing," wherein "more or less persistently, more or less violently, the police appear wherever political protest is set in motion, to break down initiative and to determine 'proper' pathways for protesters."[16] This is achieved by imposing blockades, dispersing crowds, and dragging bodies. The purpose of choreopolicing, Lepecki argues, is "to de-mobilize political action by means of implementing a certain kind of movement that prevents any formation and expression of the political."[17] All too often, peaceful Black protests are met with a tightly choreographed, well-rehearsed police force. With increasingly militarized weapons, police contain, kettle, rush, mandate movement (demanding permits and pre-routes from organizers), and restrict access to space.

BLM—TO resists this choreopolicing by anticipating, diverting, and often outwitting our opposition. We recognize there are real political implications to the assemblage of Black people en masse. By choreographing our communities, we show force and remind our political leaders that Black folks will mobilize. We will move our whole selves to disrupt anti-Blackness, whether by showing up in civic meetings or downtown intersections, along highways or parade routes, at police headquarters or at the home of the premier.

Ultimately BLM—TO recognizes the ability of mass convergences of Black people to destabilize white Canadian liberalism. Our actions enact continued resistance to a societal apparatus designed to dictate how we assemble. They are deliberate choreographic projects that incorporate visual, rhythmic, and tactical Black-centricity to challenge the belief that Black folks taking to the streets are unruly and lawless, and to remind people of our humanity—and our collective history of well-coordinated mass resistance. Through our work we pose the question: *whose streets?* With our movement we challenge not only the ownership of public space, but also the control of those same sites. By asserting our right to justice we recognize that when Black people come together, we must be bold, unapologetic, and militant.

BLM—TO's work challenges non-Black and Black people alike to grapple with the claim that Black people coming together affirms: Black lives, they matter here.

NOTES

1 Anusha Kedhar, "Choreography and Gesture Play an Important Role in Protests," *The New York Times*, 15 December 2014, www.nytimes.com/roomfordebate/2014/12/15/what-does-the-style-of-a-protest-say-about-a-movement/choreography-and-gesture-play-an-important-role-in-protests.

2 On the impacts of Trayvon Martin's death on Black resistance movements today, see Trymane Lee's "Analysis: Trayvon Martin's Death Still Fuels a Movement Five Years Later," NBC News, 26 February 2017, www.nbcnews.com/news/nbcblk/analysis-trayvon-martin-s-death-still-fuels-movement-five-years-n725646.

3 Janet Dench, "A Hundred Years of Immigration to Canada 1900–1949," The Canadian Council for Refugees, May 2000, ccrweb.ca/en/hundred-years-immigration-canada-1900–1999; Bee Quammie, "The Black Women Who Helped Build Canada," The Establishment, January 18, 2016, http://www.theestablishment.co/the-black-women-who-helped-build-canada-ed8e08e2dfde; Lindsay Van Dyk, "Immigration Act, 1910," Canadian Museum of Immigration at Pier 21, 2017, http://www.pier21.ca/research/immigration-history/immigration-act-1910; Heritage Community Foundation, "Black Settlers come to Alberta," Canada's Digital Collections, March 19, 2001, http://www.collectionscanada.gc.ca/eppp-archive/100/200/301/ic/can_digital_collections/pasttopresent/opportunity/black_settlers.html.

4 Rachel Décoste, "The Racist Truth About Canadian Immigration," Huffington Post Blog, July 2, 2014, http://www.huffingtonpost.ca/rachel-decoste/canada-immigration_b_4747612.html.

5 Eli Yarchi, "Order-in-Council P.C. 1911-1324: The Proposed Ban on Black Immigration to Canada," *The Canadian Encyclopedia*, http://www.thecanadianencyclopedia.ca/en/article/order-in-council-pc-1911-1324-the-proposed-ban-on-black-immigration-to-canada/.

6 Dench, "A Hundred Years of Immigration"; Van Dyk, "Immigration Act, 1910."

7 "Census Profile, 2016 Census." Statistics Canada, March 20, 2018, www12.statcan.gc.ca/census-recensement/2016/dp-pd/prof/details/page.cfm?Lang=E&Geo1=PR&Code1=01&Geo2=PR&Code2=01&Data=Count&SearchText=Canada&SearchType=Begins&SearchPR=01&B1=Visible%20minority&TABID=1.

8 Environics Institute for Survey Research, "The Black Experience Project in the GTA: Executive Summary," The Black Experience Project, July 31, 2017, https://www.theblackexperienceproject.ca/wp-content/uploads/2017/07/Black-Experience-Project-GTA-OVERVIEW-REPORT-4.pdf.

9 Susan Leigh Foster, "Choreographies of Protest," *Theatre Journal* 55, no. 3 (2003): 395–412, https://doi.org/10.1353/tj.2003.0111. For more on the twelve variants of 'physical intervention,' see Gene Sharp's *The Politics of Nonviolent Action: Power and Struggle* (Boston: Porter Sargent Publishers, 1973).

10 Malcolm Harris, "Tactical Lessons from the Civil Rights Movement," *Pacific Standard*, March 9, 2017, psmag.com/news/tactical-lessons-from-the-civil-rights-movement; Nicolas D. Mirzoeff, "#BlackLivesMatter is Breathing New Life into the Die-In." *The New Republic,* August 10, 2015, newrepublic.com/article/122513/blacklivesmatter-breathing-new-life-die.

11 Laurent Dubois, "Avenging America: The Politics of Violence in the Haitian Revolution," in *The World of the Haitian Revolution*, David Patrick Geggus and Norman Fiering, eds. (Bloomington: Indiana University Press, 2009), 11–25. For more on the Ferguson uprisings, see Moni Basu et al.'s "Fires, Chaos Erupt in Ferguson after grand jury doesn't indict in Michael Brown case," CNN, November 25, 2014, http://www.cnn.com/2014/11/24/justice/ferguson-grand-jury/index.html.

12 For more, see Foster, "Choreographies of Protest," 412.

13 Christopher Norris, "He Co-Founded the Black Panther Party and Made Discipline a Pillar," The Good Men Project, March 29, 2016, http://www.goodmenproject.com/featured-content/he-co-founded-the-black-panther-party-and-made-discipline-a-pillar-cnorris/.

14 Kedhar, Anusha, "'Hands Up! Don't Shoot!' Gesture, Choreography and Protest in Ferguson," *The Feminist Wire*, October 6, 2014. https://thefeministwire.com/2014/10/protest-in-ferguson/.

15 Kedhar, "'Hands Up! Don't Shoot!'"
16 André Lepecki, "Choreopolice and Choreopolitics, or the Task of the Dancer," *Drama Review* 57, no. 4 (2013): 16, https://doi.org/10.1162/DRAM_a_00300.
17 Ibid., 20.

REFERENCES

Dubois, Laurent. "Avenging America: The Politics of Violence in the Haitian Revolution." In *The World of the Haitian Revolution*, edited by David Patrick Geggus and Norman Fiering, 111–25. Bloomington: Indiana University Press, 2009.

Environics Institute for Survey Research. "The Black Experience Project in the GTA: Executive Summary." The Black Experience Project, July 31, 2017, https://www.theblackexperienceproject.ca/wp-content/uploads/2017/04/Black-Experience-Project-GTA-OVERVIEW-REPORT-4.pdf.

Foster, Susan Leigh. "Choreographies of Protest." *Theatre Journal* 55, no. 3 (2003): 395–412. https://doi.org/10.1353/tj.2003.0111.

Harris, Malcolm. "Tactical Lessons from the Civil Rights Movement." *Pacific Standard*, March 9, 2017, psmag.com/news/tactical-lessons-from-the-civil-rights-movement.

Kedhar, Anusha. "Choreography and Gesture Play an Important Role in Protests." *The New York Times*, 15 December 2014. www.nytimes.com/roomfordebate/2014/12/15/what-does-the-style-of-a-protest-say-about-a-movement/choreography-and-gesture-play-an-important-role-in-protests.

———. "'Hands Up! Don't Shoot!' Gesture, Choreography and Protest in Ferguson." *The Feminist Wire*, October 6, 2014. https://thefeministwire.com/2014/10/protest-in-ferguson/.

Lepecki, Andre. "Choreopolice and Choreopolitics, or the Task of the Dancer." *Drama Review* 57, no. 4 (2013): 13–27. https://doi.org/10.1162/DRAM_a_00300.

Mirzoeff, Nicolas D. "#BlackLivesMatter is Breathing New Life into the Die-In." *The New Republic*, August 10, 2015. newrepublic.com/article/122513/blacklivesmatter-breathing-new-life-die.

Shakur, Assata. *Assata: An Autobiography.* Chicago: Lawrence Hill Books, 1999.

Sharp, Gene. *The Politics of Nonviolent Action: Power and Struggle.* Boston: Porter Sargent Publishers, 1973.

PART IV

THEORIZING BLACKNESS: CONSIDERATIONS THROUGH TIME AND SPACE

12

THE NEED TO ROOT DISABILITY JUSTICE INTO MOVEMENTS

SARAH JAMA

As a child I was convinced that I was struggling to maintain my sanity.

My teachers varied significantly in their treatment of me, either treating me like a savant or like someone with zero ability to learn independently. At one point educators enrolled me into a class for children with autism, unsure of my ability to perform in mainstream classes. As I got older, people mistook my friends for helpers. I was seen as too angry when I spoke my mind and too disabled and without agency when I didn't. It meant being fetishized for my Blackness and desexualized because of my disability. It meant never fitting into the Black communities around me; it meant being too visibly disabled, which made aunties and uncles uncomfortable. It meant never fitting into the disability communities around me because my Blackness made it harder for the white disabled people around me to ignore their role in the project of white supremacy. To some, being disabled meant the erasure of all privilege, full stop. Being Black and disabled meant going through the medical system believing, for years, that my tolerance for pain was higher than average, a sort of superpower, instead of what it really was: a tolerance for pain built through years of doctors denying my reality of living with cerebral palsy. It meant doctors attempting to convince me to redo surgeries for aesthetic purposes, enduring months of rehabilitation. While eating in public I have been prayed for by strangers, and by my age-mates on school grounds.

For a long time I believed I was struggling to stay rooted in reality because the ways people had chosen to interact with me varied so much that I would have to engage in a twisted game of role playing in order to get through the day. If I fell down in front of an able-bodied white man, as I often did while learning to balance my movements as my height changed, I learned it was easier to let them try to help me than to get up on my own—not because I needed it, but because to try and deny this help would be perceived as violence or ungratefulness, leaving me in a more vulnerable position. I learned that asking more questions and allowing teachers to feel like they were walking me through a gateway of understanding would make them feel accomplished and they would grade my tests higher. I began to see this as a sort of code-switching,[1] a necessary survival tool, and carried these skills with me into post-secondary education. It required an erasure of the self on a daily basis that I really didn't learn to undo until my introduction to organizing.

My organizing started off with a group called the Young Communist League (YCL) in Hamilton, Ontario. It was run primarily by students at McMaster University; in its formative years its members were mostly white, and during my time there, mostly people without disabilities. I was in my first year of university, and they were the only group on this relatively conservative campus willing to listen to my frustrations about funding cuts that hemorrhage special education departments in schools across Ontario. I was driving by their table in my electric wheelchair in the student centre one random day in the spring and they stopped me to hand out one of their magazines, Rebel Youth. We stayed in touch. As Marxist-Leninists, they taught me more about intersectionality and oppression than any class on sociology did. They also, on a theoretical level, helped me to begin to see the ways in which capitalism, understandings of productivity, and the treatment of disabled bodies are linked, something I had never connected before. Though not perfect, the club taught me to identify when I was internalizing ableism and anti-Black racism, giving me space to learn about building community power and to apply my anger toward change-making instead of languishing in apathy. I was introduced to the Fight for $15 & Fairness campaign through the Worker's Action Centre in Toronto and canvassed with them every weekend in Hamilton, even before the local large labour unions decided to endorse the campaign. I was then introduced to community-based organizing through the campus-based Boycott, Divestment and Sanctions (BDS) campaign against Israeli apartheid, where I watched, for the first time in almost thirty years, over 700 people congregate in a tiny campus gym to vote—a vote that university administration tried to prevent over and over again. These victories and experiences taught me that, when done correctly, organizing in groups and in coalitions to work toward a common goal is much more effective than an individualized approach to activism.

At the recommendation of one of the YCL members, and on a whim, I ran for the students union and was elected as a representative. I sat on the council amongst students who embodied wealth and privilege and were the exact personification of everything I wanted to challenge.

Right away there were challenges. Many of the people around me on council assumed I was incompetent and that I was only invested in one single issue: anti-ableism on campus. By the end of my first term, they voted me the most passionate/theatrical representative because of their perception of my words as angry or overly emotional. For example, I would get up to speak about how I thought tuition should be free and our electoral processes should be more open and democratic. The student representatives around me often were ableist in response and language, consistently responding with the argument that I didn't understand our bylaws and constitutions—documents I spent hours poring over.

I used these perceptions steeped in ignorance to gather intel needed for organizing on campus, be it to push for certain budget allocations or when to fill the room to vote something down. For example, I was able to convince the student union to send me to the Ontario Undergraduate Student Alliance (OUSA) general assembly, twice, where I learned just how deeply the organization was tied to partisan Liberal and Conservative organizing. I also engaged in discussions with the Canadian Federation of Students around how to organize on campus to leave OUSA. I did this knowing full well that people in positions of power always assume I have something to learn from them and that I crave community and acceptance because I am left out in so many facets of society. The thing is, people like me are very good at being isolated, mentally, emotionally, and physically.

I never craved building community on campus with those who fundamentally believed I was less than because of what I stood for. So I organized like-minded peers to run in our students union elections, to create a polity of student unionists committed to progressive ideals. I ran a slate of progressive candidates that I spent hours training how to run a political campaign. The level of intimidation I experienced and the number of back-room meetings I was pushed into was unimaginable, but I always had friends in the YCL to talk me through it and to help me focus on using my position to bring information back to the campus to use in progressive organizing. At one point, the vice president of education of the students union pulled me into a meeting room to tell me he was worried that I was being manipulated by the president of Solidarity for Palestinian Human Rights (SPHR) because I ran in a slate with her during my re-election. He thought I was being manipulated, never assuming that the idea was mine, because, to him, I lacked agency. Being in these spaces as a person with a disability and as a Black woman was characterized by dismissal, gaslighting, and exploitation.

Organizing outside of this space, however, continued to feel liberatory. I navigated spaces that made me feel as though people were working with me to end the root causes of my struggles. For four years I honed my organizing skills with the YCL. Still, over time I noticed many frustrating parallels between that group and the students union. Though the group members in the YCL claimed to appreciate Blackness, they did not understand how to organize with Black people. They would write statements on Black Lives Matter while excluding Black people from the writing process. They would critique Black women, me included, for organizing vigils for victims of police brutality because it did not fit their exact line of organizing. I was told that I was wrong for not yelling "fuck the police," out of concern for my safety as the only Black woman holding the microphone. They would exhibit frustration at mass-movement-building work when it wasn't rooted in academic theory that they were familiar with, to the extent that it prohibited them from actually being able to organize in the Hamilton community, a working-class city where many of the people who are the most oppressed do not have a background in academic theory. Though, as someone who has been homeless, lived in shelters, struggled to survive and faced Islamophobia, racism, sexism, and ableism on a consistent basis, I had the most experience in understanding the failures of the current structures of our systems, my organizing capacity was constantly delegitimized because I did not yet know how to ground these experiences with the language of Leninism. In the same way that the students' union delegitimized my intelligence and capacity, so too did some of the very privileged members of the YCL.

The members of the YCL failed, again and again, to adequately respond to issues relating to Black people or people with disabilities. They consistently fell, perhaps ironically, into a capitalist narrative around accessibility. For example, I was called un-Marxist for asking for an accessible meeting space when an emergency meeting was called in response to my allegations around racism in the group. Their conversations around disability in these spaces were also often limited to that of ensuring a makeshift ramp was created for the fundraiser locations. The dangers of a focus on access that isn't grounded in the idea of liberation or a critique of power is that it quickly turns into a focus of ensuring people with disabilities have the ability to execute purchasing power or become an economic benefit to society. Access is predicated on the notion that people with disabilities all wish to have access to locations for the sole purpose of being productive. Had I not been in the group, this bare minimum of ramps provided at fundraisers might not have even been met because the productivity value of a person with my kind of disability would be absent, thus negating the need for the access. This in the city of Hamilton, the city with the highest density of people with disabilities in Ontario.[2] This was mirrored by the liberalism in the students' union, in which there were also conversations around accessibility and the importance of people with disabilities, but the engagement always ended at the conversation. Their practice remained staunchly ableist.

Many organizers make the mistake of fixating on this idea that productivity and outcomes are the most important steps to liberation, concluding that those who cannot be productive must no longer be given space to build in movements. This is an individualist way of thinking, forced onto us by very system we work to dismantle. We hear often that movement-building looks different for people with various disabilities, but I would caution organizers to think about the ways in which we cater to people with disabilities that are palatable, easy for the non-disabled to handle or understand. We do not do enough to create space for people who communicate in a way that is different than the standard. What roles can people with intellectual disabilities or who rely on communication devices, or people with mental health concerns that extend beyond the mainstream of anxiety or depression play?

We see this problem too in our labour circles . Unions protect the rights of workers. At the same time, the labour movement in Canada has a long history of being born from xenophobia, with labour groups at times formed to protect the rights of white workers from the threat to jobs that immigrants were believed to pose. We see this replicated today, where in Hamilton, Ontario, there are almost no Black members or people of colour on the executive of the Hamilton District Labour Council or the United Steelworkers. On the ground, stories of people being subject to anti-Black racism, called slurs in the workplace, or experiencing toxic work environments are rampant. Unions are, in many cases, unsafe for Black people. Yet to be considered progressive, we are expected to support unionism wholeheartedly, without critique. We are told that our attempts to address anti-Blackness endanger the strategy of labour and are not a priority, a trap that puts the theory of unionism, without much assessment of its impacts, in praxis. I was told, in an organizing meeting with a labour group, that to bring issues of race and disability into the conversation about workers' rights could be divisive, and that in their eyes "to be hired and fired meant you were working class." Though Black people and people with disabilities are working class, and often have access to the least resources in everyday life and in organizing spaces, this phrase meant that we were all equal, a dangerous liberal idea that would frame the struggles of a white worker with a six-figure salary in a union as the same as the struggle of people with precarious contract positions. In this space too, I felt my whole self be dismissed.

These erasures of people with disabilities or the stipulations on productivity are no mistake and are rooted in a history in Canada steeped in ableism and colonialism. We know that slavery and white supremacy were founded upon the physical imprisonment of Black people, as well as psychological warfare. Throughout history Black people continued to be told that we were mentally inferior, language used as justification of slavery and language that led to the development of eugenic practices against people with disabilities.[3] In Canada, the Alberta Sterilization Act, created in the early 1920s, stated that any Indigenous women or disabled persons could be sterilized against their will or knowledge and without their consent, and it was a law that helped to inspire the Nazis' 1933 Law for the Prevention of Hereditarily Diseased Offspring.[4] Black people in particular were labelled with all kinds of disabilities or mental health challenges in order to keep them subjected to white control. Black men were often labelled as having drapetomania for claiming to be free,[5] and later on in history as having schizophrenia for fighting for their right to vote through means of protest.[6]

The impact of generations of this violence against Black people with disabilities in Canada is still present. The link between anti-Black racism and police violence is grossly under-reported. According to a comprehensive study done by the CBC, "more than 460 people have died in encounters with police across Canada since the year 2000, and a substantial majority suffered from mental health problems or symptoms of drug abuse . . . . 70 percent of the people who died struggled with mental health issues or substance abuse or both."[7]

An example of this was the attack on Abdirahman Abdi, an Ottawa Somali man with autism who had the police call on him due to a noise complaint. The police brutally beat him to death for being noisy in a coffee shop. This violence enacted on disabled people in a public space epitomizes the use of force against disabled bodies by the police system in Canada. The medical-industrial complex also preys on poor people with mental health challenges or disabilities. If you're poor, you're more likely to struggle to access expensive medications suited to your needs, or to access services that require large amounts of money, such as therapy. In addition, if you are living in poverty this can increase your likelihood of developing a mental health diagnosis or disability, as well as increase your likelihood of experiencing homelessness. As discussed in Poverty and Policy in Canada: Implications for Health and Quality of Life, "people experience economic hardship as a result of a variety of difficult life situations, such as divorce, a death in the family, loss of job, etc. The resulting loss of income may lead to poverty in other essential resources, such as housing, education, and employment." As well, evidence indicates that "poverty—and the material and social deprivation associated with it—is a primary cause of poor health among Canadians."[8] Policing systems are set up to eliminate any aneurotypical expressions of mental health concerns or disabilities, increasing the likelihood of arrest when people with disabilities interact with police. Black people in America and Canada were subjected to drug experimentation for the advancement of gynecology, advancements in cures for syphilis and more by the state,[9] in the same way the pharmaceutical companies today experiment on working-class people with disabilities, who, in order to survive, in turn rely on various free trial-and-error medication samples they are given.

These realities are coupled with legislative ableism. For example, prior to 2018 Canada could deny citizenship applications on the basis of personal disability or a disability in the family that could cause "undue financial hardship" to the Canadian medical system.[10] The case of thirteen-year-old Nico Montoya, who was born with Down syndrome, was widely reported in the media: even though his family had been living in Canada for years, his family's permanent residency application was denied due to his disability.[11]

While the legislative change overturning this rule is a move in the right direction, the generational trauma that predates this decision has left many Black families and people with disabilities to cope with their disabilities in silence, afraid to access services for fear of immigration-related repercussions. This fear of accessing medical support, I believe, still exists, despite the fact that many people are dealing with disabilities that have been caused by their immediate environments.

I now believe, through my experience of erasure in many different organizing spaces, that we will not see liberation from the systems that oppress us in this country unless we shift our movement-building to also focus on the protection and liberation of disabled people. I say this because people with disabilities fit every race, religion, geographic location, and LGBTQ+ spectrum. Disabled people are thus the antithesis to the capitalist system that continues to base the value of human beings on our ability to compete and produce, because many people with disabilities cannot work and do not choose to work. The leading cause of disability is age, which affects everyone. We are the largest category of people in the world. If we can figure out a way to build a society that fundamentally includes and supports people with disabilities, we will have built a society that is no longer reliant on capitalist philosophies and will have moved closer to a global liberation for all.

The answer to achieving all of this is for every organizer to use a disability justice framework.

The term "disability justice" was coined by a group of artists and social justice organizers known as Sins Invalid, a collective of queer, disabled women and non-binary people of colour.[12] To Sins Invalid, disability justice means understanding that our liberations are tied together and that it is not enough to focus on my experiences of being Black or disabled in an intersectional way, but we must also think about these experiences as connected. It means not just thinking about access as an end goal, but instead examining all of the ways in which our organizing in different communities provides justice and supports a right to live for everyone, including those with disabilities. This is a framework that is missing from a society built through colonialism and imperialism.

For example, most Canadian legislation around accessibility focuses on consumerist language, foregrounding the need to allow people with disabilities the ability to purchase goods and services and participate in society publicly. This is evident in the Accessibility for Ontarians with Disabilities Act and the new Accessible Canada Act being pushed for by our federal government. Much of this focus on consumerism comes from the idea that we as people only have value if we contribute to the economy. It discusses access to space and employment, but does not discuss the right to accessible housing, the right to accessible education, and more. What is worse is that many politicians refuse to discuss what should happen to people with disabilities who cannot work or who do not aspire to be employed. Do they too have the right to exist in public space? Sins Invalid is pushing people to think of people with disabilities outside of capitalist narratives around productivity and to start thinking about all anti-capitalist struggle as connected to disability justice.

This is a framework that is missing from most of the groups wanting to liberate our society from these oppressions. If we cannot remember to build spaces where those who have multiple experiences of oppression can be their full selves, instead of taking on predefined roles based on tokenism or what fits in the moment, we will never attain liberation as people.

Coalition-building is a central tenet of the disability justice framework, and coalition-building can only happen when we begin to understand that all of our struggles are rooted in this overarching desire to be free of the notion that our humanity is defined by our economic purchasing power or controlled by it. This is the desire that drives the fight for environmental justice, racial justice, queer liberation, and every other successful movement. Coalition-building is the ability to see the connection between multiple kinds of struggle. It is the reason that the Black Panthers and the Butterfly Brigade—a group of gay men who patrolled city streets on the lookout for gay violence[13]—supported the 504 protests in the United States, a fight for accessible spaces for people with disabilities. It is also the reason that the Black Panthers pushed for healthcare reform across the entire United States as it related to the screening of sickle cell anemia. In order to fight for liberation for one oppressed group, we cannot operate in silos. No one organizer has all of the answers or holds all of the necessary experience to make change. This means we must also translate our theoretical understanding of intersectionality into action, which includes figuring out the gaps that our organizing is missing and finding who is out there to fill it.

As I get older and begin to understand my disability more, I have decided that my place in movement-building and organizing is no longer on the front lines. I am much more useful in other capacities than I am holding a picket and organizing a physical disruption. Instead, I am attempting to find the best way to connect different movements in Hamilton that already exist, such as connecting the local disability justice organizers with environmental activists, teaching environmental justice activists about environmental racism, teaching Black youth about state violence, and challenging people with disabilities in my city to imagine a world where we are all free to be.

I also believe that the way organizing spaces, and society in general, had, over time, convinced me that I belonged nowhere—that I was too different or disabled, or not academic enough, or too radical—was purposeful. It was done, over and over again, to make me doubt what I already know to be true: that only those who have failed to fit in have the capacity to see organizing from a bird's-eye view. In order to take down a building, you have to understand the blueprint of it first, lest it fall on top of you, crushing your purpose. I have the ability to see and connect causes and organizers to one another because I understand that, in order to have an impact on those with the least resources in our society, none of our struggles should ever be seen as disconnected. We need to stop thinking about intersectionality as simply a descriptor of one who carries multiple identities, and shift its approach to one of action, calling us to dismantle oppressive systems.

NOTES

1 Chad Nilep, "'Code Switching' in Sociocultural Linguistics," *Colorado Research in Linguistics*, 19 (2006), DOI: https://doi.org/10.25810/hnq4-jv62.

2 Jennifer Mak. *Disability Demographics - Gender, Poverty, and Age.* Report submitted by the Access and Equity Office of the City of Hamilton, ON, 2010. www2.hamilton.ca/NR/rdonlyres/1DF82911.../0/2006Disability Demographics.pdf.

3 Shaun Grech and Karen Soldatic, "Disability and Colonialism: (Dis)encounters and Anxious Intersectionalities," *Social Identities* 21, no. 1 (2015): 1–5, DOI: 10.1080/13504630.2014.995394.

4 "Timeline," Eugenics Archives, http://eugenicsarchive.ca/discover/timeline.

5 Michael D. Naragon, "Communities in motion: Drapetomania, work and the development of African-American slave cultures," *Slavery & Abolition* 15, no. 3 (1994), DOI: https://doi.org/10.1080/01440399408575139.

6 J.M. Metzl, *The Protest Psychosis: How Schizophrenia Became a Black Disease* (Boston: Beacon Press, 2009).

7 Katie Nicholson and Jacques Marcoux, "Most Canadians killed in police encounters since 2000 had mental health or substance abuse issues," CBC News, April 4, 2018, https://www.cbc.ca/news/investigates/most-canadians-killed-in-police-encounters-since-2000-had-mental-health-or-substance-abuse-issues-1.4602916.

8 Dennis Raphael, *Poverty and Policy in Canada: Implications for Health and Quality of Life* (Toronto: Canadian Scholars' Press Inc., 2007), 223.

9 Allen M. Hornblum, Judith Lynn Newman, and Gregory J. Dober, *Against Their Will: The Secret History of Medical Experimentation on Children in Cold War America* (New York: St. Martin's Press, 2013).

10 Brian Hill and Andrew Russell, "Trudeau Liberals to overhall 'discriminatory' immigration law targeting people with disabilities," Global News,

April 16, 2018, https://globalnews.ca/news/4142592/trudeau-liberals-overhaul-discriminatory-immigration-law-disabilities/.

11 Michelle McQuigge, "Ontario family denied residency over son's Down syndrome," *Toronto Star*, March 20, 2016, https://www.thestar.com/news/canada/2016/03/20/ontario-family-denied-residency-over-sons-down-syndrome.html.

12 Sins Invalid website, https://www.sinsinvalid.org/.

13 Susan Schweik, "Lomax's Matrix: Disability, Solidarity, and the Black Power of 504," *Disability Studies Quarterly* 31, no. 1 (2011), http://dsq-sds.org/article/view/1371/1539.

REFERENCES

Grech, Shaun, and Karen Soldatic. "Disability and Colonialism: (Dis)encounters and Anxious Intersectionalities." *Social Identities* 21, no. 1 (2015): 1–5. DOI: 10.1080/13504630.2014.995394.

Hornblum, Allen M., Judith Lynn Newman, and Gregory J. Dober. *Against Their Will: The Secret History of Medical Experimentation on Children in Cold War America*. New York: St. Martin's Press, 2013.

Joseph, Ameil J. "Empowering Alliances in Pursuit of Social Justice: Social Workers Supporting Psychiatric-Survivor Movements." *Journal of Progressive Human Services* 24, no. 3 (2013): 265–288.

Mak, Jennifer. *Disability Demographics - Gender, Poverty, and Age*. Report submitted by the Access and Equity Office of the City of Hamilton, ON, 2010. www2.hamilton.ca/NR/rdonlyres/1DF82911.../0/2006DisabilityDemographics.pdf.

Metzl, J. M. *The Protest Psychosis: How Schizophrenia Became a Black Disease*. Boston: Beacon Press, 2009.

Naragon, Michael D. "Communities in motion: Drapetomania, work and the development of African-American slave cultures." *Slavery & Abolition* 15, no. 3 (1994): 63–87. https://doi.org/10.1080/01440399408575139.

Nilep, Chad. "'Code Switching' in Sociocultural Linguistics." *Colorado Research in Linguistics*, 19 (2006). https://doi.org/10.25810/hnq4-jv62.

Raphael, Dennis. *Poverty and Policy in Canada: Implications for Health and Quality of Life*. Toronto: Canadian Scholars' Press, 2007.

Schweik, Susan. "Lomax's Matrix: Disability, Solidarity, and the Black Power of 504." *Disability Studies Quarterly* 31, no. 1 (2011). http://dsq-sds.org/article/view/1371/1539.

13

BLACKNESS IN THE ATMOSPHERE

DANA INKSTER

Blackness absorbs all the colours of the visible spectrum and reflects none of them to the eyes.

It is an achromatic colour; literally a colour without hue.

To my eye, Black is not a void. It is everything.

Atmosphere is the air we breathe. Beyond the "Black is beautiful" rallying cries of the 1960s civil rights movement, Blackness has carried a burden of optimism for imminent change or progress in our cultural history, one that is at odds with what I call cultural agency; others refer to cultural agency as cultural capital. I define cultural agency as a currency bestowed by institutions such as academic learning and civic engagement. Simply put, it is power: power to promote divergent, new ways of thinking within the arts and humanities in the service of solutions to real-life problems. In cultural studies, agency refers to a given subject's ability to have social impact. One's agency is one's social power, the capacity of an individual to act independently and to make (relatively) free choices. Art is a force that drives innovation in everything from education, science, law, and political leadership, to business.

Blackness in the atmosphere facilitates a consideration of activism as a means to an end of enlightened compassion as we navigate cultural difference with others in our community. Atmosphere refers to the dominant mood or tone of a work of art. It creates a distinctive quality within a place or character. My study of this atmosphere of Blackness in Canadian culture conjures ambiguity of voice. In the context of this writing, the notion of agency is at the centre of this possibility of the freedom to define one's own experience of Blackness that may be at odds culturally expected norms and notions. My experience of Blackness is so rooted in the reality of being violently displaced and forced into a life of migration. To survive displacement, I wander and my itinerancy is a place, not a void. My experience of wandering is expansive and, to my mind, gives way to Afrofuturistic possibilities of what could be with regard to freedom and cultural agency.

BLACK NOISE

Within the scholarly paradigm of audiology, Black noise may refer to complete silence, or a complete lack of noise, or noise at a frequency that cannot be heard or measured, but that still affects the environment or the outcome of statistical experiments. Black noise is also referred to as silent noise.

I am a media artist. Within my practice, I have become consciously aware of the impacts of my creative decisions; specifically how they might simultaneously benefit some viewers at the expense of others. I hope that while I have prioritized giving voice to lost cultural histories I have not sidelined the histories of others. The production notes from the producers of my mainstream documentary, *24 Days in Brooks,* suggested that the prioritization of the lives and experiences of the African-Canadian settling in rural Alberta in 2005 cannot be fully appreciated by Canadian television audiences without the perspective of white residents. I respectfully disagreed with producers throughout the production process. I disagreed with the producers' often reiterated belief that the audience will not understand unless everything is spelled out. This impulse quashes the very power of what art brings to the expression. Art is in the multiplicity of reading. I am aware of my marginalized cultural perspective in relation to the vast majority of Canadian broadcast media I have consumed. My hypothesis in all contexts is: in the face of confusion, articulated questions can create meaning. Consensus about and agreement on meaning does not equate creation of knowledge. Consensus does not reflect a new way of seeing—which is my priority. Consensus reflects a whittling down of ideas.

The power dynamics of being contracted by a producer and entering into a collaborative process of film-making can be considered along the axis of voice and silence, or prioritization and dismissal. There is still much to gain from analyses of power dynamics, with specific focus on dominant and non-dominant voices, in the sector of media production. Who has the agency to ask and answer?

My media art practice is a site in which questions are posed for the purposes of sparking conversations. Theorizing the motivations of my own practice, production, process of reaching audiences, and their reception of my work facilitates an articulation of my vision for this creative life that is transparent and accountable. Audiences who view work formulate meaning by articulating their opinions about the work for themselves or others, in a collective viewing content.

GOOD NEIGHBOURS

Adult education theorist Ron Norman made an important presentation about the development of the narrative capacities of the mind, its use of metaphor for sense-making, and its overarching imagination. He says that these narrative capacities are of educational importance because they are so central to our general capacity to make meaning out of our experience. The educational possibilities of narrative that trigger the human capacity to imagine a cultural experience which we have not experienced first-hand is an essential consideration within my artistic engagement and my work with audiences.

In conversation about media art and cultural practices, Mi'kmaq writer and director Bretten Hannam says, "Respect is the cornerstone of good relationships, and protocols fall into that . . . I guess you can sum up the worldview in the phrase Msit No'kmaq that means 'all of my relations.'" Hannam acknowledges that we are all related: people and animals, land and water. And those relationships are treated with respect. Hannam says, "If I find a feather I don't just take it, I leave an offering in exchange, or sing a song; there's never just taking, there's always giving back as well. It's the same if I ask to learn something from an elder, I'll give her tobacco or a gift of some kind to acknowledge the information and time she's giving me." This is customary for both Indigenous and non-Indigenous artists who have that worldview built into their practice. It is an acknowledgement that if they have community or cultural involvement they need to give something back to receive guidance or teachings. The offering can be an honorarium, as well as a gift of tobacco, or whatever else might be fitting for that individual or community.

Being a good neighbour runs the gamut from common sense to survival. It makes so much sense and really resonates deeply with my experience of an Afro-Canadian diasporic tradition. My Blackness, my visibility in communities founded by settlers of European descent has situated moments in my life where, to my absolute disbelief, my life has been at risk. Skinheads tried to beat me; homophobes tried to burn my house down while my partner and baby slept. I'm invested in finding a peaceful path to peace while I wander. When I am seen, when I invite you and others into my home, I set the terms for my expectations of good neighbours. There is a consideration of interdependence and trust. I aspire for my documentaries to be used to facilitate transformative learning for the purpose of cultural competency. If I, as an artist, can weave a tale that transforms or shifts an opinion about a particular individual who represents a different demographic from the viewer, and effectively suggest, to quote the words of Maya Angelou, "We are more alike . . . than unalike,"[1] then I have been successful in my goal. This possibility of intercultural exchange between Black and Indigenous communities is central to understanding my creative intentions as a female media artist.

I WENT DOWN TO THE CROSSROADS

Cross Road Blues is a song written and recorded by American blues artist Robert Leroy Johnson in 1936. Johnson performed it as a solo piece with his vocal and acoustic slide guitar in the Delta blues style. The song has become part of the Robert Johnson mythology as referring to the place where he supposedly sold his soul to the Devil in exchange for his musical talents.

I have always heard my works before I've seen them. Everything begins with music. The foundation of my creative work in all its form is predicated on the premise that recognizing racial difference offers a way of thinking about social power structures through which we can contemplate the world in which we live.

My Blackness is important to anyone seeking understanding of my worldview. As the writer and director of *24 Days in Brooks*, Blackness, in a contemporary context, is particularly important as a social phenomenon, not just a biological one. Race is metaphor for difference. And yet, there is tangibility to race. You can see it. Touch it. It is in the skin. Toni Morrison argues,

> the fabrication of an Africanist persona is reflexive; an extraordinary mediation on the self; a powerful exploration of the fears and desires that reside in the writerly conscious. It is an astonishing revelation of longing, of terror, of perplexity, of shame, of magnanimity. It requires hard work *not* to see this.[2]

Much has been written about the worldviews of different peoples living in North America and how friction and racial tensions occur when people do not know how others view the world. As a Canadian-born person of African descent, my ancestral connection to histories of oppression and enslavement steels me to resist submission to authority when it comes to my creative practice. I am armed with the vocabulary to insist upon inclusion of underrepresented voices in public histories. Angela Y. Davis's *Blues, Legacies and Black Feminism: Gertrude "Ma" Rainey, Bessie Smith, and Billie Holliday* (1998) encapsulates an essential theorization of traditional Marxist feminism to appreciate the economy of race and power. Davis underscores the manner in which women of African descent developed artistic and folkloric means to produce cultural histories. This is the tradition in which I participate in a contemporary context.

My practice and contemplations of African-Canadian histories is not an academic exercise. The tone of my body of work is inextricably linked to audience readings of the fiction and non-fiction film, photography, and writing I create and, similar to Davis's discussions of blues music, the "possibility of knowledge production that suppresses neither the individual at the expense of the general welfare, nor feelings at the expense of rational thought. The participatory character of the blues affirms women's community without negating individual readings."[3] My trust in the value of multiple, diverse, and independent readings of the work I create is an integral part of my interest in cultural production.

For Canadian audiences, as for me, imagining and realizing new work is not a passive act. My intention is activist. Realizing this activist ambition by means of media production parallels the goals of transformative learning. Transformative learning is based on the principle that personal experience is an integral part of the learning process. A person's interpretation of the experience creates meaning, which leads to a change in behaviour, mindset, and beliefs. Its power lies in the potential that, when transformational learning occurs, a learner may undergo a shift that directly impacts future experiences. Creative collaboration is required because of the team-oriented nature of media production. From my position of Blackness, I seek to engage in acts of intercultural exchange with racially diverse audiences in a manner that reflects communication between members of different groups, where a vibrant exchange of ideas and cultural beliefs occurs, with the goal being that each group or individual representing a group has something to learn from the others. Hopefully this is a positive act of transformation; an act of becoming for all involved, whatever you want to become; becoming whatever the world, your parents, your lovers, or your children have planned for you. An in-depth curiosity about human behaviour is essential for survival as a writer and director because of the collaborative nature of production. It involves an innate investment in understanding, facilitated by curious observation, listening, and artistic articulation skills.

My relationship to the work of blues performers such as Gertrude "Ma" Rainey, Bessie Smith, and Billie Holliday is reflected in the manner in which I rely upon creative interpretation of oral history. In their observations about emotional engagement, these artists' works infuse folklore with a specific mood and tone. I have often said to my contemporaries in the art world that I hear the stories I tell before I see them. The African diasporic tradition of oral history in song informs my artistic approach. I am propelled by my mood and tone. If I could write music and master the piano or guitar, I would compose songs rather than make media art videos. However, I use the means available to a person of my ability. The social patterns of music that originated in African culture act "as forms of expression handed down by generations and firmly rooted in the Black community[;] these sounds offer an expressive potential that enables individuals to appropriate the English language and transform it according to their needs."[4] It gives voice to formerly unspeakable occurrences and offers a redemptive potential for misplaced histories.

BLACK NOISE IN THE ATMOSPHERE

Black noise. I can hear it. It's bass. It's Al Green's bonus track "Eli's Game." It's Daniel Lanois' instrumental "Smoke." It's Me'Shell Ndegeocoello. It's quiet. It's the storm.

I have had the freedom to pursue these creative objectives due, in part, to the support of Canadian arts councils. This freedom has permitted me to promote consideration of race metaphorically, and my propensity to employ the language of documentary cinema in its very symbolic nature may be perceived as no more than a failure to produce realistic, clear, and accomplished film-making by those who occupy positions outside of the artists' sphere. "The cards are readily shifted so as to turn a limit, if not an impoverishment of dominant thinking into a virtue, a legitimate stance in mass communication, therefore a tool for political demagogy to appeal widely to naturalized prejudices."[5] This financial support from Canadian arts councils insists that the individual artist retain creative freedom to determine the structure, tone, and creative intention of the works. While media production itself is a highly collaborative process, I have established a body of work in which I have retained creative control over the final cut.

With this freedom I have chosen my production priorities. As a media artist, I write a narrative of the experience as a tribute to oral history and storytelling traditions of the African diaspora. Pre-eminent education scholars Clandinin and Connelly note that "humans are storytelling organisms who, individually and collectively, lead storied lives. Thus, the study of narrative is the study of the ways humans experience the world."[6] In other words, people's lives consist of stories. One value of narrative is that it gives us a way to connect past, present, and future, both as individuals and as societies. The often-quoted Barbara Hardy details narrative's role in individual lives: "We dream in narrative, daydream in narrative, remember, anticipate, hope, despair, believe, doubt, plan, revise, criticize, gossip, learn, hate and live by narrative."[7] The development of the narrative concern is, arguably, educationally relevant to any intercultural exchange. I am specifically invested in how narrative manifests itself in documentary as illustrations that promote pedagogical ends. As in documentary film-making, narrative inquiry is founded on the process of gathering information for the purpose of research through storytelling.

This justification of pedagogical terms of production has an additional consideration in the context of my creative practice. Intangible, yet powerful, imagination has the potential to bring about tremendous rewards, enhancing the quality of life for oneself and others. To be productive, the imagination needs to be fed. "Imagination is indispensable to understanding the unknown. We imagine alternative ways of seeing and interpreting."[8] This possibility is universally available to each human. Interacting with other creative artefacts, such a narrative in documentary, is a source of feeding one's imagination. Documentary works that elaborate on a person or society's understanding of difference lend themselves very well to analysis of documentary as learning. "Simply stated . . . narrative inquiry is stories lived and told."[9] This genre contributes to the generation of knowledge about the human experience in formal and informal learning contexts. Viewing of documentary films brings a contemporary perspective on oral tradition and its ability to facilitate learning.

The work I make must have a function in facilitating transformative learning in its production and exhibition because "educators are interested in life [and] life, to borrow from John Dewey's metaphor, *is* education."[10] This establishes a foundational term of production for me. This intercultural exchange after viewing artistically composed documentary texts is an effective means of transformative learning. This is how we structure a life story that is coherent and that justifies who and what we currently are. It also enables us to envision a future that is credible, the further development of the story of who we are. Narratives are dynamic. They are like videos, capturing movement, growth, change, and the ever-unfolding plots of our lives.[11] A function of this temporal character of narrative is its ability to make process visible. Through multiple means we can interpret the inner workings of the narrative, examining it from many perspectives.

Creative practice permits a sense of autonomy and empowerment to pose questions for which I have not received institutionally sanctioned answers. Becoming conscious of our cultural position promotes an evolution into a culturally competent educational content producer. There is considerable potential for documentaries to facilitate intercultural exchange toward the end of transformative learning, and this potential is greatest when producers are explicit about and accountable to not only their creative but also their pedagogical intention, or lack thereof.

Negotiating power dynamics between the producers and me often boiled down to my relationship to the ethics of power in media production. I was eager for each viewer to bring their own reading to the stories of the individuals behind the headlines in my documentary. This diversity of readings was precisely what concerned my producers. I did not share the cultural experience of race with my producers or crew. As visible minorities of African descent living in Canada, this was a cultural shorthand that I shared with the primary participants in the documentary. Given the culturally loaded nature of producing media, I wanted to honour this shared experiential knowledge as a priority. I acknowledge and understand my producers had an array of creative intentions for this documentary that were often different from my own regarding the role of representing the racialized and cultural experience of the African-Canadians in this film.

Despite the invitation from mainstream documentary producers, who possess constitutionally entrenched rights "to reflect Canada to Canadians," to collaborate, I have to appreciate my collaboration was not an invitation for Canadian film-makers of colour to write the rules that dictated the terms of production. My production process involved what has to be construed as a financial exploitation of the writer/director. As a contracted employee of the National Film Board of Canada (NFB), I of course had to accept the institution's terms of employment. I accepted early on that creative compromise was central to the production of this documentary. What confounded my efforts was the sense that, while I was contracted to tell the story I submitted as a treatment, the creative collaboration did not facilitate the presentation of the story that was mine to tell. For a significant period of this production I was unclear of my role in this creative collaboration.

Ultimately, *24 Days in Brooks* was conceived as an articulation of the representation of self-determination among African-Canadians as agents of their own future in contexts of intercultural exchange.

As the writer/director, I grant that the creative process definitively did not reflect my cultural consciousness individually or diasporically, nor the interests of any other culture. Due to the fact that *24 Days in Brooks* was the product of considerable collaborative compromise, on my part and that of producers, I do not feel this documentary holds any definitive cultural value with regard to critical race theory, which I had hoped for.

It took this experience with the NFB to transform my worldview and accept that my goals as an African-Canadian media artist could not be, and perhaps cannot be, realized in the context of creative collaboration with an institution so steeped in a colonial legacy, despite its efforts to include and represent diverse voices and perspectives. A documentary, which is relevant to a larger lived context, becomes a vital means of reflecting upon the nature of society and social existence. Perhaps the same can be said of a documentary production.

NOTES

1 From Maya Angelou's famous poem, "Human Family."

2 Toni Morrison, *Playing in the Dark: Whiteness and the Literary Imagination* (Cambridge, MA: Harvard University Press, 1992), 17.

3 Angela Y. Davis, *Blues, Legacies and Black Feminism: Gertrude "Ma" Rainey, Bessie Smith, and Billie Holiday* (New York: Pantheon Books, 1998), 57.

4 Lars Eckstein, "A Love Supreme: Jazzthetic Strategies in Toni Morrison's *Beloved*," *African American Review* 40, no. 2 (2006), 272.

5 Trinh T. Minh-ha, "All-Owning Spectatorship," in Hamid Naficy and Teshome H. Gabriel, eds., *Otherness and the Media: The Ethnography of the Imagined and the Imaged*, vol. 3 (Reading, UK: Harwood Academic Publishers, 1993), 191.

6 D. Jean Clandinin and F. Michael Connell, *Narrative Inquiry: Experience and Story in Qualitative Research* (San Francisco: Jossey-Bass, 2000), 27.

7 Barbara Hardy, "Towards a Poetics of Fiction: An Approach through Narrative," *Novel: A Forum on Fiction* 2, no. 1 (Autumn, 1968), 5.

8 Jack Mezirow, *Transformative Dimensions of Adult Learning* (San Francisco: Jossey-Bass, 1991), 83.

9 Clandinin and Connelly, *Narrative Inquiry*, 20.

10 Elizabeth McIsaac Bruce, "Narrative Inquiry: A Spiritual and Liberating Approach to Research," *Religious Education: The Official Journal of the Re-*

ligious Education Association 103, no. 3 (2008), 325.

11 John M. Dirkx, Jack Mezirow, and Patricia Cranton, "Musings and Reflections on the Meaning, Context, and Process of Transformative Learning," *Journal of Transformative Education* 4, no. 2 (2006), 127.

REFERENCES

Aitken, Ian. *Film and Reform: John Grierson and the Documentary Film Movement.* London: Routledge, 1990.

Armstrong, Stephen A., and Robert C. Berg. "Demonstrating Group Process Using *12 Angry Men.*" *The Journal for Specialists in Group Work* 30, no. 2 (2005): 135–136. https://doi.org/10.1080/01933920590925986.

Boghal, Preet. "Interview with Filmmaker Dana Inkster: Breaking through Canadian Isolation." *Xtra*, May 7, 2009, https://www.dailyxtra.com/filmmaker-dana-inkster-24878.

Bruce, Elizabeth McIsaac. "Narrative Inquiry: A Spiritual and Liberating Approach to Research." *Religious Education: The Official Journal of the Religious Education Association* 103, no. 3 (2008): 323–338. https://doi.org/10.1080/00344080802053493.

Bush, Christopher. "The Other of the Other?: Cultural Studies, Theory, and the Location of the Modernist Signifier." *Comparative Literature Studies* 42, no. 2 (2005): 162-80. https://www.jstor.org/stable/40247474.

Clandinin, D. Jean and F. Michael Connell. *Narrative Inquiry: Experience and Story in Qualitative Research.* San Francisco: Jossey-Bass, 2000.

Davis, Angela Y. *Blues, Legacies and Black Feminism: Gertrude "Ma" Rainey, Bessie Smith, and Billie Holiday.* New York: Pantheon Books, 1998.

Dirkx, John M., Jack Mezirow, and Patricia Cranton. "Musings and Reflections on the Meaning, Context, and Process of Transformative Learning." *Journal of Transformative Education* 4, no. 2 (2006): 123-139. https://doi.org/10.1177/1541344606287503.

Druick, Zoë. (2007). *Projecting Canada: Government Policy and Documentary Film at the National Film Board.* Montreal: McGill-Queen's University Press, 2007.

Dyer, Richard. "Whiteness." *Screen* 29, no. 4 (1997): 44-5.

———. *White: Essays on Race and Culture* (6th ed.). London: Routledge, 1997.

Eckstein, Lars. "A Love Supreme: Jazzthetic Strategies in Toni Morrison's *Beloved.*" *African American Review* 40, no. 2 (2006): 271–283. https://www.jstor.org/stable/40033715.

Ellis, Jack C. *John Grierson: Life, Contributions, Influence.* Carbondale, IL: Southern Illinois University Press, 2000.

Evans, Gary. *In the National Interest: A Chronicle of the National Film Board of Canada from 1949 to 1989*. Toronto: University of Toronto Press, 1991.

Freire, Paulo. *The Pedagogy of the Oppressed*. New York: Herder and Herder, 1970.

———. *Teachers as Cultural Workers: Letters to Those Who Dare to Teach*. Boulder, CO: Westview Press, 2005.

Friend, Marilyn. "Myths and Misunderstandings about Professional Collaboration." *Remedial and Special Education* 21, no. 3 (2000): 130–160. https://doi.org/10.1177/074193250002100301.

Hardy, Barbara. "Towards a Poetics of Fiction: An Approach through Narrative." *Novel: A Forum on Fiction* 2, no. 1 (Autumn, 1968): 5–14.

Hodge, Carroll. "Film Collaboration and Creative Conflict." *Journal of Film and Video* 61, no. 1 (2009): 63–72. https://www.jstor.org/stable/20688613.

Marchessault, Janine. "Amateur Video and the Challenge for Change." In *Mirror Machine: Video and Identity*, edited by J. Marchessault, 13–25. Toronto: YYZ Books, 1995.

Mayer, Richard E. *Multimedia Learning*. Cambridge, UK: Cambridge University Press, 2001.

Mezirow, Jack. *Transformative Dimensions of Adult Learning*. San Francisco: Jossey-Bass, 1991.

Minh-ha, Trinh T. "All-Owning Spectatorship." In *Otherness and the Media: The Ethnography of the Imagined and the Imaged*, vol. 3, edited by Hamid Naficy and Teshome H. Gabriel, 189–204. Reading, UK: Harwood Academic Publishers, 1993.

Morrison, Toni. *Playing in the Dark: Whiteness and the Literary Imagination*. Cambridge, MA: Harvard University Press, 1992.

National Film Act, R.S.C. 1985, c. N-8. https://laws-lois.justice.gc.ca/eng/acts/N-8/index.html.

Nobles, Wade W. "African Philosophy: Foundations for Black Psychology." In *Black Psychology*, edited by Reginald L. Jones, 46–63. New York: Harper and Row, 1972.

Norman, Ron. "Cultivating Imagination in Adult Education." Paper presented at the Adult Education Research Conference, University of British Columbia, Vancouver, BC, June 2000. https://eric.ed.gov/?id=ED452417.

Purdy, Sean. "Framing Regent Park: The National Film Board of Canada and the Construction of 'Outcast Spaces' in the Inner City, 1953 and 1994." *Media, Culture, and Society* 27, no. 4 (2005): 523–49. https://doi.org/10.1177/0163443705053975.

James, C. Rodney. *Film as National Art: The NFB of Canada and the Film Board*

Idea. New York: Arno Press, 1997.

Ryan, Judylyn S. *Spirituality as Ideology in Black Women's Film and Literature*, Charlottesville: University of Virginia Press, 2005.

Watson, Mireille. *A Review of Programs and Policies Regarding Documentary Production in Canada*. Toronto: Documentary Policy Advisory Group, 2005. www.onf-nfb.gc.ca/publications/en/pdf/ctf_programs_and_policies_report_en.pdf.

Wayne, Mike. "Reflections on Pedagogy." *Journal of Media Practice* 4, no. 1 (2003): 55–61. https://doi.org/10.1386/jmpr.4.1.55/0.

14

FIRST-GENERATION TRIBULATIONS

QUEENTITE OPALEKE

THINK DEEPLY // DEEPLY THINKING

Anti-Black Racism
Capitalism
Sexism
Colonialism
So very many isms
Watch them dance with no rhythm

Is this how we bun babylon each and every day
Is it just(us) feeling some type of way?
Is there justice for the person of colour today?

Let it be known—
the power of Black Love combined
immediately removes subversive paradigms
Breaks mental chains used to confine
Relax & Unwind
Discarded thoughts that no longer bind
Melanin so dark, so brilliant, so divine
this beautiful Black life of mine

consciously removes fear
conjuring it into energy
Manifesting that energy into dynamic a force
that force becomes momentum
that momentum brings about action
The action of the Movement for Black Lives
Which once in motion
infinitely exists
consistently resists
proudly throws up the black fist
Heals you with a passionate kiss
protects you as
You are the essence of life's bliss.

This.
Is.
Black.
Love.

Abundant Love that I saw—and saw me
Radiance birthed undetected,
then affected my realm
ma rue, ma vie.
Together we are . . .
Black Love Black Magic Black Light
Rulers of the Night
Melanin Royalty
Third eye sight

Together we will join a united fight
against racism—capitalism—and colonialism
Natural mystics we bun mad ism
connections based upon differences of multiculturalism
balanced by praise and constructive criticism
Teachings of higher eyes and stolen smiles
I still cry for you
in past lives elders stood on the front lines
and died for you
Reincarnated into your child

so I may ride for you
Stand by your side for you
In past lives have you laughed at fear
and died for me
allowing the Most High to reincarnate you
into my tribe for me
Ride for me
Stand by my side for me
I always knew, Black Love
Black Magic
Black Light
It was you.

• • •

Poet Thomas Gray originally coined the phrase "ignorance is bliss." Do we ponder upon the veil of ignorance, or the illusion of bliss? The majority of Canadians live their lives with this veil of ignorance around their lives. There is a similar but different ignorance that some migrants arrive in Canada with. This beautiful ignorance is a true blessing. For the most part, Black migrants have a gauge, a foundation as to what a Black-led nation looks like, feels like, operates like. Then they come to Canada, the land of hope and opportunity, land of the nice people, the subtly racist fake smiles, and affirmative-actioned opportunities; the Promised Land. The result of this ignorant bliss is what I consider first-generation tribulations. Black Canadians face the brunt of anti-Black racism. Being one of the first-generation children growing up in Canada, all of my challenges, oppressive moments in the sea of white privilege, were not experienced by my parents/caregivers in their youth. They could not relate. Their main socio-economic challenges were whether they were rich or poor, as everyone was Black. As a Nigerian/Jamaican hybrid raised in central Canada, I faced an unjust amount of negative experiences due to the colour of my skin. In the fourth grade my brother and I, the only Black students in the class, were called "nigger" by our teacher. Not one person in the class said anything in response, except me. I stood up from my chair, youngest student in the class, and said, "You can't talk to us like that." Us being my brother BamiDele and me. The teacher told me to sit down; I did not. I grabbed my brother and told him we had to call our mom. Something in my spirit knew what was happening was unjust. I didn't know what injustice, discrimination, or oppression were, but I learned what it felt like that day. My inherent reaction was to reject and deny it. As it was not my truth, only my experience. So we marched passed that teacher, straight to the office, and called our mother. This petite Jamaican force arrived no more than ten minutes later and I never saw that teacher again. He was replaced with an Asian woman named Ms. Wong. She, as a woman of colour, hugely impacted the next years of my existence in ways that are still seen today. She nurtured my differences until I saw their beauty, as she too was different. Representation matters. She wasn't Black, but she wasn't Caucasian, and that made all the difference in my life.

This was the '80s; I wasn't sure that I had a right to say anything. That teacher was fired that day due to the diligent advocating of a Black mother, my mother, who quickly learned her rights, as well as those of her children.

Think about the trauma that that experience caused. Reflect upon the damage that derogatory words have upon a young mind. Imagine the negative image one can begin to associate with brown skin colour. Imagine if every faculty member of the school was white, including the man who called you a nigger. Just imagine how it would feel to enter that school each day, to be taught by these people. Sadly, this is but one day in the life of a Black youth born in Canada. These traumatic, mentally damaging, soul-draining events forcibly shape one's existence.

Viola Desmond, the first Black person to be featured on Canadian currency, was a trailblazer. Growing up she saw a lack of haircare and skincare products for Black women and decided to address that need. She not only started a hair salon and barbershop catering to people of colour, but in addition to the salon Desmond opened The Desmond School of Beauty Culture so that Black women were provided with the skills required to open their own businesses and provide jobs for other Black women within their communities. As her school grew each year, up to as many as fifteen women graduated from the school in every class. Her story of courage, triumph, loss, and racial gains is a blueprint for the constant fight against anti-Blackness every Black Canadian faces. There are so many more stories of the migrant, the newcomer, the international student, the refugee that are unheard. There is a certain familiarity to every story that I hear from every Black Canadian I meet: resistance. Resisting the urge to retaliate, resisting the need for validation, resisting the approval of white society. Resisting the oppression white privilege creates; and so we continue to resist.

Within this resistance is rage, love, pain, and an abundance of Black joy. Black Love is what we were created in and with. It is a divine birthright that leads effortlessly. It is intimidating, mysterious, alluring, and awe-inspiring. There is value in our words, our art, our existence, our resistance. There is duty in our spirits to guide, to love, to create, to unite, and to be unmoved in our dedication to the liberation of Black Lives. This is our rite of passage, honouring our journey, our ancestors' journey, and the lineage that follows. From tribulation to testimony. In "Patience," Damien Marley speaks of a spiritual DNA etched inside our essence that will always be ours.[1] And so I digress with one of my poems about being real and truthful with one's self. This poem is my mantra for my life. I look in the mirror and I state my intentions proudly, loudly, and truthfully. It's not always pretty, no. It at times is magnificent, yes. But it is always real. Nothing more, nothing less. Just enough. Because I am, you are, we are ENOUGH.

REAL

Teach the youths to stand up tall
However big or small
Fighting for human rights and justice for all.

Whether you are brown, Black, gay, queer
Hybrids in shapes and forms from near and far
I was born a natural siSTAR
Beaming and gleaming
Kinda like afro sheening
Back tattooed with tribal meanings
Just, real.

And as I stare into the depths of my mind
As inspiring spirits infest me with rhyme
I know that at this very moment in time
ALL this power is Mine.
Divine.
Spontaneous.
Influence all in full shine.

know it's as easy as being heard
But I also need you to ovastand the meaning of each of my words
From the look of my eye to the body language that I speak
My ups and my downs
My weakness and my freak.

I am not a simple woman
it's rather complicated
Some of them they love me
and to others I am hated
Memories they keep getting faded and faded
You keep those you want to keep
Dreaming is sweet
But when you're dreaming, you're really not asleep.
In my dream I was running, when I awoke I was tired
In my dream I was writing, when I awoke I was inspired.

Inspired to rise to the highest of heights
Spreading my wings
Allowing my dreams to take flight
Leaping faithfully in the depth of my own fright
Ooh I feel cooler than the darkest of night
and in that space
I AM Stealth
with an abundance of soulful wealth
Here, I rise
and to I this climb is no surprise
It was predestined in my book of lIfe.

and in this book,
I teach the youths to stand up tall
However big or small
Fighting for human rights against the injustice system for all
Whether you are brown, black, gay, queer
Hybrids in shapes and forms from near and far
We were all born natural brother and siSTARS
Beaming and gleaming
Kinda like how my mom stays afro sheening
Kinda like how my back's tattooed with tribal meanings
Just real.
Yeah, just real.

NOTES

1 "Patience," written by Nasir Jones (Nas), Damien Marley, Amadou Bajayoko, and Mariam Doumbia.

15

IT'S IN US TO GIVE: BLACK LIFE AND THE RACIAL PROFILING OF BLOOD DONATION

OMISOORE DRYDEN

In July 2018, I received a text message from a colleague who was travelling in South Africa. The message included a picture of a large red silo located in a large open grassy space. The silo is imprinted with a message (advertisement) from the South African National Blood Service which states, "Our Blood Saves Lives. Donate Blood Today."

At first this may seem like an obvious statement. Of course our blood saves lives. However, to read this along the backdrop of Blackness, anti-Black racism, and the experiences of Black people, this statement, for me at least, takes on added significance. In the larger public imagination, Black people are rarely thought of as belonging in Canadian society.[1] In fact, Black people often experience this unbelonging through seemingly benign questions such as "where are you *really* from?" As a result, Black people are stereotypically thought of as recent arrivals from the Caribbean region, Africa, and the United States. This often stands against the exception of Black people who came to Canada in the 1800s through the Underground Railroad. While some of this is factual, its overwhelming performance as the single Black-people-in-Canada narrative occludes our long history both pre- and post-slavery. The interrogations into the mysteries of the body, including blood, did not occur as objective examinations. Scientific investigations into the body, and its blood, occur within the tapestries of anti-Black racism, colonialism, religiosity, and white supremacist logics. These same logics frame the parameters of citizenship and belonging within Canada and frame the systems of blood donation. As a result, Black people are often associated with having/possessing bad bodily fluids, in particular blood and semen. Through these logics, HIV and AIDS has become a "natural association" with Blackness. As such, Black people and their blood and semen have been a site of contention, containment, and concealment. Although HIV and AIDS impact marginalized populations differently, the criminalization of HIV has negatively impacted Black people. Rinaldo Walcott writes in his book *Queer Returns: Essays on Multiculturalism, Diaspora, and Black Studies*, "in the age of HIV/AIDS, the Black dick has emerged as an instrument as dangerous as the gun."[2] My focus is how the racist (and racist-homophobic) narratives of disease (including HIV and AIDS) inform the "truths" about blood. These racist "truths" are in turn deployed against Black people in Canada. Public blood donation has been the responsibility of two agencies: the Canadian Red Cross Society (from 1940 to 1998) and the Canadian Blood Services/Héma Québec (1998 to the present). Anti-Black racism and "afro-phobia" have impacted public blood donation policies and practices in Canada from its inception in 1940. The Canadian Red Cross Society (CRCS) was an auxiliary to the government's military medical services in wartime and held its first public, non-military blood donor clinic in 1940 in Toronto. With the slogan "Make a Date with a Wounded Soldier,"[3] Canadians were urged to donate blood, with all donations reserved for use exclusively within the military. In other words, all blood collected was earmarked for military use only.

Dr. Charles R. Drew (1904–1950), an African-American cisgender man, developed procedures for collecting, storing, and transporting large quantities of blood. He began the development of these procedures while studying at McGill University, and these methods and procedures became the basis for national blood collection programs in Canada, the United States, and Britain.[4] "The first blood transfusion recipients were white American and British soldiers, and following the direction of the American Red Cross Society, all blood collected in Canada and the US was racially catalogued with the purpose of ensuring that white soldiers did not receive blood from not-white [people]."[5]

As the creator of the modern blood donation system, Dr. Charles Drew rigorously objected to this practice of the racial segregation of donated blood, arguing that there was no scientific evidence to support such a practice. However, the practice prevailed. Between 1940 and 1942, women, who largely ran the clinics, were not allowed to donate blood, as it was suggested that women would not be able to handle the physical process of donation. Once women were allowed to donate, the practice of racial segregation was applied to their blood. The first peacetime blood donor clinic happened in 1947, with blood now used for non-military use.

These blood narratives of racial segregation and gendered exclusion were understood to fall within the parameters of "safe" blood and thus framed the early practices of blood donation in Canada; they constituted the social determinants, the very conditions, of safe blood and optimal health. Public health discourse has often framed the body as dangerous and problematic, as ever threatening to run out of control, to attract disease, and to pose imminent danger to the rest of society. And in response to this framing, numerous measures have been taken to confine people and to control their environments, movements, and interactions.

HIV, AIDS, and the tainted blood crisis renewed the dominance of science in systems of social control, particularly in dictating appropriate behaviours, thus creating a connection between these behaviours and one's true nature as a human being. The contamination of the blood supply signalled a significant breach—one in which dangerous bodies (homosexual, Haitian, heroin users, and hemophiliacs—the 4 H) and their blood—infected the general public. HIV and AIDS marked an important moment in blood donation in Canada.

Canada reported its first case of AIDS in March 1982. To keep the blood supply safe, North American health officials placed a ban on men who have sex with men from donating blood. AIDS was considered to be exclusively a gay-related disease. The homophobia embedded in the early detection of AIDS included assumptions of lack of moral correctness and lack of self-control among men who have sex with men. To keep the blood supply safe, men who have sex with men were called on to "take 'ownership' of and assume 'responsibility' for the virus."[6] In March 1983, the Centers for Disease Control and Prevention (CDC) in the United States released a list detailing the "dangers" of HIV contamination by naming four vectors for its transmission—homosexuals, heroin addicts, hemophiliacs and Haitians.[7] Blood donor clinic operators were asked to bar these groups of people from donating blood, but also to put them under surveillance. Haitian people, regardless of citizenship, were included in this ban. Concurrently with the political activism of gays and lesbians in the 1970s and 1980s, the political situation in Haiti was catastrophic. In the 1970s Haitian people were fleeing the poverty and repression in a dictator-led Haiti, finding their way to nearby Caribbean countries, the United States, and Canada—specifically Quebec. Anti-Black racism is not a new phenomenon in Canada or in Quebec, but it is important to note that this influx of Haitian people during this time was met with xenophobic fears. As newcomers to Canada, Haitians faced challenges including racially motivated violence, racial harassment, and racial discrimination. It is not surprising, then, that when HIV/AIDS began to be diagnosed within Haitian communities, the desire to find the origin of HIV/AIDS shifted to include Haitian people. As a result, not only was Haiti framed as a place riddled with HIV and AIDS, but also all Haitian people were considered to be carriers of this deadly disease. Stereotypes and fiction were presented as medical and scientific objective study. Haitian people were described as "mysterious, isolated, disease-ridden, blood-maddened and engaging in exotic, violent voodoo rituals."[8] These racist stereotypes existed long before the advent of AIDS and the "scientific" blaming of Haitian people in North America and in Haiti.

Not only did the CDC release a list detailing the 4 H club in March 1983, but the Red Cross also issued a pamphlet asking persons at "high risk" of getting HIV/AIDS (in this case gay and Haitian people) to refrain from donating blood.[9] Predictably, these actions were met with outrage and protest.

On April 20, 1990, about 80,000 Haitian people marched across the Brooklyn Bridge in protest of the decision by the United States Food and Drug Administration to outright ban Haitian people from donating blood. Photos from the protest show New York streets overflowing with protestors holding signs ranging from "Proud of our Blood" or "International Criminals like FDA Scientists Belong in

Prison. They Try to Kill African Race" to "Find a Cure for AIDS."[10] Overall, 150,000 Haitian people protested the ban on Haitian people from donating blood.[11] This action tied up traffic for hours while simultaneously shutting down Wall Street trading.[12] The ban was overturned later that month.

Racism and homophobia led public health officials to believe that simply by banning Haitian people and men who have sex with men from donating blood, the blood supply would remain untainted. And it was within this climate that the tainted blood scandal was framed—the inability to bar the vectors of disease: the 4 H club.

From the mid-1980s to the 1990s, blood donation recipients became infected with HIV and hepatitis C through tainted blood products. This was a public health disaster, an outcome of inadequate screening procedures and a new and (at the time) undetectable sexually transmitted infection.

The panic regarding HIV/AIDS is conflated with the panic regarding homosexuality and the continuing colonial panic about miscegenation. As has been stated elsewhere, HIV and AIDS is an epidemic on multiple simultaneous levels: it is an epidemic of a transmissible lethal disease as well as an epidemic of meanings or significations.[13] It is in this climate that the Canadian federal government established the Royal Commission of Inquiry on the Blood System in Canada (otherwise known as the Krever Commission) in 1993. The Krever Commission's report, which was tabled in the House of Commons in 1997, concluded that, although it was inevitable that there would be a blood contamination crisis, this crisis was much larger than it needed to be. Believing that the Canadian Red Cross Society had now become itself too tainted and contaminated from its failures to effectively and properly protect the innocent victims of this blood crisis, the Krever Commission's report instructed the government to remove the responsibility of the blood supply system from the Red Cross.

In 1998 the federal government created the new organization: Canadian Blood Services. Canadian Blood Services is a not-for-profit, charitable organization responsible for the regulatory frameworks related to donors, the blood supply, blood safety, and the distribution of blood products. In addition, Canadian Blood Services is also responsible for the surveillance and monitoring of all aspects of the blood system/supply; thus, it is argued, Canadian Blood Services will be able to respond quickly if another blood-borne disease should ever threaten the general public.[14] In response to a recommendation from the Krever Commission (and to fulfill its commitment in providing a clean and healthy blood supply), Canadian Blood Services developed and implemented a new donor questionnaire as part of the larger screening process. With the establishment of Canadian Blood Services, the creation of the ideal blood donor became an earnest endeavour. However, there was an already-established perception that the only way to protect the blood supply was through the cultivation of white, heterosexual donors. And this perception found its way into the new organization.

Canadian Blood Services' slogan, "It's in you to give," stands alongside a detailed and in-depth donor questionnaire that operates to weed out bodies deemed to be already diseased and, ultimately, a threat to the system. The scope and breadth of the questions on the donor questionnaire are important to note, for each question does not simply exist as a separate and distinct "moment" with its own historical specificity; each question is also conjunctural—connected and hinging upon one another—part of a larger vibrant discursive exchange. Canadian Blood Services argues that its required donor questionnaire is specifically designed to effectively screen potential blood donors. The questionnaire asks a number of questions regarding travel, medical background, drug use, sex, and sexual encounters. Also included are questions regarding geographic locations, ostensibly to determine where one is "from," where one has been (and for how long), and the range and scope of sexual contact potentially engaged in whilst there. The donor questionnaire is supposed to facilitate the identification of potential blood-borne diseases, but in practice the questions have been most closely directed at preventing a recurrence of an HIV and AIDS outbreak.

Between 1998 and 2016 the donor questionnaire was a printed document reminiscent of multiple-choice questions on school exams, with participants invited to provide answers that best reflect their location, position, and place. Divided into two sections, the participant fills out question numbers 1 to 13 directly, and question numbers 14 to 30 are asked of the participant by the nurse/clinic worker.

Earlier practices of blood donation in Canada focused on not-white people (1940), and Haitian people (from 1983 to 1990).

However, contemporary donation practices focus on Africa. Up until 2005 the following questions were asked on the donor questionnaire:

- Were you born in or have you lived in any of the countries listed here since 1977: Cameroon, Central African Republic, Chad, Congo, Equatorial Guinea, Gabon, Niger, Nigeria?
- Have you had sexual contact with a male, even one time since 1977, who was from Cameroon, Central African Republic, Chad, Congo, Equatorial Guinea, Gabon, Niger, Nigeria?
- When traveling to any of the above countries since 1977, have you received blood or treatment with a product made from blood?[15]

At this time, Canadian Blood Services argued that this type of "geographic deferral" was necessary since people who lived in these countries may have been exposed to a new strain of the virus HIV-I, group O. As such, they were not eligible to donate blood. CBS also stated directly, "this is not based on race or ethnicity but possible exposure to HIV-I Group O."[16]

The over-identification of Blackness with HIV and AIDS occluded additional information regarding this strain of HIV, specifically its presence in the predominantly white countries of France, Belgium, Spain, Germany, and the United States.[17] It would seem that, if this strain was beyond testing capabilities of the day, all countries where the strain was present would be included in the ban. In other words, the questions would read instead:

- Were you born in or have you lived in any of the countries listed here since 1977: *Belgium*, Cameroon, Central African Republic, Chad, Congo, Equatorial Guinea, *France*, Gabon, *Germany*, *Spain*, Niger, Nigeria and the *United States*?
- Have you had sexual contact with a male, even one time since 1977, who was from *Belgium*, Cameroon, Central African Republic, Chad, Congo, Equatorial Guinea, *France*, Gabon, *Germany*, *Spain*, Niger, Nigeria and the *United States*?
- When traveling to any of the above countries (*Belgium*, Cameroon, Central African Republic, Chad, Congo, Equatorial Guinea, *France*, Gabon, *Germany*, *Spain*, Niger,

Nigeria and the *United States*) since 1977, have you received blood or treatment with a product made from blood?

Instead, in 2005, Canadian Blood Services changed the questions to read:

- Were you born in or have you lived in *Africa* since 1977?
- Since 1977, did you receive a blood transfusion or blood product in *Africa*?
- Have you had sexual contact with anyone who was born in or lived in *Africa* since 1977?[18]

In 2015, Shannon Ryan, Executive Director of Black Coalition for AIDS Prevention (Black CAP), Debbie Douglas, Executive Director of the Ontario Council of Agencies Serving Immigrants (OCASI), and I had the opportunity to meet with representatives of Canadian Blood Services, specifically the medical director of donor and clinical services, Dr. Mindy Goldman, and the manager, stakeholder relations, Don Lapierre. In this meeting I asked about the shift from eight specific African countries to the inclusion of all of Africa (all fifty-four countries) in the blood donor questionnaire. Goldman informed us that this shift was to make the donor questionnaire easier to administer. She stated that it was too difficult to name each country separately and that Canadian Blood Services and Health Canada felt it would be better to instead name "Africa."

As the justification for asking the question initially was about a specific strain of HIV in those eight specific countries, I asked if the impetus for the question had changed. After all, the continent of Africa is not riddled with HIV and AIDS. Goldman informed us that HIV-I, group O, remained the reason for the question.

The shift from including eight countries in Africa to including all fifty-four countries demonstrates how anti-Black racism informs the construction of the donor questionnaire. Although the "science" relied upon by CBS identified only eight countries with this particular strain of HIV, this did not stop the agency from disregarding this data.

I have spoken across the country about my research. White people have shared with me that they also have been barred from giving blood. And yet, white people have also shared with me that, even though they were born in Africa, they were instructed by the Canadian Blood Services' employees to answer "no" to this question. This is just one example of how these questions are not about geography; the questions are operationalized based on anti-African/anti-Black racist stereotypes.

In 2013, Canadian Blood Services moved to an electronic donor questionnaire, uploading the questions to an interactive computer screen. Not only were the questions now voiced, generic pictures of African landscapes accompanied the questions. For example, the lifestyle question asks, "Have you had sexual contact with anyone who was born in or lived in Africa since 1977?," while the travel question, accompanied by an image of an African elephant, wants to know if you have received a blood transfusion or blood product while in Africa since that same year. One would assume that the images added to the donor questionnaire are used to augment understanding of the questions—to further inform the viewer of what the questions actually mean.

During my 2015 meeting with Goldman and Lapierre, I asked about the use of the image of the African elephant and asked them to clarify that Canadian Blood Services was actually asking if people had received blood donation from people.[19] I also wondered about the use of an image of the acacia tree to accompany the question regarding sexual contact. Were donors to assume that folks were/are having sex in trees, and if so, if this was a particularly risky African practice: one that resulted in transmission of an untestable strain of HIV?

When I asked Goldman about the choice of these images, she informed me that they felt these images would elicit feelings of nostalgia in African people attempting to donate blood.

In fact, the use of these pictures is reminiscent of the imagery described in Joseph Conrad's *Heart of Darkness* and the early affectations of tropical medicine. Disease in Africa is considered natural. It is imagined that African people live in dirt, side by side with animals and vegetation. These are the kinds of images that facilitate Black people being "scienced into degradation."[20] To realize that the senior administrative body of Canadian Blood Services felt these images most appropriately represented the question being asked is astonishing, yet for many expected. These are the realities and contradictions of anti-African/anti-Black racism in Canada.

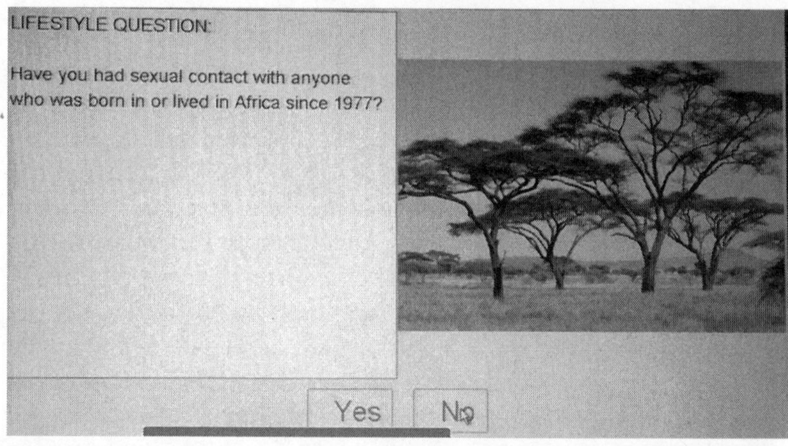

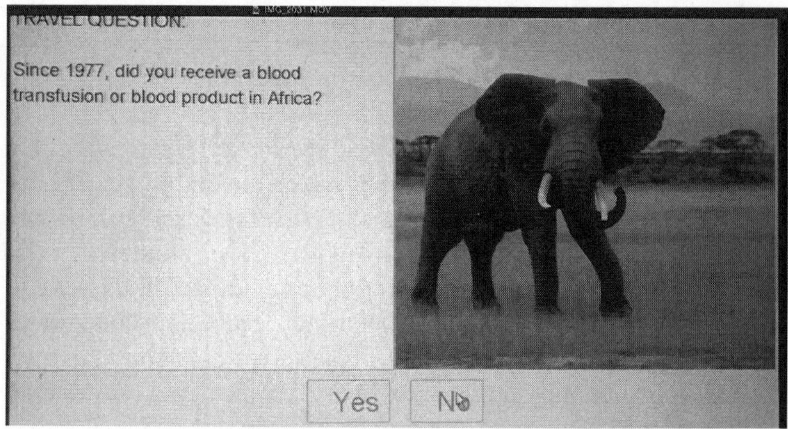

Lifestyle Question and Travel Question from CBS touch screen questionnaire. SOURCE: Screenshots taken and shared via personal correspondence by SR, Facebook friend.

It is important to note that a reliable test for HIV-1, group O, existed and was approved for use in 2009; however, Canadian Blood Services kept this ban in place until 2015—another six years.

In 2015 the blood donor questionnaire questions changed once again. Instead of reading "African," they now read "Togo and Cameroon." The online questionnaire still used images to further accompany the written questions; the elephant has been removed, yet the acacia tree remains. However, the acacia tree is not indigenous to

Togo or Cameroon. These trees are indigenous to the southeastern region of the continent (in the countries of Mozambique, Botswana, and Swaziland, for example), not the west, where the countries of Togo and Cameroon are located.

Canadian Blood Services relied on these images to communicate and deliver messages about risky behaviour and sources of tainted blood and in doing so perpetuated racist stereotypes about Black people and Blackness. These stereotypes both simultaneously exceed the limits of science while also engaging in the domain of scientific racism.

I return one last time to my 2015 meeting with Canadian Blood Services, where I asked about the changes from (all fifty-four countries in) Africa to (just) two, Togo and Cameroon. Goldman shared that these countries were included in case new strains of HIV were to develop. If this were the case, the agency would need time to develop effective testing. Of course, this presupposes that new strains of HIV can only develop on the African continent.

In May 2018, Canadian Blood Services ended the direct ban on African people from blood donation, but the impact of anti-Black racism remains. Since Canadian Blood Services has refused to acknowledge how racism informed their determination of what constituted safe blood, the blood agency has not taken any steps to repair or reconcile with Black communities in Canada. In this way, attempts to erase this history of racism (by removing questions and erasing the images) does not diminish its effects, but instead the silence regarding this racism works to preserve and continue it. This long history of the degradation of Black people and their blood remains. To be clear, this is not perceived racism; this is the real and operationalized racism in the blood system.

I share this history of anti-Black/anti-African blood donation practices in Canada not so that we can simply hope to have our blood included. When a disease is aligned, even in part, with one of the politically and socially constructed categories of race, it both defines and is defined by that category and inevitably reinforces its existence. Hope of inclusion does not ultimately disrupt the anti-Black practices of racism, homophobia, and sexism.

The racist experiences with blood donation and the signification of HIV/AIDS have impacted Black people from across the Black diaspora. Blood donation systems in Canada have treated Black people as the "fruit of the poisonous tree." This legal metaphor, used in the United States, positions the source of the information, in this case the tree, as tainted. And as such, any fruit from this tree must be tainted as well. In terms of blood donation, the tree is Africa (remember the use of the acacia tree). And the fruit are her people—African-descended (Black) people. As such, any blood (information) collected from this tree is inadmissible. This process of racialization ascribes racial subjectivity to HIV, blood, and disease.

Canadian Blood Services has become a barrier in the stories told about HIV and AIDS and "high-risk" Black communities. Removing the ban does not account for Canadian Blood Services' continuing silence on their racist practices. Black liberation includes Black health, wellness, and healing. And this is the type of intervention needed at this blood agency. Are we able to imagine healthy Black people, and if so, how does this inform the path to Black healing?

NOTES

1 Rinaldo Walcott, *Queer Returns: Essays on Multiculturalism, Diaspora, and Black Studies* (Toronto: Insomniac Press, 2016).

2 Walcott, *Queer Returns*, 206.

3 André Picard, *The Gift of Death: Confronting Canada's Tainted-Blood Tragedy* (Toronto: Harper Collins, 1995).

4 Charles W. Carey, Jr., *African Americans in Science: An Encyclopedia of People and Progress* (Santa Barbara, CA: ABC-CLIO, 2008).

5 OmiSoore H. Dryden, "'A Queer Too Far': Blackness, 'Gay Blood,' and Transgressive Possibilities," in *Disrupting Queer Inclusion: Canadian Homonationalisms and the Politics of Belonging*, OmiSoore H. Dryden and Suzanne Lenon, eds. (Vancouver: University of British Columbia Press, 2015) 116–32.

6 Georges E. Fouron, "Race, Blood, Disease and Citizenship: The Making of the Haitian-Americans and the Haitian Immigrants into 'the Others' during the 1980s-1990s AIDS Crisis," *Identities: Global Studies in Culture and Power* 20, no. 6 (2013), 707.

7 Régine Michelle Jean-Charles, "The Sway of Stigma," 64.

8 Paul Farmer, *AIDS and Accusation: Haiti and the Geography of Blame* (Berkeley: University of California Press, 2006), 3.

9 Commission of Inquiry on the Blood System in Canada, 1997, xxiv.

10 Retrieved from *Haïti Liberté* June 15, 2018, https://haitiliberte.com/haitians-form-coaliton-and-plan-jan-19-demonstration-to-answer-trumps-racism/.

11 "Now, No Haitians Can Donate Blood," *New York Times*, March 14, 1990, https://www.nytimes.com/1990/03/14/us/now-no-haitians-can-donate-blood.html.

12 "F.D.A. Policy to Limit Blood is Protested," *New York Times*, April 21, 1990, https://www.nytimes.com/1990/04/21/nyregion/fda-policy-to-limit-blood-is-protested.html; Unite Press International Archives, April 20, 1990, retrieved June 15, 2018, https://www.upi.com/Archives/1990/04/20/Haitians-protest-blood-ruling/7480640584000/.

13 Paula Treichler, *How to Have Theory in an Epidemic: Cultural Chronicles of AIDS* (Durham, NC: Duke University Press, 1999).

14 "Blood donor recruitment," Canadian Blood Services, October 12, 2010, http://www.bloodservices.ca/CentreApps/Internet/UW_V502_MainEngine.nsf/page/E_faq_Recruitment?OpenDocument.

15 Canadian Blood Services Donor Questionnaire, 1999.

16 Ibid.

17 Behring-Diagnostics, August 1997.

18 Canadian Blood Services Donor Questionnarie, 2005.

19 I know that humans and elephants are mammals, but I have not come across anything that has stated that they currently share compatible blood products.

20 Katherine McKittrick, "Science Quarrels Sculpture: The Politics of Reading Sarah Baartman" in *Mosaic* 43, no. 2 (June 2010): 117.

REFERENCES

Carey, Jr. Charles W. *African Americans in Science: An Encyclopedia of People and Progress*. Santa Barbara, CA: ABC-CLIO, 2008.

Dryden, OmiSoore H. "'A Queer Too Far': Blackness, 'Gay Blood,' and Transgressive Possibilities." In *Disrupting Queer Inclusion: Canadian Homonationalisms and the Politics of Belonging*, edited by OmiSoore H. Dryden and Suzanne Lenon, 116–132. Vancouver: University of British Columbia Press, 2015.

Farmer, Paul. *AIDS and Accusation: Haiti and the Geography of Blame*. Berkeley: University of California Press, 2006.

Fouron, Georges E. "Race, Blood, Disease and Citizenship: The Making of the Haitian-Americans and the Haitian Immigrants into 'the Others' during the 1980s–1990s AIDS Crisis." *Identities: Global Studies in Culture and Power* 20, no. 6 (2013): 705–719. https://doi.org/10.1080/1070289X.2013.828624.

Jean-Charles, Régine Michelle. "The Sway of Stigma: The Politics and Poetics of AIDS Representation in *Le président a-t-il le SIDA?* and Spirit of Haiti." *Small Axe* 15, no. 3 (2011): 62–79.

McKittrick, Katherine. "Science Quarrels Sculpture: The Politics of Reading Sarah Baartman." *Mosaic: An Interdisciplinary Critical Journal* 43, no. 2 (June 2010): 113–130. JSTOR, www.jstor.org/stable/44030627.

Picard, André. *The Gift of Death: Confronting Canada's Tainted-Blood Tragedy.* Toronto: Harper Collins, 1995.

Treichler, Paula. *How to Have Theory in an Epidemic: Cultural Chronicles of AIDS*. Durham, NC: Duke University Press, 1999.

Walcott, Rinaldo. *Queer Returns: Essays on Multiculturalism, Diaspora, and Black Studies*. Toronto: Insomniac Press, 2016.

16

FROM *CHEECHAKO* TO *SOURDOUGH*: REFLECTIONS ON NORTHERN LIVING AND SURVIVING, WHILE BEING BLACK

PAIGE GALETTE

Surviving winter is hard enough.

The dry skin, the wet feet, the feeling of perpetual cold. I could try to be cute, but my nose will still leak.

I would often catch myself daydreaming of the hot August sun caressing my shoulders.

While shivering at the bus stand, I close my eyes, imagining the freshness of an ice-cold lemonade while my skin breathes in spite of the sweat and is caressed by a soft breeze.

Or I think of spring, and I remind myself of days I will be looking out my bedroom window, admiring the budding flowers, the cherry trees, the lush of green, the smell of lilacs in gardens, and visiting farmer's markets.

But all I see is snow.

I'm exhausted.

I'm hopeless and I don't feel the end coming.

Each morning I hit snooze again and again, knowing I will soon have to gather up the energy to go outside, take transit, endure work.

Surviving winter is hard enough.

Surviving Blackness is hard enough.

Put the two together and I'm already on the ground.

Those were my winters in Ontario. They sucked the life force out of me. The winters were harsh, and compounded with the stresses and pace of urban life—it was almost too much to take. I would leave my apartment and go to work, feeling so fraught I would be gasping for air. I needed to breathe. I needed space to be alone for a bit, to think, to laugh on my own, to be me! I couldn't breathe. Even in summertime, laid back on a blanket in Christie Pits Park in Toronto, alone. I should have been relaxed, admiring the scene. But I couldn't breathe.

The pace of the city was unbearable. I'd ride my bike, hoping for some relief from the exercise . . . . But I would constantly worry about drivers passing by who might harm me or the other cyclists and pedestrians. I would meet up with friends and get dressed up for an event, only to waste forty-five minutes in a line-up for only one or two hours at the actual event.

It always amazed me that, in a city of millions, I always felt alone. With this loneliness, depression crept up on me and decided to tag along. It tagged along with me to work, to outings with friends, and found ways to ground itself comfortably in my activism.

I used to be described as fun and bubbly. Now I was angry and pissed off, 24/7.

Depression made me unrecognizable. I needed to breathe.

• • •

Back in 2014, friends of mine invited me to visit them in the Yukon.

"The Yukon?" I thought. "What the fuck am I going to do there? Black people don't go north, let alone the Yukon."

But with a heart full of love for these friends, who assured me that the Yukon was a magical place, I left for my first visit to the North; my first time travelling on my own. I still remember boarding the flight to Whitehorse on Air North, which I later found out was owned by a First Nation in the territory.

I was nervous. I thought to myself, "What the hell am I doing, going to a place so far north and by myself?" The friends I was visiting weren't Black. So, as much as I believed them when they said the Yukon was magical, I began to panic. All I knew is that I was heading to a hunting area . . . Would I get shot? Would I be asked questions about my Blackness and forced to contend with inappropriate stares? Would I be the only Black person in town? What if my friends lured me into a place where their whiteness and privilege prevented them from seeing the dangers that were present for Black and racialized folks? The experience of travelling to somewhere new is often fraught for Black people. Wherever we go, we need to consider whether or not we will be treated with dignity. Add the fact that I am a woman, queer, and unapologetically outspoken; I was truly nervous. But I needed to leave the city.

While leaving the airport in my friend's car, I looked in the rearview mirror and gasped at the multitude of mountains looking back. "If you think these mountains are pretty, just wait until we take the road to Skagway (Alaska)," my friend said. As I walked in the streets of Whitehorse, I couldn't help but notice the number of Indigenous people. Suddenly I didn't feel so alone. Yukon is home to fourteen First Nations, eleven of which are self-governing. This is a fact that is barely discussed in Canadian history, politics, or education. I hold a bachelor's degree in social sciences and political science. Never did we learn about Indigenous governance. But I was required to learn about the colour of the carpet in the House of Commons and the Senate. Am I surprised? Absolutely not. This country is founded on colonialism, racism, and genocide. I was ashamed that I had assumed that white people had power and control in this land simply because that's what I was used to seeing.

Needless to say, my visit was spectacular. I ate berries from backyards and public trails; I was taught to forage for Labrador Tea; I saw northern lights for the very first time. I did things I hadn't done in a really long time, but that I loved: camping, hiking, exploring. On my last day in Whitehorse, I hiked up a mountain with my friends to see the sunset; I sat down on the fresh ground, cracked open a beer, and tears started flowing. At first I thought it was because of the winds and the fact that I was going back home and probably wouldn't see my friends again in a while. I thought I was sad. But when I took the plane back home to Ottawa the next day, I started to sob uncontrollably. I cried tears of joy, I cried tears of sadness, but most of all I cried because I was able to breathe! That was it! I knew I'd be back.

The following winter I was invited to come up to Yellowknife, Northwest Territories, to visit a friend. I figured if I was going all the way up there, I might as well stop by Whitehorse in the Yukon. And there I was, so far north, only this time in the beginning of winter. I was so "misplaced," even my phone would die from the cold as soon as I took it out of my coat. I was cold. But I didn't care. I was facing mountains. The same ones that had taken my heart a year prior. The sun would rise near 11 a.m. and go back down near 3 p.m. The sun was almost nonexistent, yet the darkness was calming, soothing, and best felt with a burning fire. That year, winter was different; during my Yukon visit we played in the snow all day, went tubing in the Carcross Desert. I wasn't once cold. I was glowing. I felt like a kid again.

I remembered being a kid in London, Ontario, building houses made out of snow on our front lawn. I'd invite my neighbours for "lunch" in my made-up kitchen. Most of the other kids couldn't sustain the cold and would make up an excuse to run back home. I didn't really have that many friends growing up, and as a result I realized that it was nice to not have to share my "snow house" with anybody else. I hadn't played in the snow for such a long period of time in so long until that Yukon visit. Growing up I often cursed the snow. As an adult living in Canada I'd ask myself why the hell was I still living in this cold-ass place. Yet, after one experience of Yukon winter, I had a different, a very different view: She (winter) was gorgeous! A wonderland to discover, so inviting. With fauna that seemed so mysterious, like out of a fantasy novel. There was caribou, elk, bison, arctic fox and lynx. Due to the lack of humidity, I felt this winter visit was so much warmer than winter in

Toronto, Ottawa, or Montreal—all places that made me despise winter. People here were laughing, always wanting to do things outside and be cozy inside. I'd meet up with a friend of mine, who is visibly racialized, and I allowed myself to ask the real questions: Are there Black people here? Other racialized people? Could I move here? Would I be happy? Could I find community? Sure, I give credit to my friends: they were the ones to invite me up to visit in the first place. But the greater credit goes to my friend Reem: she inspired me to be who I am and to embrace my love for camping and hiking and loving the North's winter while still being true to myself. She showed me that we POCs can enjoy life not fitting "the norm." We can still do those outdoor sports and activities and not let ourselves down or betray ourselves. I decided to take a bold step and move north.

Leaving Toronto was easier than I thought. Sure, I was rattled with anxiety, depression, and fear, but my activism had always pushed me in unfamiliar territory. At this time in my life, the price of my activism was catching up to me—I was receiving real threats from people with power and influence, as well as your average asshole trolls. I read descriptions of me online that were so vile in ways I had never seen or imagine possible. I'd be belittled with the most hurtful words, criticisms of my Blackness, my queerness, and my intelligence. People who I had never seen or met before wished ill on my well-being and pain on my friends and family. I saw darkness everywhere I went. I couldn't breathe. I knew I needed to leave, to go. If I were to survive in this world, I needed a place that allowed me to be me, to love myself, and a place where I could escape when things would get wild again. I say "wild again," because (a) being Black in Canada, you can't seclude yourself from racist bullshit. There is no place, not even one as big and diverse as Toronto, that will protect you from haters, racists, misogynists, and white supremacists. Our country is founded on white supremacy, and its roots run so deep. It is everywhere. And I say "wild again" because (b) being unapologetically outspoken means shit will sometimes pop off, no matter how hard I try. And trust me . . . I've tried! Being Haitian, I like to think that I can never be tamed in my activism, in my quest for social justice. It's in my blood, it's in my history, and it's in the generations of my ancestors and in the generations of my futures. I need to be able to speak my mind.

And so I packed my car and drove across the country, refusing to look back. I couldn't look back. The view in front was too sweet to take my eyes off of it. However, the decision to move was complex. Firstly, I needed to acknowledge that it was complex to move and create a life for myself on land that isn't mine. I often think about whether or not I'm participating in a modern-day colonialism, one where I chose to move somewhere, without being invited or consulting the First Nations community in that place. I truly believe in decolonization and that by decolonizing, Indigenous people will be free. But I also feel like a fraud for settling in a location where I wasn't invited. I'm still conflicted by this. Modern-day settlerism. It doesn't feel good. Second, I am extremely privileged to have been able to move away. I left my family, my friends, my community. Leaving made me feel so selfish. I was fortunate enough to have the funds, to find employment, and to have friends to take me in while I found a place to live. But leaving is not that easy. As Black people, it can be hard to leave a place you know has all your needs, your community—especially for a place so unfamiliar, so unknown. I think of the displacement of refugees seeking a place to live, to be alive, to be free, to breathe. I think of the barriers that borders place in front of people seeking refuge. I think of the tests that migrants have to go through and pass in order to prove they are able to "conform" to the white supremacy already rooted in this country. Leaving and coming, travels and migrations: they are hard processes and complex ones.

I left Ontario with absolute peace of mind, and I left no one—not family, child, dependant—behind. I left without the need to conform or to prove and declare patriotism. I left easy, while my people, Haitian people, are at the United States–Canada border seeking refuge, a promise of a better future and opportunities, while facing sacrifices, a generous colder weather, and isolation.

I'd be a great liar if I were to say I'm living a perfect life in Whitehorse, free to be me, to show my Blackness, to live carefree. My new life in Yukon has still been marked by anti-Blackness. For example, at my work, when I straighten my natural hair, I still get reactions from colleagues: "I didn't recognize you." There are only two Black people at my workplace of over 300 employees. I am short (four feet, eleven inches), with a very distinguishable tattoo on my forearm and a nose piercing. And yet I was still "unrecognizable" because my hair was straight. Similarly, as president of a not-for-profit's board of administration, I get questioned every day about my intentions and actions. I get undermined constantly, even by fellow board members. All of this is steeped in anti-Blackness. When meeting new people, I get asked how "my people" react to X, Y, and Z. I get questioned about the fact that I've never been to my homeland, Haiti, when Becky, Julie, Chad, and Matt all went on at least three to four "missions."[1] And yes, I *still* get told that my anger with white people wearing so-called dreads at music festivals is unwarranted. Don't let my Instagram account fool you—anti-Blackness is alive and present in Yukon.

But there are also lots of great things, worth taking into account, about living in the North. First off, the impact of the self-governing First Nations people is tremendous. I've never lived in an area where people, white people, question their own actions and impacts with the intention of respecting First Nations people. Living in Yukon is living on recognized First Nations territory. A lot of this is due to policy changes and implementations as well as consultations with and directions from First Nations peoples. Their strength, tenacity, and resilience has made it that the North is a much more welcoming place for racialized people as these changes positively impact the lives of people from marginalized communities.

In Whitehorse, a government town, instead of seeing buildings and streets named after Wilfrid Laurier, Mackenzie King, and other nonsense slave owners, as I've experienced in Ottawa, there are names of First Nations people, and there are First Nations cultural centres able to host a variety of events and feature the First Nation's history, art, and culture. Hunting, trapping, and fishing season are done with intention, and with recognition of and respect for First Nations culture. For a Black person like me, who may feel displaced, it's quite comforting to know white people don't own everything. It permits me to feel safe and hopeful, as reconciliation with Indigenous people will bring liberation of other racialized people, including Black people, on Turtle Island.

I moved in May of 2017, and finding community, let alone Black community, proved difficult. I left Toronto with other people's fears put onto me. From close friends to family members to co-workers and bosses, everyone seemed to have an opinion on how I was going to live in the North. Yet most of them had never visited or lived there. Alone, scared, and constantly questioning this move, I left friends and family with very little warning. I knew I was going to be told not to leave or that opportunities, such as work or partnerships, too good to pass up would suddenly arise, as they had done before. I especially didn't tell my Black friends until much later because I knew I would be made a fool of. "You going where there's snow? The hell? Where are you going to get shea butter? You gonna be dusty as hell!" Well, to my surprise, most Black friends offered to send up care packages, which was so touching. I felt cared for and, in a sense, permitted to go. I did feel like I was leaving my Black fam behind, to suffer alone rather than to experience pain together, at a political time when friends and close family members were being attacked in the public eye in the media or social networks. It was nice to know that, even though it wasn't up to them, I was to go and my leaving was accepted, and that if things didn't work out, I'd be allowed back. That's a tough one with community. Leaving is hard, but not being allowed to come back, that's heart wrenching.

Because Yukon, especially Whitehorse, gets filled up with tourists in the summer, most Yukoners are gone during the months of May through August, camping, exploring, anywhere away from the tourists! Others, who stay, don't want to get emotionally attached to tourists who are just passing through. To this day, I get asked if I plan on moving back, even though I have changed my health card, license plate, and gotten a (real cute) puppy and continuously make my apartment a home. It wasn't until autumn, when winter started creeping back, that people started opening themselves and their homes to me.

And suddenly, I was introduced to Black people! That's the thing about winter; she can be real sweet, if you're ready to welcome her. But she can cut you real deep if you neglect her, speak ill of her, or don't welcome her! People would ask me what equipment I had for winter, and because I had already visited in wintertime, I was prepared. What I wasn't prepared for was finding my Black community. You can have all the warmest gear for winter. If you don't have your people, your Black family to enlighten you and make you happy, people to trust and keep you cozy, it's as though you have nothing.

The Black people I have met were also people who, like me, lived in big cities, mostly Toronto, and left with a need for adventure and the need to breathe! When meeting Black people, I wasn't offered clothing or winter gear, but rather hair products, well-seasoned food, talks on and reviews of Black culture/Black movies, and invitations to family gatherings. This also was offered by First Nations people I met. My first Christmas in Whitehorse was definitely not lonely. I was invited to a multitude of family gatherings and dinners and met extended family members of new friends and acquaintances. That's the thing with community, it's rooted in culture and love. Because I was welcomed in such manners, I feel the necessity to continue doing the same for others. Whenever I see Black people, I don't offer clothing and winter gear—I know they'll find such things with ease. What they won't find easily is community. We are so spread out, all over the territory, it can be months before we meet each other. The times I had seen the most Black people were in gathering places, such as public talks with Lawrence Hill, author of *The Book of Negroes*, who is currently writing about and researching the history of Black soldiers who helped build the Alaska Highway and their encounters with First Nations people. Or meeting Auntie Antoinette. I put the "Auntie" in front of her name, as she really has been an auntie to me, even if we've mostly encountered each other across great distances. When asked if there are Black people in Yukon, one of the first names to pop up is Antoinette. Owner of Antoinette's Caribbean restaurant and very involved in the Yukon community, she shares her story with Black people she barely even knows while welcoming them to her "Northern" life. Another place I've found Black people are community centres and gyms! Winter hits hard with thirty-five to forty degrees below Celsius. We have to stay motivated and active, even despite the lack of sun! The first time I walked in the Canada Games Centre (a gym/community centre), my jaw dropped as I had never seen so many Black people and Black babies in Whitehorse! I'm sure they were equally shocked when they saw me. We'd exchange smiles so big with a feeling of hugging each other, similar to the scene in *The Colour Purple* when Celie is reunited with her sister and family. But instead, cognisant that white people are constantly watching (and probably with the RCMP on speed dial, 'cause you know . . . white people!), we exchange nods and smirks à la Black Panther, and carried on our workout or whatever business we had going. Every time I leave a Black person's presence without making conversation, internally I melt, hitting myself in the forehead, like, "gahh, what are you doing, go back, go back!" But unless they were visiting, I am relieved with the thought that we will see each other really soon!

That's the thing, Black people, we are everywhere! Even in the smallest of towns, in the furthest of lands, in the coldest of winters: we are here. And we've been here for a long time. In the Yukon, Black history goes as far back as the Klondike gold rush, and even includes their contribution to the construction of the Alaska Highway.[2] Yet, Black history in Canada is not taught and barely shared from a northern perspective. Which is not surprising when Black people's reaction to northern living is fear, confusion, and angst. We tend to fear the unknown. And when we are in a country that openly celebrates its racist history and refuses to acknowledge and remedy its practices, policies, and laws rooted in white supremacy, the fear of the unknown is doubled. We fear for our lives, and we tend to limit ourselves by missing what could be another way of living: one that is guided by First Nations practices, culture, and rituals. A way of living that would lead us to decolonization, progress, and thus, liberation.

In Alaska and Yukon, a term used to describe a new person in the North is *Cheechako*. A Cheechako is a person who has yet to survive a winter. As you continue to live in the North—some will say after have had survived one winter, others will say five years, and still others will say over ten-plus years—you become a *Sourdough*. Legend and history have said that the term comes from settlers who would come through the North for the Gold Rush and would carry their sourdough starters through the harsh winters, in order to keep their culture alive.[3] In other words, to become a Sourdough you need to survive and earn your right of passage, so to speak, by surviving winter.

I would argue that being a Black in the North, not only do we survive every day, but we also face the winter's challenges in addition. If I am able to write, to speak, to breathe, today, it's because my ancestors have survived. Northern living for Black people, in my opinion, is just a testament that we are far more resilient than what others make of us. We shouldn't fear moving to the North because of the winter; we have, and continue to, survive much worst. This is an ode to northern Black people, such as myself, who continue to defy all odds put against us.

TEN WAYS TO SURVIVE AS A BLACK SOURDOUGH

1. Learn and respect the land you are on. Its history, struggles, and wins are important factors that permit you to live and breathe. Recognize this and ensure that all your actions are made with good intentions, good practices, and openness to change, if and when corrected by a First Nations elder.
2. Playlists and podcasts: Whether you play Amanda Parris' Marvin's Room, on CBC, all day, every day, or listen to Sandy and Nora's podcast to give you some political umph, we are so connected!
3. Support members of CUP-W. Not only are you supporting the public service of postal workers, you are able to get your blackass needs, such as shea butter, jojoba oil, head wraps, black subscription boxes, music, and films via mail.
4. Appreciate what nature provides. Our ancestors knew what was good. White people saw a profit and continue to do so (castor oil is one of Haiti's gold, back off my "Lwil Maskreti"). Foraging, hunting, trapping, and fishing are all great trades to learn and participate in. Participate responsibly with the mind that this land is not yours.
5. Listen to the aurora borealis. Your ancestors speak and root for you every day. Listen when they speak and trust their guidance. Watch them dance, they dance for you.
6. Take care of your community. They too, may feel alone, displaced, or constantly watched. Take care of each other, as Black love is real love and powerful love.
7. Call out anti-Blackness! Just because people don't live the "southern way" doesn't mean they can be excused for their anti-Blackness. This will require much patience and can hurt, but it's important, especially for the Black babies who are living various forms of anti-Blackness and may feel alone and unsupported.
8. Get out there and explore! Dare to be different and try things you may have never had the opportunity to try before. The North offers experiences that are unique. Black people DO camp, DO hike, DO ski, DO sup, DO swim. Remember, we were hunters, foragers, gatherers too, before and after we were displaced.

9. Take time to breathe! You are privileged to be in the North where mountains hold your every move and fresh air fills your lungs.
10. Love yourself! You aren't any kind of Sourdough. You're a BLACK Sourdough. Which means your survival of the winter is deeper and greater than other non-racialized sourdoughs.

NOTES

1 In Haiti there is a long-standing history of Christian missionaries coming to the country with intentions to "change the country" for the better. This is usually based on criteria founded on non-Haitians principles and ways of living, leaving the country in a worse state.

2 "The Early Years," Hidden History: Black History of the Yukon, accessed 2007, http://tc.gov.yk.ca/archives/hiddenhistory/en/early.html.

3 Liz Jackson, "Cheechako, Sourdough and Other Alaskan Terms," Hatcher Pass Bed and Breakfast, accessed 2017, http://hatcherpassbb.com/news/cheechako-sourdough-and-other-alaskan-terms/.

17

MOTHERING IN THE MOVEMENT

SILVIA ARGENTINA ARAUZ

writ·ing /'rīdiNG/
noun: **writing**

- *The ability to write—to bring forward from the spirit and flesh, ancestral teachings that give life to movements and legacies.*
- *A magical, and often maddening process of remembering and reclaiming.*
- *Strengthening human connections through shared experiences of struggle, resistance, and radical transformation.*

It has been years since I last wrote a personal reflection for public consumption. I was once a poet who wrote every day; once a spoken-word activist who performed on the front lines; once a young women who felt she had to get it all out—because she didn't expect to live to see twenty-one. I wrote to be free of everything inside me that told me I wasn't free to live and neither were my people.

In preparing to write about my journey as an activist-mother for this book, I asked my sixteen- and seventeen-year-old sons, "What's one thing people should know about my life as an activist and mom?" My youngest son answered, "You want everyone to succeed." My eldest son responded with "You don't sleep." Their responses have me thinking about how much women of colour, but in particular Black women, give of ourselves as individuals to see the birth and rebirth of the collective. As my eldest son accurately identified, organizing in the movement, creating new movements, and mothering has resulted in loss of sleep.

Conversations with my children revealed that they understood the public and private roles I play in the movement, and that they see me as inspiring. I knew this because, from a young age, they repeatedly chose me as their hero to write about in classroom assignments and have shared with me many times how much they are proud of me. What I didn't know was their repeated worries for my well-being and overall safety. It hurt me to learn that my sons see my work as sacrifice that harms me. I have been working so much that I've forgotten to stop and ask my family (not just my sons) how my choices as an activist have impacted them. I had forgotten to ask myself, What is this all about? How does this serve me? This was not the image of an empowered and freed mother that I hoped to reflect for my sons. As such, I have been deliberately unlearning the self-sacrifice narrative that has become endemic within the movement and mothering. Writing this chapter is a part of this unlearning.

This writing process has brought up many questions for me, much like the ones that arise while organizing a protest or an important meeting with accomplices or allies: How do I honour my experience and that of others? How do I pay homage to the energy of the Black Lives Matter movement? What does the reader want to know?

I then turn to considerations about my approach: Do I offer the reader strategy for their own campaigns? Do I offer emotional insight through the story of my life as an African Indigenous Latina from Nicaragua helping to activate a movement for Black Latinx peoples in Toronto? Does my audience want organizing techniques for street protests? Are you interested in discussing my work in social enterprise and shared platforms?

I switch to considerations about my relevance: Will you want to hear from me? How will I impress upon you that I am in the best place to tell this story? Maybe you want to know how a teenage mother goes on to raise two amazing Black Latino sons on her own.

I consider how people will read me and how I want to identify myself. I'll share with you that I am a racialized woman of African, Indigenous (of the south), and Spanish ancestry. I acknowledge that in Toronto I am read as light-skinned and hold privilege in my proximity to whiteness in an anti-Black, colonial society that centres and celebrates proximity to whiteness. This privilege affords me deferential treatment from darker-skinned kin. I also recognize that in most spaces I navigate I am too Black and brown, often having to call on the mother within to affirm I am enough. I identify with the gender pronouns 'she' and 'they' after exploring the fluidity with which I can feel both male and female as I move through this world. I learned faith through Catholicism but feel most authentic spiritually in my connection to Land and the Four Elements. I do identify within the 2SLGBTQIA+ spectrum, and identify as a pan-lovist, a personal term that defines my love for the spirit within the human. If I love you and can see you as my life partner, then your gender and biological assignment are irrelevant to me.

I have humble beginnings in a low-income community in Nicaragua and have lived in Toronto since my family fled the civil war in the 1980s. I was raised mainly near the intersections of Markham/Eglinton, Neilson/Sewells, and Jane/Finch.

I can haphazardly describe my culture through musical fusions of Hip-Hop, R&B, Salsa, Merengue curated by BET, TeleLatino, *Fresh Prince of Bel Air, Family Matters, In Living Color* and MuchMusic's *RapCity*. I regard Tupac Shakur, Selena Quintanilla, Mariah Carey, Brandy, Monica, Lil'Kim, TLC, and Aaliyah as my role models growing up. Today, Sandy Hudson, Janaya Khan, Patrisse Cullors, Leroi Newbold, Rodney Diverlus, Pascale Diverlus, and Andrea Vásquez Jiménez are my role models.

My connection to family has been one of unconditional love for our dysfunctionally functional dynamics. They have never truly understood my commitments to activism, but they support me in their own ways and I regard this as a privilege. I have lived the life of a single mother, student-mother, and activist-mother. I have three university degrees but financial literacy was never taught to me. I write today, living in struggle, holding privilege, and facing many opportunities to pull myself, my sons, and my community further away from the labels of "poor" and "low income."

My ancestral name is still unknown to me, but the name given to me by my parents has been deemed worthy of discrimination in this society. I've been afraid to be thought of as "too much" because I have too many names that are too hard for Anglo-Saxon tongues to pronounce and they lash out when corrected much too often. I take pride in ensuring that the names I bear, the names of my aunt and grandmother, live on.

LET ME START WITH MY NAME

You can call me Silvia Argentina Arauz Cisneros

I mean Silvia Argentina Arauz

NO. Actually I mean Silvia Argentina Gabriela Arauz Cisneros Madriz de Godoy

21 syllables but really 18 if you:

Remember to roll your r, soften your n, pronounce the g as an h, g as a g, d as a d, and d as dth

Rinse and repeat as needed.

You know what, let's leave it at first name Silvia Argentina, last name Arauz, and you can call me SA for short if I know you and tell you so.

Those who love me know I love my name.

I'm excited to say my name.

I get butterflies in my tummy when you say my name.

My heart fills with warmth when effort is made to mimic my tongue.

And appreciation when you're ok with my correction(s);

Yet, I dread the question: *What's your name?*

What's my name? Who Am I? Why Am I Here?

Responses include:
Refugee of War
Nicaraguense
Daughter
Sister
Teenage Mother

Domestic Abuse Survivor
Sexual Assault Survivor
Afro-Indigenous Latina
Spoken-Word Activist
Organizer
Leader
Follower
Light
Darkness
Libra
Shape-Shifter
Shit-Disturber
Moon Magic
Child from the Stars . . .

Mothering in the movement has been as much about creating and reclaiming language and space for myself as it has been about curating for others. I felt driven to mother movements by performing spoken-word pieces that spoke out against injustices that I saw happening around me like over-policing of Black and brown bodies, unjust deportations, violence against women, etc. I had many ideas for supporting racialized and marginalized youth and families, but I was often overlooked as "entertainment" within activist communities. I began to believe that I had to choose to either "grow up" and learn to code-switch my way into critical decision-making spaces or continue to play in my poetry. I chose to close myself off to poetry and non-academic writing. Such is the story of many of us in the diaspora that feel we have to erase connections to our culture so that we might infiltrate and find a way to free our people or just survive. It is living the life of "by any means necessary."

At 21, mothering in the movement by any means necessary meant taking my sons and leaving an abusive relationship, and the financial stability he brought me; move out of a community that had been my childhood home because it was a place people needed to "make it out of"; and most memorably, never let anyone see me cry. I learned all I could about the boogeymen and their systems called capitalism and white supremacy. I would sleep every other night so I could complete my university degrees; writing to demand change from the boogeyman. Some nights, I would be overwhelmed with the pain of knowing my sons, my youth could be the next victims of police violence. The 'Year of the Gun' introduced zero-tolerance tactics executed to disproportionately impact Black people. Things had been getting progressively worse in our communities, and the issues faced by my sons were not capturing the attention of media platforms, elected officials, and community members—until Black Lives Matter.

I felt like a daughter returning home when I started to attend BLM—TO events in Toronto. The spaces were non-judgemental, fierce with dedication to having Black voices heard, relentless in their demands for nothing short of liberation, and humble in the face of so many admirers. Many people will criticize without truly knowing. I've seen it with my own eyes. Black Lives Matter—Toronto mothered Toronto's present-day activism scene. They showed affection to all those who came with genuine intentions to support the community, ferociously, and quite publicly, defended their community from those wanting to do harm, and repeatedly put their lives and freedoms in harm's way in order to build new opportunities for leadership and growth.

I was mothered by BLM—TO. In 2017, I approached them as co-director of the Latinx, Afro-Latin-America, AbyaYala Education Network (LAEN) to lead a campaign that addressed the abuse of power being reported by students within the Toronto District School Board (TDSB) and the Toronto Catholic District School Board (TCDSB), and their support brought the campaign to families' living rooms all across the country. At the time, an internal report revealed that several hundreds of students had serious concerns with the police in their schools through the School Resource Officer program. With BLM—TO leading the campaign, we were able to successfully win the elimination of the program from the TDSB, the nation's largest school board.

• • •

THE ACTIVIST MOTHER, THE ACTIVIST AS A MOTHER

moth·er-ing /'məTHər/iNG
verb: **mothering**

- *A never-ending commitment to cultivating energy.*
- *The art of keeping alive a person, one's life work, or a social movement.*
- *To express and act with love above all.*

When I was preparing to give birth, I learned that a steady breath was essential to keep the oxygen flowing to the baby. I remember my senses going wild once in labour. I was drenched in sweat with encouraging voices inaudible; the room was spinning. I wanted to sleep, but the pain wouldn't let me. Survival was my focus; I knew I could not scream. I had to let the pain hit, breathe, let the tears fall, and visualize my ideal outcome.

Inhala, exhala,
Visualize.
Inhala, exhala,
Visualize
Pain.
Love.
Dedication.
Exhaustion.
Resilience.
Rebirth.
Giving birth to a child,
Giving birth to a movement.
Breathe in, breathe out,
Visualize.

Moments that alter the world as we know it. Mothering has been a laborious process, rooted in joy, gratitude, and love so deep it renews my faith in Spirit because I know I draw from the depths of the universe to deal with ghost pains from the trauma, new pains from the heartbreak. The most powerful thing that I could do in that moment to ensure our survival was to breathe and trust my body.

Similarly, the pain that comes with the labour of love in activism has caused me to lose my breath and doubt my survival at times. I have felt like I could die from the physical, emotional, and spiritual pain that has come with creating spaces where the voices of the most marginalized can live and thrive. I have often felt suffocated within the walls of a white supremacist world that lies and hides behind politeness and fake news. Like hospital walls, boardroom walls often close in on me, making me sick to my stomach.

Many times, I want to scream! At the top of my lungs every time our spaces are taken or when our hard work is undone. In Ontario, Black Lives Matter—Toronto's advocacy resulted in millions of dollars of funding committed at the municipal and provincial level, the creation of an Anti-Black Racism Directorate and countless public programs, offices, and positions; members of the BLM—TO movement organized the Black Lives Matter Freedom School, encouraging parental/caregiver involvement in abolitionist work, pushing for equity in education and police-free classrooms, and of course the win of an armed and uniformed police–free Pride. Then, in what felt like overnight, upon the election the Ford Conservative government at the provincial level, we began to see a rollback of all the hard-fought wins by BLM—TO for our communities.

In times like this I feel like I'm back in the hospital, full of pain, trying to give life, while scared for my life and that of my child. Sometimes I see red, drenched in sweat, encouraging voices inaudible, and wanting to sleep but being kept awake by the fear that my sons and I could be killed. In these frustrating moments, when I feel exhausted and ready to die, I breathe through the pain. In my third year of receiving guidance from Indigenous Knowledge Keeper Maria Montejo, I have learned again and again how to breathe new life into this world. Maria tells me I have the power to bring Spirit into the physical form. This connection between motherhood and activism, the job of manifesting joy and life in the physical form, is connected with my breath, with transformation.

It has been a year since I first interviewed my sons for this chapter. And in that time, a process of radical transformation has occurred within me. I have taken critical steps to communicate and model healthier lifestyle choices to my sons. I am practicing a radical love that centres me and confirms my worthiness. Writing this chapter helped me see how the patterns of activism—of minimal sleep, high stress, poor eating habits, and repeated exposure to unchecked abuses of power—has made me sick. Loving myself and modelling love of self for others has freed me to mother in the healthiest states of mind and spirit that I've ever felt. From this pain, through breath, will come new life. The truth is that the boogeymen will not listen to our screams because they don't care to hear us. But if we breathe, love ourselves, and transcend to the realization that we have the power to give birth to new education systems, new streams of funding, new sustainable ways of organizing, then screaming at them becomes irrelevant. By being adaptive we won't need to be screaming, because we will be busy building a world where our people hold power and are free.

I have drawn boundaries of what I am and am not willing to give of myself and my family to push forward the movement; it is not a love lost but simply a clarity around misplaced feelings of guilt, shame, anger, fear, and sadness. When I advocate for the rights of our people, I'm advocating for the little girl that has not had her needs met. I have experienced immense pressure as an Afro-Indigenous Latina, teenage mother, and organizer to prove my worth to everyone around me. The last poem I submitted for public viewing was published eight years ago,[1] in an effort to heal my inner child from that self-judgement. Today, my inner child has found her voice and she is raising herself and her sons with trust, love, compassion and permission. Permission to unlearn/relearn is to let the young girl in me play and also cry. It is permission I have vocalized with my sons and many of the youth I work with along my journey. They have now seen me cry, breathe, and process emotions many times. They in turn have felt permission to feel and even cry.

I celebrate the young spirit in me with bright lips, funky nails, large hoop earrings, and big curly hair. She is writing poetry again. Soon, I will take to the stage. I am mothering me, my sons, and my many children in the movement. My goal is our freedom; the strategy: self-love.

NOTES

1 Silvia Argentina Arauz Cisneros, "(Mis)education: Recollections of the Revolution," in *Becoming Feminists: An Anthology of How We Became Feminists*, eds. Lorena M. Gajarado and Jamie Ryckman (Toronto: Ontario Institute for Studies in Education, 2011), 2–3.

18

BLACK AND MUSLIM

GILARY MASSA

I have always had a complicated relationship with my Blackness. Growing up in an Afro-Latina household, Blackness was never really something we talked about. We are Panamanian. And while I always knew that my sister had light brown eyes because of my paternal grandfather's supposed French background, and that the redness in our skin was because of our Indigenous ancestry, we very rarely talked about our Blackness with the same boastfulness. We knew we were African. But from where? I still don't know.

During my last visit to Panama, my father, who while living in Canada would often get mistaken for Somali, was confused as to why I was so interested in going to the "Defile de la Etnia Negra," the Black history month parade in Panama. It was part of Panama's month-long festivities celebrating Afro-Panamanian History. "You want to go to Rio Abajo?" he asked. "Why? That's like the Jane and Finch of Panama City. It's where all the Black people live."

"Dad, we are Black too, you know!" I said. He laughed and joked, "Maybe you, but me, I'm just the darkest shade of white."

My mother, who I was raised by, was always a little more progressive in her acknowledgement of our Blackness. She would at least admit to our African heritage. Even still, talk about our Blackness in my home was always subtly negative. There were slight jabs here and there about the behaviour of Black kids in our neighbourhood that somehow separated us from them. Yes, we had African ancestry from way, way back, but we weren't, you know, "Black."

Questions around identity become even more complicated because of my mother's conversion to Islam. I was four years old. Her new-found religion caused tension amongst our friends and family, who had immigrated to Canada from Panama and other parts of Latin America around the same time we did. They didn't understand why my mom no longer partied like they did, or why she was now refusing to even shake hands with the men in the group. They had questions about our new modest clothing, and generally saw our Muslimness as somehow contradictory to our Latin roots.

We never talked about Blackness.

In Muslim spaces it was much of the same. Wherever I went, I felt different. At mosque it was because I was the daughter of a convert and because I didn't look like the other kids. I knew that my Muslimness and my understanding of religious practice were always under a different level of scrutiny as a result. Did I know, at the time, that I was receiving differential treatment because I was Black? Not really. That realization came to me years later.

In organized Muslim settings, I grew up surrounded mostly by the Khoja Shia Ithna Ashari Muslim community in the Greater Toronto Area. Khojas are a group of Indian Muslim converts that migrated to parts of Africa as merchants throughout the 1800s.[1] Shias are a minority sect of Islam, and as one of the very few Black Muslim families, we were a minority within a minority. It didn't always feel great. It felt like no one wanting to partner with you in Sunday-school class. It meant that my sister was really my only friend at lunchtime and that the prayer aunties paid extra close attention to me, ready to offer criticism of my prayer technique at a moment's notice. I grew up attending Quran classes and Sunday school in this community, and resented most of it. Very soon my parents also became fed up with the racism we were all experiencing and our visits to mosque became reserved for special occasions like Eid. Beyond that, we spent a lot of our time participating in halaqas or prayer sessions in the homes of other Black Muslims or non-Black Muslim community members who were also fed up with the exclusionary nature of their formal mosque settings.

We were, for the most part, unmosqued.

But my family craved community. I craved community. Even at a young age I was proudly Muslim: proud to be one of two girls to wear the hijab in my public school, proud to be Latina, proud to be Black (even though I had not yet labelled myself as that). I was proud of my multiple identities and so fiercely wanted a space where I didn't have to pick and choose which part of myself I brought into a room—which is precisely why I decided to write this article: to create space for this conversation.

Seemingly disparate parts of identity being pulled in different directions all the time was a theme that came up consistently amongst those I spoke to in the lead-up to writing this text. For this piece I spoke to Black Muslim women of varied age groups, including converts to Islam and those coming from families with long-standing adherence to the faith. The word *belonging* rang through every single conversation: the search for belonging and the struggle to exist, non-compartmentalized, in all spaces. Unconditionally.

In this chapter I tease out the tension points within many Black Muslims; through my interviewees' life stories, I heard about the challenges of feeling like they have to vacillate between their Black and Muslim identities. I draw out diverse experiences of marginalization of the Black Muslims I interviewed to facilitate a broader conversation on the Black Muslim identity and experience in Canada and globally. Ultimately these stories represent a collective refusal to separate our Black and Muslim identities. The impulse to separate these identities marks a double erasure of Black people in Islamic history and of Muslims in Black history. This forced, artificial, and problematic separation is, for me, also an indication of where we begin to dream up possibilities for Black liberation. The unspoken need to secularize present-day Black-led movements is just one example of the marginalization of Black Muslim conceptualizations of freedom, which are entrenched in faith.

This text is thus also a call for transforming the normativity of our progressive movements to create space for Black people who have ideas of freedom and liberation that are directly linked to their spirituality.

BLACK OR MUSLIM?

In my second year of university I engrossed myself in all things campus life. At York University, in Toronto, I was involved in my Muslim Students' Association, became the founding executive of a Muslim and Arab political action network called the Muslim Coalition, and ran in the elections to be a student representative in my students' union. The president of the York University Black Students' Association (YUBSA), let's call him Kwame, was running on my slate to be the president of the students' union at the time. I started university two years after 9/11, just as the United States government was getting ready to go to war with Iraq. The campus was abuzz with protests, anti-war organizing, and general activism against Islamophobia. It was formative for me, particularly because that year I had made the personal decision to spend my university years finding myself as a Muslim. I had decided that my Latinaness was to be put on the back burner as a result. Which was a bit of a constant. No one had ever racialized me as Latina anyway. My Blackness? I hadn't even fully labelled myself that yet.

Kwame was always trying to recruit new people to join YUBSA, a space that I had frequented once or twice but really felt out of place and out of touch in. He pulled me aside one day to ask me why he hadn't seen me around the YUBSA office. I was too shy to tell him that I didn't feel Black enough, so I just said I had been busy. Then came the question. One that has haunted me ever since: "Gilary, my sister, I have a question for you. Are you Black first, or are you Muslim first?" I was shocked. "Um . . . Muslim, both? Wait, I'm Latina!" I told him. He shook his head and told me, "No my friend, you are Black."

It has been over ten years since that conversation with Kwame, and I don't think that I ever fully processed it. I find myself retelling this story often, particularly when I'm in Black organizing spaces—almost as an explanation for who I am or why I seem disconnected from that part of myself. The truth is that I never feel Black enough, and while I still feel offended that Kwame would so boldly and unapologetically separated my identities and ask me to choose, choosing is really is something I have been forced to do my entire life.

In all my conversations with those that I interviewed, the feeling that we needed to separate parts of our identities in order to move in

Muslim or Black spaces was unanimous. Fatima,[2] a Muslim convert originally from Zimbabwe, found that her conversion story included an erasure of all the things she identified with as a Black woman. She explained,

> I was born to a Christian family in Zimbabwe and I came to Islam at the age of eighteen through another Black Muslim who exposed me to the faith. I really accepted the faith wholeheartedly, thinking and believing that Islam was above race. So I believed all the statements that were said [about Islam being beyond race] and I actually ended up adopting a more Arabized religious expression. I really kind of forsook all or most of my symbols of Blackness. So I let go of hip hop—I often talked about how I had kind of a borrowed Blackness that a lot of Black Canadians have from the US. I abandoned that. You know, there were so many markers of my Blackness that I just abandoned for the sake of the religion because I really felt that you had to erase parts of yourself and replace it with faith. And so Blackness and Muslimness were a process of erasure and then a process of reclamation. After many years of soul-searching and me trying to figure out who I was, I felt it was important for me to reclaim the most essential parts of me.

Imaani, who also accepted Islam when she was in university, understood early on that there was this unspoken requirement—by some Muslims, not by Islam—to erase your ethnic or cultural identity for the sake of the faith. Imaani grew up in a Caribbean family and comes from a mixed Christian background with different family members following different paths within Christianity. She explained,

> It was very challenging for me because I come from a multi-faith family within the Christian community. My aunt is an evangelist, my grandmother was Baptist, my cousins were of other faiths where they get overcome by the spirit and they clap their hands.

At the same time, she described her family as very "Black-conscious" and involved in helping their own community and those who had less than them. It was when she moved to Canada when she was ten years old that she first experienced overt anti-Black racism and a feeling of being less-than. She recalls being called the N-word just a few weeks after immigrating to Canada. She started searching for what she described as a "religion that represents me." Her path to accepting Islam is an interesting and complex one. While Imaani found that the message of Islam deeply resonated with her, her conversion story is one of a constant struggle to actively push back against the erasure of her Blackness. She described how she came to Islam at twenty-one years of age:

> It was really the whole idea of tawheed, or the oneness of God, that really struck my heart. That's when I found Islam. I was still sceptical though. I had heard and seen images and stories about the treatment of Muslim women. I needed to make sure that Islam didn't preach the oppression of women. I thought to myself, I'm not going to be one of those women that dresses all in black and is all submissive. I really had some anti-Islam ideas. So I did my due diligence and in my research found that it was really culture influencing Muslims, and that for many Muslims, especially African Muslim women, this was not the reality. They were strong, outspoken, engaged in their community. And was pleasantly surprised to read how Islam talked about women not as devils or heathens, like we are talked about in other faiths, but instead they were talked about as equals in the eyes of Allah, that paradise lies under the mother's feet, and that it offered women rights like inheritance hundreds of years ago. Once I realized that it was culture influencing how people were interpreting Islam in problematic ways, I accepted Islam and started identifying as a Black Muslim.

When Imaani began participating in the Muslim community in Canada, she came up against a range of issues that eventually led up to her formulating her identity as "Black Muslim." She explained,

> When I took my shahada [declaration of faith], I found that the Imams and people around me had a very Arabized way of teaching and practicing the faith. I remember in my heart thinking, this is not for me. I'm a Black Muslim and I come from a very Black-conscious family. And while there were many attempts from people to try and wipe away my culture, I spent a lot of time, and it took me many years, to solidify my identity as a Black Muslim. I think that upset some people. For example, I took Imaani as my Muslim name because it was a Swahili name, but also an Arabic name meaning faith . . . my husband and I never gave up our history. This often led to us being ostracized.

This question of parts of identity being pulled apart or erased in order to belong came up even when speaking with Black Muslims who did not have a conversion story. This tension came up for people like Muna, who comes from a Somali family with very deep African roots and Muslim lineage. When I spoke with Muna she recounted the racism she experienced in the Muslim community in Toronto. She said:

> I came to Canada when I was five. I did all of my schooling in Scarborough and really identified as a Somali Canadian. For me, the easiest way to answer the questions about my experience as Black Muslim is by reflecting on what it was like growing up in mostly South Asian or Arab congregations. And really, I can only describe that experience as a series of anti-Black microaggressions veiled as compliments about how not-Black I looked. It would be comments like, "You aren't really Black. You are African," or, "Oh you guys as are so pretty for being Somali," or "You can pass for this or that." It was a constant attempt to downplay our Blackness.

Muna went on to describe how the racialized structure of Muslim spaces went beyond these microaggressions. She explained:

> Even as Somalis, we internalize this [downplaying of our Blackness] in the ways we always talk about our proximity

> to Arabness. Maybe it's our way of coping. Growing up in communities dominated by Indian and Pakistani Muslims, we were surrounded by a religious practice informed by those cultures. I spent a lot of time trying to blend in. It took me a long time to realize that their way wasn't the only way. It wasn't the superior way. I could dress modestly and not have to be in a salwar kameez, and began trying to unpack how faith and identity are so interconnected. And how an emphasis on this idea of being one Ummah or a single community didn't have to be this violent erasure of Black and African culture.

Over time, as Muna related, the Somali community responded to these racialized practices of Islam by creating their own spaces where Black Muslim history and culture was front and centre:

> I know a lot of Black Muslims who stopped going to Islamic schools or going into Muslim spaces because the racism was too much to handle. I also think that it was this that triggered the creation of many of the Somali centres we have in Toronto today. We have always been Muslim. Somalis have always been Muslim. We boast about the fact that some of the companions of the Prophet were from the horn of Africa. We needed spaces that reflected our particular flavour of our Imaan [faith] and acknowledged this history.

BLACKNESS IN ISLAM

There are two stories commonly told about the Black Muslim within Muslim spaces.

The first is the story of Bilal Ibn Rabah and the second is the story of Malcolm X (may Allah be pleased with them).

The story of Bilal is a story of a slave from Ethiopia who became one of the first to convert to Islam.[3] As a slave, Bilal was owned by a wealthy Meccan idol worshipper, Umayya ibn Khalaf, and suffered terrible punishment from his master as a result of his open acceptance of Muhammed's (Peace Be Upon Him (PBUH)) message. Many biographers of Bilal describe the egregious physical violence Ibn Khalaf subjected Bilal to in an attempt to compel him to renounce Islam: Bilal was "beaten mercilessly, dragged around the streets and hills of Mecca by his neck, and subjected to long periods without food or water. Ibn Khalaf would throw Bilal on his back at the hottest time of the day and put a great rock on his chest and tell him, 'You will stay here till you die or deny Muhammed and worship at-Lat and al-'Uzza.' Bilal would not renounce Islam, and amidst his suffering he uttered only one word—Ahad (meaning One God)."[4] It is said that Bilal was drawn to Islam because of its message of justice, mercy, freedom, and the oneness of God.

The Prophet Muhammed (PBUH), upon hearing about Bilal, sent Abu Bakar, one of his companions, to buy Bilal from his master, nursed him back to health, and then freed him. Bilal soon became one of the Prophet's most trusted companions and the first person to issue the call to prayer.[5]

The story of Bilal and his rise to leadership amongst the Prophet's companions emphasizes Islam's commitment to human equality, anti-racism, and justice, and it serves as a backdrop to the last sermon of the Prophet, which took place on the ninth of dul-hajj, the month in which Muslims perform pilgrimage to the Kaaba in Mecca, in which he is said to have made the following declaration:

> O people! Your Lord is one Lord, and you all share the same father (Adam). Indeed, there is no superiority of an Arab over a non-Arab or of a non-Arab over an Arab; or of a white over a Black; nor a Black over a white, except by taqwa [righteousness].[6]

It was his participation in the Hajj that led civil rights leader Malcolm X to his conversion to Sunni Islam from the Nation of Islam. Like Bilal, Malcolm X has been a central figure in Black Muslim discourse. In *The Autobiography of Malcolm X,* he talks about being drawn to Islam because, in Mecca, for the first time he felt treated with dignity by people of all races.[7]

"The reason that I am Muslim is because I am Black," Aasiyah tells me. She is among my mother's closest friends, who converted to Islam after having read the biography of Malcolm X. She was a flight attendant working a Hajj flight to Saudi Arabia and recalls hearing the adhan (call to prayer) every time the plane took off.

She didn't understand it, but it moved her and she needed to learn more. In our conversation, she recalled her trajectory that brought together experiences of anti-Black racism with her conversion to Islam. She recounted,

> I came to Islam because I found out about Malcolm X, and reading the autobiography of Malcolm X made me want to be like him. It was really funny, because I finished the autobiography of Malcolm X while I was on an airplane in Saudi Arabia when I was working as a flight attendant right after I had graduated from McMaster University where I got my first degree in philosophy. I was sitting on a plane taxiing to India—which means we were on an empty plane heading to pick up a group of travelers, so I had a lot of time to read. We were on our way to India, coincidentally, to pick up a group of travelers heading to Hajj. Saudi Airline did this thing that, when it takes off they play a duah, and at prayer time they play the adhan. At that time I was not Muslim, so I didn't know what it was, but I remember my first time hearing the adhan I got goosebumps on the back of my neck. I was transfixed. I remember exactly where I was standing on the flight and I couldn't move any further. I just sat there listening to it and when it was over I asked one of the crew members if I could get a copy of that and he told me no, because I was a kafir (non-believer). Of course I don't know what a kafir was. I just heard "no." Anyway, I finished reading the autobiography of Malcolm X and I learned about Islam and for me it was a really nice solution to my hatred for white people.

Aasiyah described what she meant by her "hatred" of white people. She used the word deliberately to convey the severity of the racism she experienced as a child. She went on to say,

> In my childhood anti-Black racism was quite prominent and my resistance to it and my fight against it was very pronounced. I became quite disgusted with white people by the time I was eleven, and my mother was afraid for me because I was so vocal and so what they called "militant"

as a child. And it was only through Islam that I learned that it's not about white people. I must tell you, I really hated white people and I had good reason for it, honestly. Being a child in Boston, Massachusetts, in the '70s and going through the bussing system, it was common to find myself in situations where angry white mobs were lined up to overturn our school bus . . . this type of stuff happened to me . . . .

I was born in Hamilton, Ontario, but my family moved to the USA shortly after my father died. I started grade one in Massachusetts. We lived in a large ranch bungalow on a couple of acres of land with a creek behind us, and we were the only Black family in the area so we were subjected to a lot of abuse by the white racists. They would put feces and dead birds and garbage on our front porch. It was awful. And I hated them. I ended up going to grade one in an environment where there were two Black kids in the school: my sister and I. We were not popular. It didn't help that I was also very well prepared and already knew how to read, write, and count, and I was considered to be academically above my peers. I remember on my first day of school being really eager and excited to be there and then one of the other students called me a nigger. And I'm there thinking, "Wow! Mother never told me I was a nigger; she told me a lot of things about me but you never told me that."

For grade two we moved into the city and I went to a Black school. However, I went to a white school first, so I knew what white schools looked like. They were beautiful. The Black school in Dorchester, Boston, had no heat and it had mice running around the corners, and it had schoolbooks that the white schools had discarded, so pages were missing or old and shabby with turned-back yellow pages. It was awful. So I became sick. I was often too sick, you know, psychosomatically, and I couldn't go to school. My stomach hurt and I had all sorts of foolishness and I ended up spending a lot of time at home with my mother . . . and my education continued [at home].

For Aasiyah, Islam became the vehicle through which she was able to manage her "hatred."

I reflect on Aasyiah's conversion story and her admiration for Malcolm X. It's a common one. Many of my mother's friends came to Islam for similar reasons: a search for faith amidst racism and oppression. In fact, my stepfather—who is Indian South African, not Black, and moved to Canada with his family just before the fall of apartheid—also credits Malcolm X for his return to Islam. There is undoubtedly power in Malcolm's story. While these narratives are important to the story of the Black Muslim experience, they are often told as the only Black contributions to Islamic history. Blackness is often framed, by many Muslims, around a slave narrative that predates European colonialism, or a convert narrative, as if Black African communities haven't historically been part of the Muslim fabric in a similar way that Arabs or South Asians have. While there is a wealth of research that indicates that Blackness has been part of Islam for centuries, the complaint from many of the Black Muslims I spoke to was that there is a collective amnesia or outright erasure of this history when it comes to how we talk about Muslim communities in the Islamic world.

While the first recorded Muslims in Canada were James and Agnes Love, who were of Scottish descent, it is said that one of the first Muslims to come to Canada was a Black man from present-day Benin in West Africa. Mahommah Baquaqua was enslaved by Europeans and first taken to Brazil before escaping off a ship in New York and attaining his freedom at the age of seventeen. It is said that Baquaqua made his way to Canada through the Underground Railroad in the late 1850s, settling in Ontario, where he co-authored the *Biography of Mohammad G Baquaqua, a Native of Zoogoo, in the Interior of Africa*, which is "one of the few surviving narratives of individuals who were enslaved in Africa and survived the middle passage."[8]

Margarita Rosario, a Princeton PhD candidate in comparative literature, studies the untold history and experiences of enslaved Muslims during and after the slave trade. Her research suggests that between 10 and 30 percent of slaves that came to the Americas through the trans-Atlantic slave trade were Muslim, about 1.25 to 3.75 million people, with the majority of them ending up in Brazil.

But the story of the enslaved Black Muslims is not only one of slavery, it is one of Islam as a gateway to freedom. Rosario states that enslaved Muslims would have secret meetings in the middle of the night and this was when their religion classes took place. According to her research, it was in these secret Quran and Islamic education meetings that ideas for many slave revolts were born.[9]

Islam and Blackness was a dangerous combination for the Portuguese slave masters in nineteenth-century Brazil. African Muslims were strong in faith and literacy. They were inspired by Islamic and Quranic teachings of fighting against oppression, as well as by the success of the Haitian slave rebellion. On a Sunday during Ramadan in January 1835, 600 Black slaves in Bahia, Brazil, rose up against their Portuguese masters in what is known as the revolt of the Malês. The West African Yoruban Muslim slaves had managed to unify multi-ethnic African Muslims under the banner of Islam along with non-Muslim Africans under the banner of Blackness in a revolt that led to the abolishment of slavery in Brazil in 1888.[10]

The untold history of Black Muslims extends beyond that of slave rebellions and emancipation. It is also a history of kings, queens, and scholars like Fatima Fihri, who in 859 founded Al Qarrawiyyin University, the world's first academic university, or Mansa Musa of Mali, who ruled the Malian empire in the 1300s and is known for being the wealthiest man to ever have lived. However, somehow the mainstream Muslim narrative about Islam and Blackness falls into the same trap as mainstream Western narratives of Blackness. In both cases, our story starts and ends with slavery—or at best our resistance to it—with no real recognition of how we existed as leaders and scholars in our own right.

BEING MUSLIM IN NON-MUSLIM BLACK SPACES

Black Muslims are pushing back against normative Islamic narratives and against members of the non-Black Muslim community resistant to the acknowledgement of Black and African culture in the context of Muslim identity. But there is equal frustration towards the non-Muslim Black community, which normalises a separation of identities. For me, it always comes back to that haunting question posed by Kwame: "Sister, are you Black first or Muslim first?" Well, we are both. These identities are intertwined and interconnected. They are histories and stories that cannot be neatly separated.

Unsheltered from the tyranny of white supremacist ideals of Blackness, non-Muslim Black spaces often perpetuate negative assumptions about what it means to be Muslim. In our conversation, Imaani spoke to the fact that while she felt a need to always hold on firmly to her Black identity, she feels an equal need to push back against Islamophobic assumptions that exist about her within the non-Muslim Black community, that, like many Muslim spaces, these spaces often sought to strip her of her Blackness and Caribbean heritage just as forcefully.

Others I interviewed expressed feeling unwelcomed in non-Muslim Black spaces as a result of their Muslimness. For the women, their hijab or modest wear often came laden with assumptions about their supposed oppression. The often overtly secular nature of Black liberation movements in Canada leaves little room for a person of faith—a challenge for those of us who see our Blackness, our freedom, and our faith as intimately interconnected.

When someone like me, someone who is actively engaged in community work, says that I am an activist because I am Muslim, we say this not out of a matter of personal preference, but because we understand that, particularly as Black Muslims, we are descendants of people who used faith, and Islam specifically, as their inspiration as well as their tool for liberation.

For me, activism and the pursuit of justice, freedom, and Black consciousness are as much a part of my religious practice as prayer, fasting, and modesty. I consider them to be all equally part of my religious obligations. This conviction stems directly from Quranic teachings that state:

> Believers, be strict in upholding justice and bear witness for the sake of God, even though it be against yourselves, your parents, or your kindred. Be they rich or poor. God knows better about them both. Do not, then, follow your own desires, lest you swerve from Justice. If you conceal the truth or evade it. Then remember, God is well aware of all that you do.[11]

For both me and many of the Black Muslims I spoke to, whether they were born into Muslim families or found Islam later in life, it is our faith that grounds our work in community and influences our desire to pursue justice for all oppressed people.

I had lengthy conversations with all those I interviewed about the hypocrisy of Black liberation movements who put men like Malcolm X or Martin Luther King on pedestals, and yet choose to ignore the reality that, in both cases, their resistance was rooted in a belief in God; in an adherence to a faith.

Many of those I interviewed had deep admiration for present-day movements like Black Lives Matter and credited them for giving us the words and creating the space for us to have conversations about anti-Black racism in the Muslim community in ways we have never been able to before. Aasyiah told me,

> They [Black Lives Matter] mean a lot to me. I identify as an activist, so obviously their work is absolutely essential to activism around Blackness in a North American context, I know that the job that I have was framed by them. The Anti-Racism Directorate in Ontario, for example, only exists because of their pushing. I have absolute respect for the work that they have done.

Imaani echoes this:

> While I have my critiques, I defer to them. They are a group of young Black activists unapologetically fighting for our rights and demanding our dignity as Black people. No one else is doing that. We need them. We need people pounding the pavement and saying that enough is enough. Our lives matter too.

But as Black Muslim activists, artists, organizers, and community workers, we are tired. Tired, as Fatima says, of

> keeping this secret about my Muslimness when I'm trying to re-engage in Black organizing and cultural spaces. I feel sad because these places that I used to be part of don't feel like they are mine anymore, and it has become really hard

to reclaim my Blackness as a result.

We all muse about the thought of one day not having to play down our Muslimness in order to feel Black enough or down-with-the-cause enough. We muse about the day when we will stop feeling too Black for Muslim spaces.

Even as we challenge white supremacy, challenge anti-Black racism, challenge Islamophobia, we seem to adopt a colonial model of being where we are told oppressed people have to compete for attention. Imaani comments,

> I think Black people's issues have a priority, I think that LGBTQ issues have a priority, and Black Muslim issues have a priority, and we can figure out ways for all of those things to be priority number one, together, maybe sometimes in different ways, at different times, but in tandem. I don't often feel like BLM represents the Black Muslim. I know that Black Muslims support BLM, but I am concerned that sometimes they don't do a good enough job of making sure that we represent the layers and different needs of Black people.

To put down on paper that I often dream about a time where I, as a Black Muslim Latina woman, can bring my whole self into a space without toning down my faith, feels too honest and too vulnerable.

Maybe because I know them and because I can put faces to the names of the people pounding the pavement doing the hard, hard work of shifting a dialogue, it becomes difficult to say the full truth out loud. Maybe it's because I don't want sound like I discredit or downplay the work or the intention. Maybe it's because I so deeply admire them.

Even as I write this, I feel anxious.

Justice and freedom are not solely secular ideas.

They belong to all of us together.

For many of us, we can see quite clearly the line connecting Black liberation movements to Islamic religious practice. We hope one day you will see it too.

NOTES

1 *Encyclopaedia Britannica Online*, s.v. "Khoja" accessed June 2018, https://www.britannica.com/topic/Khoja.

2 I have given pseudonyms to some of those interviewed in order to protect their identities.

3 "Bilal Ibn Rabah," IslamHouse.com, accessed June 21, 2018, https://d1.islamhouse.com/data/en/ih_articles/single2/en_Bilal_Ibn_Rabah.pdf.

4 Ibid.

5 Ibid.

6 Abu Tariq Hijazi, "Bilal Ibn Rabah: The Symbol of Human Equality," *Islamic Voice*, February 17, 2015, https://islamicvoice.com/bilal-ibn-rabah-the-symbol-of-human-equality/

7 Malcolm X and Alex Haley, *The Autobiography of Malcolm X*, (New York: Ballantine Books, 2015).

8 Patrick E. Horn, "Mahommah Gardo Baquaqua," in *Encyclopedia of Muslim-American History*, ed. Edward E. Curtis, IV (New York: Facts on File, 2010).

9 Margarita Rosario, "Muslim Slave Rebellions in the Americas," paper presented at 16th MAS-ICNA Convention, December 28, 2017, accessed August 9, 2018, https://youtube/udOsbeSJg10.

10 Ibid.

11 Holy Quran 4:135, ed. Farida Khanam, (trans. Maulana Wahiduddin Khan (Hyderabad, India: GoodWord Books, 2013).

19

BLACK LIVES MATTER—TORONTO SIT-IN AT PRIDE

DR. NAILA KELETA-MAE

Over the past few years the Toronto chapter of Black Lives Matter (Black Lives Matter—Toronto) has been engaged in front-line activism that has made lofty demands of the status quo and used tactics that are attention-grabbing.[1] In July 2015 Black Lives Matter—Toronto shut down a major thoroughfare in Toronto called the Allen Road to protest the killing of Jermaine Carby and Andrew Loku by police officers.[2] In March 2016 Black Lives Matter—Toronto built a tent city in front of Toronto Police Services headquarters. Black Lives Matter—Toronto camped out there for fifteen days to protest the fact that no charges had been laid in the death of Andrew Loku. In April 2016 they brought a summary (printed in very large font) of a Special Investigations Unit report on the death of Andrew Loku to a city councillors' meeting at Toronto's City Hall, ostensibly for the councillors to read.[3] But the action that garnered Black Lives Matter—Toronto the most media coverage and incited sustained public debate occurred on July 3, 2016, when they staged a thirty-minute sit-in at the marquee parade of the LGBTQ communities' month-long festivities produced by the organization Pride Toronto.[4]

Some people were absolutely livid and seemingly unaware that front-line activism, like that undertaken by Black Lives

Matter—Toronto on that day, rarely feels good for those whose lives and worldviews are interrupted or inconvenienced by a public demonstration of dissent. Black Lives Matter—Toronto's sit-in was not intended to comfort or reaffirm the status quo—and Pride Toronto most certainly is the status quo in terms of representations of lesbian, gay, bisexual, queer, and transgender people in Toronto. The sit-in that Black Lives Matter—Toronto performed that day was a form of front-line activism enacted after years of private futile negotiations with Pride Toronto. Pride Toronto has stated, in its own words, that it "knew that for many years, the Black queer community has had to fight for their rightful place in the Pride festival—fight for space, fight for recognition and fight for support."[5] Furthermore, Pride Toronto states that it itself "did not make enough of an effort to engage with members of our black community who have worked with the organization for a very long time. We made decisions, like the location of programming by our Black Queer Youth coalition, without appropriate engagement or consultation with those affected."[6] Black Lives Matter—Toronto's front-line activism on the day of the sit-in paid close attention to the politics and aesthetics of Black performances of presence and dissent.

At the risk of stating the obvious, it is not the job of grassroots activists to make those who condone their marginalization and oppression feel as though everything is fine. Nonetheless, the undercurrent of much of the anger and frustration about Black Lives Matter—Toronto's action was the perceived audacity of the Black Lives Matter—Toronto membership to use the platform of their Honoured Group status at Pride Toronto's parade to publicly and dramatically critique the hosts—Pride Toronto. As such, there was the seemingly requisite hand-wringing from mainstream media outlets who critiqued Black Lives Matter—Toronto for drawing attention away from the culminating event of the month-long festivities that centre LGBTQ communities in Canada's most populous city. And while the details of the status quo's critiques shift from generation to generation and from organization to organization, what remains constant is that those who espouse and support dominant discourse are perennially dissatisfied with the means of protest that Black activists in North America choose. In other words, there is rarely, if ever, a time, place, or activity that those who benefit most from dominant discourse deem as appropriate for Black people to exercise our civic right to protest an institution's practices of anti-Black racism.[7] In this regard, many of the articles and media stories that covered the Black Lives Matter—Toronto sit-in at Pride were predictable and unremarkable in their queries about the appropriateness of the sit-in. This was particularly acute in a Canadian context where dominant discourse has long sought to frame Blackness as beyond the nation space.[8] Many scholars and artists have productively and eloquently traced these violent attempts to erase and omit Blackness in Canada and have mapped the fact of Blackness on this Indigenous land that is often called Canada.[9] As such, this chapter is not an explicit continuation of that important scholarship, nor does it seek to present an equitable investigation or hearing of those enraged by Black Lives Matter—Toronto's sit-in at Pride Toronto's parade. Instead, this chapter analyzes the sit-in as a thoughtful Black public performance of presence and dissent, and contextualizes it within a larger, continent-wide practice of Black public performance wherein the performance is both a site of contestation of the status quo and affirmation of the complexities of Black humanity.

PERFORMING THE SIT-IN

My research for this chapter included a telephone interview with Robin Akimbo, a person who marched with Black Lives Matter—Toronto the day of the parade and who was part of the sit-in. I was at Pride that day, specifically at Blockorama—a stage that Black organizers have produced at Pride for years. I remember seeing Akimbo at Blockorama moments after the sit-in. I remember her telling me that they (Black Lives Matter—Toronto) had shut down Pride and that it was amazing. Her energy was palpable. It seemed like in that moment something had shifted in the power structure; an interruption had happened. The scale of the impact of Black Lives Matter—Toronto's political action became evident in the days that followed as it amassed large amounts of social media and mainstream media coverage. I interviewed Akimbo months after the sit-in, and in the following extended quote she describes some of her experience as a participant in the political action that day:

> I found out there was going to be a sit-in the moment it happened. I did not know there was going to be a sit-in.

> At first I was kinda scared. It started. It was so surreal. We brought the two-spirit contingent forward so it actually started with a round dance and it started with the Indigenous leaders coming forward and smudging. Black Lives Matter [Toronto] has always included in every protest sex workers and Indigenous folks. And so, like, aligning themselves with this struggle brought a layer of intersectionality that has not been considered before.
>
> I think around the same time as the smudging was happening, right before, there was a rainbow smoke bomb explosion—it seriously sounded like a bomb. It was terrifying and amazing. It confused the police so badly and they weren't going to do shit because all eyes were on them. The circle was functional too, because it blocked the police off from what was happening. [The Indigenous leaders] were doing a round dance chanting, "I believe that we will win. I believe that we will win."[10]

After I interviewed Akimbo on the phone I studied pictures of the sit-in on social media timelines and media coverage and observed the following: There are four small coffins, each affixed to a piece of wood held by a Black person dressed all in black. One coffin is covered in three pieces of fabric—a deep purple and olive green intercut with a tan fabric with purple veining. A second coffin is covered in a fabric with multiple blue hues and features a repeated design that resembles a spider's web. The blue fabric seems overlaid at the top with black lace. A third coffin is draped in a vibrant multicoloured fabric that is overlaid at the top two-thirds with a solid white fabric. A fourth coffin is covered in two fabrics—the top third in what appears to be a fuchsia velvet and the bottom two-thirds in a solid black fabric. Each coffin is adorned with artificial flowers. There is a line of Black people behind each coffin-bearer. Most of the participant–performers wore all black with black T-shirts that said, in a large font in capital letters made from shimmering gold, "We Will Win"—words that the participant–performers also chanted and sang as they marched along the Pride Toronto parade route. "It was like a procession," said Robin Akimbo.

The notion that there is a battle being waged and that attention to the intersections of art and politics can help win it can be read as connected to the lineage of the Black Arts Movement in the United States of America. In his landmark essay "The Black Arts Movement," published in 1968, Larry Neal distinguished between the Black Arts and Black Power movements in the following way: "both relate broadly to the Afro-American's desire for self-determination and nationhood . . . . One is concerned with the relationship between art and politics; the other with the art of politics."[11] Black Lives Matter—Toronto can be read as an extension and productive re-imaging of these historical artistic and political traditions in so far as Black Lives Matter—Toronto leverages the intersections of art and politics in ways that nullify the divide that Neal identified in the 1960s. Black Lives Matter—Toronto's intervention in the discussion of the relationship between art and politics is further evidenced by the Black, queer, feminist politics that informed their performative political action during the Pride parade. As Akimbo observed,

> To me, the queers are the healers; the queers are rejected for being different. They have the key for all of our redemption. They have to fight for space and have a far greater capacity to form new family. It [the sit-in] was definitely a call to action because we're at our wits end. And also [the sit-in was] coming from a feminist history too, because we believe that we're allowed to have a response—a response that may be an unpopular one.[12]

One of the key failings of the Black Arts Movement in the United States in the 1960s is mirrored in many other organizations that were prominent during the civil rights era, and that is that, not only were elements of the movement heteronormative and patriarchal, but elements of it were also homophobic and misogynist. To be clear, even within these discriminatory organizational contexts and practices, Black LGBTQ artists, activists, and scholars continued the long-standing work of productively critiquing and shaping the direction of social justice movements. José Esteban Muñoz's theory of dis-identification offers a productive and pragmatic process through which it can be determined what is salvageable from Neal's articulation of the Black Arts Movement. Muñoz asserts that "disidentification is about recycling and rethinking encoded meaning . . . [it] is a step further than cracking open the code of the majority; it proceeds to use this code as raw material for representing a disempowered politics or positionality that has been rendered unthinkable by the dominant culture."[13] Part of what makes the activism of Black Lives Matter—Toronto compelling is that not only do they take on the expected battle with the predominantly white mainstream, but they also do what the Black Arts Movement failed to do—they challenge the heteronormativity and patriarchy of Black communities that, in this case, are in Canada. In other words, Black Lives Matter—Toronto's sit-in at Pride was a performance that disrupted the non-Black *and* Black status quo. In this regard, it can be called a disruptive performance—one that had the ability to simultaneously rupture both the non-Black *and* Black status quo. It is precisely this disruptive performance that clearly locates Black Lives Matter—Toronto's grassroots front-line activism in Toronto on July 3, 2016, both in the lineage and at the forefront of Black, queer, feminist, radical imagining. Disruptive performances like these clearly express the political, artistic, public, and private work that Black, queer, feminist, radical imagining has consistently done to undermine and nullify the insatiable demand of institutionalized whiteness that Black people understand our public interventions as circular and stagnant. The complex work of battling multiple dominant discourses through the conception and enactment of one performance is also part of a legacy of Black queer, feminist art and/as politics. And the consequences of these bold, radical imaginings include alienation and attack from multiple sides—as evidenced by even a cursory analysis of the comment sections of the articles, Facebook pages, and Twitter accounts of Black Lives Matter—Toronto and Pride Toronto. And, in keeping with the legacy of the political and artistic repercussions of Black queer, feminist interventions in Black and non-Black mainstreams, what emerges from these disruptions—often at great personal risk to those who disrupt—is the performance of presence. The sit-in received extensive local media coverage and was covered nationally. The Black Lives Matter—Toronto organizers were sophisticated in their handling of the media and, as such, the voices and, to some extent, concerns of Black queer, trans, and feminist people were centred, for a time, in mainstream spaces of local and national meaning-making. Whether or not one agrees with its methodology or outcomes, Black Lives Matter—Toronto's sit-in used creativity and calculated risk-taking to thrust Blackness and the insistence on Black life into the city's public space. In particular, their political action prioritized the expression of Black freedom on a space (Pride Toronto) that had hitherto understood itself as able to contain, control, and predict Black life.

The dramatic delivery of the group's activism was intended to unsettle the majority and empower minorities. In the space opened by its public performance of presence and dissent, Black queer, trans, and feminist people were emboldened and the larger status-quo mainstream LGBT community were silenced for a moment. And in that moment the politics of minoritized groups who have experienced institutionalized oppression by Pride Toronto held centre stage and literally halted the programming.

When Akimbo found out that Black Lives Matter—Toronto was the Honoured Group and would be marching in the parade, she said she felt

> pure happiness, because with BLM I knew there was going to be some kind of performative element. They're very committed to street art and very committed to protest art . . . . I mostly just felt really proud. It was the first time at Pride that I felt really proud . . . . The attempt for [Black Lives Matter's march] to be socially relevant and go back to the Stonewall place was really easy math for us to do, because how did it turn into this corporate bank circus? It's like the Toronto Pride police parade. It's become a cartoonish city hall display and a bit of a freak show that heteronormative people come to watch without taking on homophobia or challenging transphobia.[14]

There is a long history of grassroots Black activists, especially Black trans, queer, feminist activists, advocating for the concerns of marginalized people within mainstream efforts for equality across the continent. These moments of public performances of presence and dissent that minoritized people are routinely called upon to do are, like most performances, not for them. They are in service of the audiences, for them to witness, respond, connect with, and ideally, change. But at what cost to the performers? This is, perhaps, the central question that arises when art and politics intersect to address what the stakes of civil rights and full expressions of humanity are for Black queer, trans, and feminist people in Toronto and beyond.

From the residential school system, to the razing of Africville and the Japanese internment camps, Canada has a violent history that is fraught with painful examples of what happens when large institutions go unchecked. Black Lives Matter—Toronto, a grassroots chapter of an activist movement that spans North America, is part of a long tradition of Black front-line activism that spans generations, cultures, and issues. In Canada, the historical context of activism that Black Lives Matter—Toronto belongs to includes the Coalition for the Truth About Africa. This coalition protested the Royal Ontario Museum's 1989–1990 exhibit *Into The Heart of Africa* and denounced it as racist in its glorification of colonization and demeaning in its portrayal of Africans. Some of the coalition's weekly demonstrations included confrontations between protesters and the police, with arrests and criminal charges being laid. The coalition's Black grassroots front-line activism posed real-life risks and had lasting consequences for those who were willing to publicly express dissent with a large and influential organization. Governor General's Award-winning playwright Djanet Sears went on to write the play *The Adventures of a Black Girl in Search of God*, which weaves in a storyline that is an artistic re-imagining of the existence of and resistance to the Royal Ontario Museum's *Into The Heart of Africa* exhibit.[15] Black art and/as politics is an ongoing act in Canada that the state is only beginning to acknowledge. In November 2016, twenty-seven years after the exhibit in question opened, the Royal Ontario Museum issued a formal apology for its exhibit to the Coalition for the Truth About Africa.[16] In 2016, Arshy Mann, a reporter from Daily Xtra (one of the city's local lesbian and gay-focused newspapers), wrote that Black Lives Matter—Toronto "may be the most effective LGBT-led protest movement in Toronto today."[17] And later that year the City of Toronto awarded Black Lives Matter—Toronto the William P. Hubbard Award for Race Relations.

During the sit-in at the Pride Toronto parade, Black Lives Matter—Toronto organizers unveiled a scroll of demands that they presented to Pride Toronto's then executive director, Mathieu Chantelois. Chantelois signed it before media cameras with a large, dramatic black-feathered plume supplied by Black Lives Matter—Toronto. The demands, that he later retracted his agreement to, were as follows:

1. Commit to BQY's (Black Queer Youth's) continued space (including stage/tents), funding and logistical support.
2. Self-determination for all community spaces, allowing community full control over hiring, content, and structure of their stages.
3. Full and adequate funding for community stages, including logistical, technical, and personnel support.
4. Double funding for Blockorama + ASL interpretation & headliner funding.
5. Reinstate and make a commitment to increase community stages/spaces (including the reinstatement of the South Asian stage).
6. A commitment to increase representation amongst Pride Toronto staffing/hiring, prioritizing Black trans women, Black queer people, Indigenous folk, and others from vulnerable communities.
7. A commitment to more Black deaf & hearing ASL interpreters for the Festival.
8. Removal of police floats/booths in all Pride marches/parades/community spaces.
9. A public townhall, organized in conjunction with groups from marginalized communities, including, but not limited to, Black Lives Matter—Toronto, Blackness Yes and BQY to be held six months from today. Pride Toronto will present an update and action plan on the aforementioned demands.[18]

When the Black Lives Matter—Toronto founders returned to their fellow performer–participants at the sit-in with the signed scroll, they modified their chant to "I believe that we have won" and began to do a version of the Electric Slide all the way down the street.[19] And while there were general murmurings from LGBTQ community members and mainstream media about all of the demands, the most palpable anger came from people who were vocal online and who fixated on one thing: Black Lives Matter's demand for the "removal of police floats /booths in all Pride marches/parades/community spaces." The irony of people rising up in 2016 to defend the police presence at Pride Toronto lies in the organization's history. When Pride Toronto started in 1981 it was as a riot against 150 police officers that raided gay bathhouses and arrested more than 300 men. The foundation of what is now known as Pride Toronto was essentially a sit-in. It was a protest. Thirty-five years later, Black Lives Matter—Toronto staged a sit-in at the sit-in; they advocated within an advocacy group. In this regard they did what Black LGBTQ people in Toronto have done for a very long time in the city's queer communities, queer organizing, and queer activism. Ali Greey's media analysis of the coverage of the Black Lives Matter—Toronto sit-in locates the group's front-line activism in a history of Black insistence on presence at Pride and anti-Black racism in LGBTQ communities in the city:

> Systemic racism from within the Toronto queer 'community' is a familiar experience for many Black queer and transgender individuals. The Caribbean queer masquerade band, *Pelau,* is a popular Carnival-inspired masquerade group which marches every year during the Toronto Pride Parade (Valelly, 2015). In July 2003, *Fab Magazine*, a now out-of-print, Toronto LGBTQ weekly magazine, included a photograph of the *Pelau* group in its annual *Pride Postmortem* review. Above the photograph of the Caribbean Pride performers read [sic] the heading: 'Wrong Day. Wrong parade . . . . Caribana stray' (Kirstein et al., 2003, p. 148, as cited in Calixte, 2005). Under the photograph a caption reads, 'Is this a voodoo or a voo-don't?' These quotations reinforce the ideology that a Blackness which refuses to cohere to White, homonormative values is exotically peripheral to queerness, an ideology that BLM—TO's sit-in and list of demands actively sought to dismantle.[20]

The work of advocating within advocacy groups is familiar terrain for Black people who have participated in social justice movements. Black people's involvement in mainstream LGBTQ, feminist, and nationalist movements has routinely exposed fundamental blind spots in the politics of these movements and institutions. Not only have Black people exposed these areas of omission and obfuscation, Black people have also pointed to the possibilities of a more just, humane, and thus radical imagining of the world. Black trans, queer, and feminist people in particular have done the work of performing presence in movements and institutions so that understandings of humanities from purveyors of dominant discourse are interrupted and silenced for moments at a time. These radically imaginative performances also allow Black people to rupture the Black status quo in ways that permit new expressions of Blackness to be performed and celebrated in the public sphere. To this end, regardless of the extent to which anti-Black narratives are adapted and rewoven into dominant discourses, public spaces for dynamic, complex, rich expressions of Blackness evolve and further nourish the uncontainable expressions of Black liberation in Toronto and beyond.

NOTES

1 Black Lives Matter—Toronto, Facebook, July 3, 2016, https://www.facebook.com/blacklivesmatterTO/photos/a.319994704862693.1073741829.313499695512194/519230751605753/?type=3&theater.

2 Jackie Hong, "Black Lives Matter Protesters Shut Down Allen Rd.," *Toronto Star*, July 27, 2015, https://www.thestar.com/news/gta/2015/07/27/black-lives-matter-protesters-shut-down-allen-rd.html; Adam Miller and Andrew Russell, "Black Lives Matter Protesters Shut Down Section of Allen Expressway," Global News, July 27, 2015, https://globalnews.ca/news/2134082/hundreds-protest-deaths-of-jermaine-carby-and-andrew-loku-in-toronto/; Amy Grief, "Black Lives Matter Protest Shuts Down Allen Road," Blog TO, July 28, 2015, http://www.blogto.com/city/2015/07/black_lives_matter_protest_shuts_down_allen_road/.

3 Luke Simcoe, "Black Lives Matter Toronto Responds to Andrew Loku Inquest," *Metro News Toronto*, April 13, 2016, http://www.metronews.ca/news/toronto/2016/04/13/black-lives-matter-toronto-andrew-loku-inquest.html; "Fatal Police Shooting of Andrew Loku Inspires Black Lives Matter Chant," CBC News, July 9, 2015, http://www.cbc.ca/news/canada/toronto/fatal-police-shooting-of-andrew-loku-inspires-black-lives-matter-chant-1.3145049.

4 Joe Clark, "Black Lives Matter vs Pride Toronto," Black Lives Matter vs. Pride Toronto, July 12, 2016, https://blmpride.wordpress.com/.

5 Pride Toronto Board of Directors, "Update: Statement from Pride Toronto," Pride Toronto, http://www.pridetoronto.com/town-hall-meeting/, accessed December 6, 2016.

6 Ibid.

7 See coverage of Beyoncé's performance of the song "Formation" at the National Football League's Super Bowl in 2016 and also coverage of

Colin Kaepernick kneeling during the playing of the United States' national anthem at NFL games. Lee Siegel, "Why Kaepernick Takes the Knee," *The New York Times*, September 25, 2017, https://www.nytimes.com/2017/09/25/opinion/nfl-football-kaepernick-take-knee.html.

8 Katherine McKittrick, "Nothing's Shocking: Black Canada," in *Demonic Grounds: Black Women and the Cartographies of Struggle*, ed. Katherine McKittrick (Minneapolis: University of Minnesota Press, 2006), 91–119; Andrea Davis, "Diaspora, Citizenship and Gender: Challenging the Myth of the Nation in African Canadian Women's Literature," *Canadian Woman Studies* 23, no. 2 (2004): 64–9; Lorena Gale, *Angélique* (Toronto: Playwrights Canada Press, 1999); Djanet Sears, "nOTES oF a cOLOURED gIRL," in *Harlem Duet* (Winnipeg: Scirocco Drama, 1997), 11–16.

9 Zainab Amadahy and Bonita Lawrence, "Indigenous Peoples and Black People in Canada: Settlers or Allies?" in *Breaching the Colonial Contact: Anti-Colonialism in the US and Canada*, ed. Arlo Kempf (Toronto: Springer, 2009), 105–36; George Elliot Clarke, "'Indigenous Blacks': An Irreconcilable Identity," in *Cultivating Canada: Reconciliation through the Lens of Cultural Diversity*, ed. Ashok Mathur, Jonathan Dewar, and Mike DeGagné (Ottawa: Aboriginal Healing Foundation, 2011), 399–406; Robyn Maynard, *Policing Black Lives: State Violence in Canada from Slavery to the Present* (Halifax: Fernwood Publishing, 2017); Joshua Ostroff, "Colonial Canada Had Slavery For More Than 200 Years. And Yes, It Still Matters Today," *Huffington Post*, June 17, 2017, http://www.huffingtonpost.ca/2017/06/17/slavery-canada-history_n_16806804.html.

10 Robin Akimbo, personal communication to author.

11 Larry Neal, "The Black Arts Movement," *The Drama Review: TDR* 12, no. 4 (1968), 29. See also, Arts Against PostRacialism, https://mcgill.ca/aapr/.

12 Akimbo, personal communication.

13 José Esteban Muñoz, *Disidentifications: Queers of Color and the Performance of Politics* (Minneapolis: University of Minnesota Press, 1999), 31.

14 Akimbo, personal communication.

15 For archival information from the exhibit, see "Into the heart of Africa," Archive.org, https://archive.org/details/intoheartofafricooroya.

16 For news coverage of the apology, see Jackie Hong, "ROM apologizes for racist 1989 African exhibit," *Toronto Star*, November 9, 2016, https://www.thestar.com/news/gta/2016/11/09/rom-apologizes-for-racist-1989-african-exhibit.html.

17 Arshy Mann, "Why Black Lives Matter is Toronto's Most Effective LGBT Movement," *Daily Xtra*, April 28, 2016, http://www.dailyxtra.com/toronto/news-and-ideas/news/black-lives-matter-torontos-effective-lgbt-movement-191488.
18 Black Lives Matter—Toronto, Facebook post.
19 Akimbo, personal communication.
20 Ali Greey, "Queer Inclusion Precludes (Black) Queer Disruption: Media Analysis of the Black Lives Matter Toronto Sit-In during Toronto Pride 2016," *Leisure Studies* 37, no. 6 (2018), 10.

REFERENCES

Amadahy, Zainab, and Bonita Lawrence. "Indigenous Peoples and Black People in Canada: Settlers or Allies?" In *Breaching the Colonial Contact: Anti-Colonialism in the US and Canada*, edited by Arlo Kempf, 105–36. Toronto: Springer, 2009.

Clarke, George Elliot. "'Indigenous Blacks': An Irreconcilable Identity." In *Cultivating Canada: Reconciliation through the Lens of Cultural Diversity*, edited by Ashok Mathur, Jonathan Dewar, and Mike DeGagné, 399–406. Ottawa: Aboriginal Healing Foundation, 2011.

Davis, Andrea. "Diaspora, Citizenship and Gender: Challenging the Myth of the Nation in African Canadian Women's Literature." *Canadian Woman Studies* 23, no. 2 (2004): 64–9.

Gale, Lorena. *Angélique*. Toronto: Playwrights Canada Press, 1999.

Greey, Ali. "Queer Inclusion Precludes (Black) Queer Disruption: Media Analysis of the Black Lives Matter Toronto Sit-In during Toronto Pride 2016." *Leisure Studies* 37, no. 6 (2018): 662–76. https://doi.org/10.1080/02614367.2018.1468475.

Maynard, Robyn. *Policing Black Lives: State Violence in Canada from Slavery to the Present*. Halifax: Fernwood Publishing, 2017.

McKittrick, Katherine. "Nothing's Shocking: Black Canada." In *Demonic Grounds: Black Women and the Cartographies of Struggle*, edited by Katherine McKittrick, 91–119. Minneapolis: University of Minnesota Press, 2006.

Muñoz, José Esteban. *Disidentifications: Queers of Color and the Performance of Politics*. Minneapolis: University of Minnesota Press, 1999.

Neal, Larry. "The Black Arts Movement." *The Drama Review: TDR* 12, no. 4 (1968): 28–39. http://www.jstor.org/stable/1144377.

Sears, Djanet. "nOTES oF a cOLOURED gIRL." In *Harlem Duet*, 11–16. Winnipeg: Scirocco Drama, 1997.

PART V

AND BEYOND: BLACK FUTURITIES AND POSSIBLE WAYS FORWARD

20

POWER TO ALL PEOPLE: BLACK LGBTTI2QQ ACTIVISM, REMEMBRANCE, AND ARCHIVING IN TORONTO

SYRUS MARCUS WARE

This chapter was originally published as an article in Transgender Studies Quarterly *4, no. 2 (May 2017): 170–180.*

INTRODUCTION

I consider the erasure of racialized and Indigenous histories from white trans archives, timelines, and cartographies of resistance. I examine interventions by Black queer and trans historiographers, critics, and activists who have attempted to re-inscribe Blackness into the history of LGBTTI2QQ[1] space in Toronto. Lastly, I consider how power and privilege influence what is allowed to be remembered and what is considered archivable. This paper was created through several collaborative feedback sessions with the Marvellous Grounds collective and draws on the emerging Marvellous Grounds archive project.[2] In particular, I draw on the writing of contributors Monica Forrester, a Black trans activist from Toronto who has worked doing sex-worker outreach for the past two decades; Richard Fung, artist and activist and one of the founders of Gay Asians of Toronto; and Douglas Stewart, a Black activist and organizer who co-founded Blockorama[3] and other key Black queer and trans organizations in the city.

The classic archive structure—and I'm speaking here primarily about white trans and queer archives—is the allegedly neutral, disembodied collection of objects that create and inscribe a narrative of struggle and resistance that always begins with whiteness and that is used too often in the service of homonationalism, gay imperialism, and the vilification of the less progressive other.[4] As Haritaworn argues in *Queer Lovers and Hateful Others*, the queer timeline we are describing/critiquing suggests a seamless march towards rights, with anti-hate-crime activism as the apex of history that the rest of the world must be forced into.[5] Instead, I am suggesting that we start with a Black trans and queer history as a way to orient us towards different pasts and futures, as well as a radically different account of the present and what needs to change. As I will illustrate in this text, we need to consider what we want to remember and how we want to remember it, building an archive of our movements going forward to ensure that intergenerational memory can inform our activism, community-building, and organizing. By tracing the histories of QTBIPOCs[6] in Toronto, and the omissions of these narratives in mainstream archives, we can begin to do this work.

I would like to begin by calling names, following in the line of author Courtnay McFarlane and his important commitment to remembering the great legacy of Black queer and trans folks in Toronto over the past several decades.[7] I want to call names to bring the spirit of these activisms into the room with us, to remember that it is ongoing and enlivened by a consideration of the past, present, and (Afro) future.[8] I'd like to call into this space the important work of trans women of colour and Indigenous trans and two-spirited folks, who are often omitted from the archives—from official records and collective memories of what has happened in this place. And so I call names: Mirha-Soleil Ross,[9] Yasmeen Persad, Monica Forrester, and Nik Redman, the names of those with us, but also those who have already passed on, including Sumaya Dalmar, Duchess, and countless others. I call these names as an act of remembrance and reverence, but also as a suggestion for where to begin looking for our trans people of colour archive—in names called and stories shared.

COMING OUT AS TRANS AND BLACK

When I entered the largely white trans community in Toronto in the late 1990s, coming out as a Black trans person felt incredibly isolating. The 519 Church Street Community Centre's trans programs were in their infancy, and though they did a lot to promote early trans visibility, the ephemera they created tended to reproduce the idea that there were few (if any) Black trans people. Online resources like FTMI[10] and the Lou Sullivan Society did not do a good job of connecting with/to/creating work by trans folks of colour, something that would eventually change after years, if not decades, of trans folks of colour mobilizing and organizing. And so, I came out and felt quite isolated. But through organizing within Black queer spaces, I met other people. I got to work with Yasmeen Persad through The 519's Trans Shelter Access Project; I got to connect with Monica Forrester through my work at PASAN. We shared information and resources. I found out through researching sex reassignment surgery (SRS) in North America that one of the first trans people to have SRS inside America was Delisa Newton, a Black trans jazz singer. I learned about Storme DeLarverie, a Black gender-variant performer and activist who set the stage for countless future trans artists of colour. Where was I to go to find out about Black trans history in Toronto? Historical and grassroots queer archives often don't do a good job at actively participating in the documentation and preservation of the artefacts, stories, and materials of Black and African diasporic cultural production and activism despite a stated desire by community members to have their work be part of a visible archive.[11] This erasure is part of a larger conceptualization of the Black queer subject as a new entity whose history is built upon an already-existing white LGBTTI2QQ space and history.

A MARVELLOUS ARCHIVE: BLACK AND TRANS COMMUNITIES THROUGH TIME AND SPACE

Trans lives of colour follow a different temporality—we fail the progress narrative espoused by the white trans movement (as advancement is typically reduced to acquiring "rights" that are inaccessible to most and in fact are wielded against so many on the margins of the margins through the prison-industrial complex, the war on terror, and the development industry).[12] At the same time, trans lives of colour open up different futures that are not just a reproduction of/diversification of/assimilation into the same. As Sylvia Rivera explains, trans folks of colour were at the front lines in part because they experienced rampant marginalization and, as a result, they "had nothing to lose."[13] Our relationship to the law changes our relationships to space and organizing and creates a certain set of freedoms, and also restrictions, in our work.[14] Rivera and her communities put everything else on the line to fight for systemic change and to fight for self-determination because of these relationships. Here, I am pointing to a different set of activist ancestors that create a tension and challenge to what and how we remember collective struggle.

By starting with QTBIPOC narratives, we gain a different entry point into trans and queer collective archives and timelines of resistance, and we interrupt the ways that these omissions produce a whitewashed canon. Starting with our stories and reading them alongside more mainstream narratives, we can inform trans theory, guide future activism, and set the stage for new ways of working for change. Derrida, in his seminal work *Archive Fever: A Freudian Impression*, argues that we produce something through these acts of re-remembering, or sharing stories: we create a sense of physical, liminal, and phenomenological space to consider our past, presents, and futures.[15] In contrast, the prioritization of white queer and trans people's history by white historiographers suggests that all LGBTTI2QQ community organizing and development was created by and for white people.[16] Instead, we offer a type of counter-archiving, as conceptualized by Jin Haritworn in the introduction to *Marvellous Grounds*.[17] Counter-archiving highlights the problems of a presentist agenda that selectively highlights and erases subjects, spaces, and events in order to expand its own power in the present into the future, without letting go of either the past or the future. It further questions what acts, subjects, and inscriptions legitimately constitute an archive. The question thus becomes not where is the archive, but rather why are Black subjects always already conceptualized as new additions? The stories of the resistance that Black peoples have enacted since being on Turtle Island are continually forgotten and erased.

WE'VE BEEN HERE: BLACK TRANS ORGANIZING IN TORONTO AND BEYOND

Contrary to the claim of newness, countless artists, activists, poets, and community mobilizers within Black queer and trans communities in Toronto have done the work of documenting our stories. This archive of Black movements over time and space exists and is exemplified, for example, by Debbie Douglas, Courtnay McFarlane, Makeda Silvera and Douglas Stewart's 1997 anthology that brought together queer Black authors in Canada, entitled *Má-Ka Diasporic Juks: Contemporary Writing by Queers of African Descent*;[18] the piles of historic video; the vivid textile banners and art by Black queer and trans people created for Blockorama[19]—currently housed in local activist Junior Harrison's basement, highlighting a large gap in the municipal archive; and in the embodied interpersonal storytelling that happens when we get together in community: at Blockorama; outside of a Black queer dance party by local DJs Blackcat, Nik Red, and Cozmic Cat; in the park outside of the queer community centre, The 519 Church Street Community Centre. There is, in fact, a big literature on the Black queer and trans experience already, and here I'm thinking of the important work of Omise'eke Natasha Tinsley, Rinaldo Walcott, OmiSoore Dryden, CasSandy Lord, and so many others.[20]

The discourse of the "new" QTIBPOC subject is further belied by the long history of activism by QTBIPOCs across this north part of Turtle Island. Toronto in the 1970s and 1980s was brimming with activism by QTBIPOCs organizing around homelessness, LGBTQ activism, HIV/AIDS, education, anti-apartheid activism, disability justice, and challenging racism and other forms of systemic marginalization and oppression, to name but a few examples. Folks were getting together to write letters in support of activists fighting against apartheid on the continent, including South African gay rights activist Simon Nkoli. Artists were coming together to form political arts initiatives like Desh Pardesh, a festival of queer and trans South Asian arts and culture in Toronto; the MayWorks Festival of the Arts, a labour arts festival that makes intersectional links between class, race, and gender through an understanding of labour arts; and the Counting Past Two festival, one of the first trans film festivals in North America. Mainstream LGBTQ records and municipal archives have omitted these initiatives, yet they exist in our community and persist in an oral tradition of telling and retelling, embodied in our activism. These tellings and retellings are self-directed and draw on what Eve Tuck has conceptualized as desire-based research: the need to root our considerations in a "framework . . . concerned with understanding complexity, contradiction, and the self-determination of lived lives" in order, she elaborates, to

> document . . . not only the painful elements of social realities but also the wisdom and hope. Such an axiology is intent on depathologizing the experiences of dispossessed and disenfranchised communities so that people are seen as more than broken and conquered. This is to say that even when communities are broken and conquered, they are so much more than that—so much more that this incomplete story is an act of aggression.[21]

Indeed, these archives interrupt the neoliberal insistence on the forced telling and retelling of a one-dimensional narrative by those on the margins—a telling that is obligatory in what Tuck contrasts as damage-centred research. Instead, these shared memories tell of a deep, intersectional knowing that can inform our understandings of our own lives today, direct our future activism, and help us build stronger communities rooted in care and justice. These lived movements and collective memories are described by Marvellous Grounds contributor Monica Forrester, who talks about her entry into activism in the 1980s. She helps us understand the different relationship that young Black trans women of that time had to archivable ephemera: keeping the kinds of objects that mainstream archives value as proof of value/worth was hard, given what they were up against. She states:

> the corner was the only community that existed. At that time, it was the only place where we could share information. And, that's where I've learned a lot . . . the determination to make change . . . . And when I was thinking about history, and archiving, I thought, "Oh! I wish I took pictures" . . . Because we were in such a different place back then. I think survival was key. No one really thought about archiving, because we really didn't think we would live

> past 30. Our lives were so undetermined that no one really thought about, "Oh, should we archive this for later use?"[22]

Forrester's text references an urgency of activism that aimed to prolong life and chances of survival in a white supremacist and transphobic world, but that frequently eludes dominant queer narratives of space and time. Thus, QTBIPOC organizing happened not in the village, but at the corner. Forrester's story informs our understanding of subsequent activisms in the city, for example, shaping our understanding of how to organize to stop sex workers from being pushed out of the LGBTQ village in Toronto as part of ongoing gentrification processes and anti-sex-worker stigma. By situating our understanding of the corner as being a community centre, a home, a classroom, and the other sorts of places described by Forrester, we can build a fight that ensures that the access points the corner represents are intact when we are done fighting.

Furthermore, as Forrester describes, in the face of ever-present systemic violence, "no one really thought about archiving, because we really didn't think we would live past 30." Just because Black trans people didn't keep ephemera doesn't mean we don't have an archive and things to remember. The obsessive collecting of posters and memorabilia—think of the elaborate pin button project[23] launched at the Canadian Lesbian and Gay Archives, a national archive of queer culture that was founded in 1973, and that now is the largest independent queer archive in the world. Despite claims that it represents and reflects queer culture across Canada, many have critiqued the archive's lack of racialized historical content, the lack of a visible trans archive, and its anachronistic name, "Lesbian and Gay Archives." Groupings such as the display of thousands of pin buttons mean nothing without the embodied memories and stories that contextualize their creation. We might speculate what the archives of Monica Forrester would have looked like and how they'd differ from the elaborate pin button project. What would the archives of Monica Forrester have looked like, had there been the capacity to create such documents at that time of great struggle? What would have been created or changed through the process of such recording? What would the community have had to look like and who would have had to be in power to foster an interest in the creation of such an archive? What would power have had to look like in the village at that moment for the lives of Black trans women to be considered worthy of archiving or remembering? We can reflect on Forrester's words to help us understand recent QTBIPOC interventions in the city, such as the Black Lives Matter—Toronto (BLM—TO) shutdown of the Toronto Pride parade in June 2016 and the subsequent anti-Black racist backlash and violence that followed within Toronto's queer and trans communities.[24] Her articulation of who gets to hold power and have ownership over the directions and decisions of these communities—in essence, who is remembered as being here and part of the fight—is brought to life in the BLM—TO moment. Their presence in the parade was seen by many to be unexpected, and their political analysis considered divergent and unwanted, with some white community members chanting, "Take this fight to Caribana,"[25] suggesting that Black queer and trans organizing was not "of the village," as this is an always already-white space, and that our organizing belonged in an explicitly Black space: Caribana. BLM—TO's leadership, largely made up of queer and trans members, and their role as Pride Toronto's Honoured Group still did not afford them belonging in the (presumed to be all-white) queer and trans community.

Forrester's words tell of the need for an intersectional understanding of what has happened within Black queer and trans communities in Toronto in the past four decades. She urges us to consider sex workers, poor and working-class trans women, and others who are marginalized within larger Black queer and trans organizing, as historical subjects. At the same time, her historical narrative does not simply "bring Black trans ephemera to the archives." It raises larger questions about who can interpret our histories and who can understand our embodied repertoires.

CONCLUSION

I began this chapter by calling names. I will end it by sharing an encounter that illustrates, or perhaps embodies, the problem with the archive. Memory is a fascinating process. The more we recall, or perhaps repeat, our memories of events, the more we begin to remember the memories more than the events.

I recently met with a self-proclaimed elder, a white gay activist whose account of the Toronto bathhouse raids is widely cited. He asked me for an interview, and I was telling him about my own organizing and my desire to build on the important work of trans women of colour leading our movements. He leaned forward and said, matter-of-factly, "You know, it's not true. People nowadays say that trans women of colour were there, but they weren't. I was there. I would have remembered." He was so certain that he was a more accurate witness of what had happened in the Toronto and New York histories that he could discount the living stories of trans women. He felt such confidence in his own memory as being *the* memory—*the* archive, *the* impartial record of human history. We simply were not there in his mind, and thus we were ripped from the fabric of time and space. The memories of this elder, for a variety of reasons including anti-Black racism, transphobia, and the active marginalization of trans Indigenous and racialized people from these movements, do not recall our presence at these events and eventually become "*the* event."

But we were there; we are, as Miss Major says, *"still fucking here."*[26] And we already exist in the beautiful (Afro) future. By beginning here, by starting with *these* genealogies, we can re-remember that we are here, that we will continue to exist, continue to fight, to struggle for change, and to win, as Assata Shakur urges us.[27] Black trans archives live in the moments of shared story, of names called, of gatherings and celebrations in public space. Our archives live in our bodies and minds, and they span across time and space.

NOTES

1 LGBTTI2QQ: Lesbian, Gay, Bisexual, Transgender, Transsexual, Intersex, Two-Spirited, Queer, and Questioning.

2 Marvellous Grounds is a Social Sciences and Humanities Research Council and Early Researcher Award–funded forerunning collection of art, activism, and academic writings by queers of colour in Toronto. It is a book and web-based project and is co-edited/curated by Jin Haritaworn, Alvis Choi, Ghaida Moussa, Rio Rodriguez, and Syrus Marcus Ware at York University in Toronto.

3 Blockorama is an eleven-hour Black queer and trans arts festival that runs on Pride Sunday in Toronto. The event is in its twenty-first year as of 2019.

4 On homonationalism and gay imperialism, see Jinthana Haritaworn, Tamsila Tauqir, and Esra Erdem, "Gay Imperialism: Gender and Sexuality Discourse in the 'War on Terror,'" in *Out of Place: Interrogating Silences and Queerness/Raciality*, ed. Adi Kuntsman and Esperanza Miyake (York: Raw Nerve Books Ltd, 2008); Rinaldo Walcott, Foreword to *Disrupting Queer Inclusion: Canadian Homonationalisms and the Politics of Belonging*, eds. OmiSoore H. Dryden and Suzanne Lenon (Vancouver: University of British Columbia Press, 2015), vii-x. On the vilification of the less progressive other see Diana Taylor, *The Archive and the Repertoire: Performing Cultural Memory in the Americas*, (Durham, NC: Duke University Press, 2003); Ann Laura Stoler, *Along the Archival Grain: Epistemic Anxieties and Colonial Common Sense* (Princeton: Princeton University Press, 2010); Edward Said, *Culture and Imperialism* (New York: Vintage Books, 1994); Kusha Dadui, "LGBT Refugees and Canadian Border Imperialism," in *Marvellous Grounds: Queer of Colour Histories of Toronto*, eds. Jinthana Haritaworn, Ghaida Moussa, and Syrus Marcus Ware (Toronto: Between the Lines Press, 2018).

5 Jinthana Haritaworn, *Queer Lovers and Hateful Others: Regenerating Violent Times and Places* (Chicago: University of Chicago Press, 2015); "Marvellous Grounds and the Belated Archive," Roundtable plenary at the Trans Temporality Conference, University of Toronto, Toronto, April 1, 2016.

6 QTBIPOC stands for queer, trans, black, Indigenous, and people of colour.

7 Courtnay McFarlane, speech given at Blockorama town hall meeting, The 519 Church Street Community Center, Toronto, April 16, 2007.

8 Lisa Yaszek, "Afrofuturism, Science Fiction, and the History of the Future," *Socialism and Democracy* 20, no. 3 (2006): 41-60, https://doi.org/10.1080/08854300600950236; Octavia E. Butler, *Parable of the Sower* (New York: Open Road Media, 2012).

9 These trans activists contributed greatly to the development of trans community during the 1990s and early 2000s in Toronto. Mirha-Soleil Ross is a trans artist, sex worker, and activist who has led seminal research and organizing in Montreal and Toronto from the early 1990s to the present day. Yasmeen Persad is a Black trans woman in Toronto who has worked for over 10 years to create access programs for trans women of colour through The 519 Church Street Community Centre and the Sherbourne Health Centre. Monica Forrester is a Black trans woman who has spent several decades doing street outreach and organizing amongst trans sex workers in Toronto. Nik Redman is a Black trans man in Toronto who has worked for two decades to create trans-specific programming and

resources for queer trans men, trans parents, and filmmakers of colour. Sumaya Dalmar was a black Trans woman who died in 2015 in Toronto. The handling of her case by the Toronto Police Services came under fire when her death was not initially reported. Duchess was a well-known Black drag queen in Toronto who died suddenly of meningitis in the early 2000s in Toronto.

10 Female To Male International. Found online at FTMI.org on May 31, 2016.

11 Andrew Flinn, Mary Stevens, and Elizabeth Shepherd, "Whose Memories, Whose Archives? Independent Community Archives, Autonomy, and the Mainstream," *Archival Science* 9, no. 1-2 (2009): 71–86. The lack of adequate archiving and a desire to create a Black queer and trans archive has come up several times; for example, it was the theme and focus of the Toronto Queering Black History gathering at Ryerson University in 2010 that featured talks on the subject by Notisha Massaquoi , Rinaldo Walcott, Courtnay McFarlane, and Syrus Marcus Ware. The gathering was organized by a student collective led by Lali Mohamed and has become an annual event.

12 Jinthana Haritawon, Adi Kuntsman, and Silvia Posocco, "Murderous Inclusions," *International Feminist Journal of Politics* 15, no. 4 (2013): 445–52, https://doi.org/10.1080/14616742.2013.841568.

13 Sylvia Rivera, "Sylvia Rivera's Talk at LGMNY, June 2001 Lesbian and Gay Community Services Center, New York City," *CENTRO: Journal of the Center for Puerto Rican Studies* 19, no. 1 (2007): 116–23, https://www.redalyc.org/pdf/377/37719106.pdf.

14 Rivera, "Sylvia Rivera's Talk"; Syrus Marcus Ware, Joan Ruzsa, and Giselle Dias, "It Can't Be Fixed Because It's Not Broken: Racism and Disability in the Prison Industrial Complex," in *Disability Incarcerated: Imprisonment and Disability in the United States and Canada*, eds. Angela Y. Davis, Chris Chapman, and Alison C. Carey, 163–184 (New York: Palgrave Macmillan: 2014); Julia Oparah Chinyere/Sudbury and Margo Okazawa-Rey, eds., *Activist Scholarship: Antiracism, Feminism, and Social Change* (Boulder, CO: Paradigm Publishers, 2009); Lena Palacios, Rosalind Hampton, Ilyan Ferrer, Elma Moses, and Edward Lee, "Learning in Social Action: Students of Color and the Québec Student Movement," *JCT: Journal of Curriculum Theorizing* 29, no. 2 (2013): 6–25, http://journal.jctonline.org/index.php/jct/article/view/469.

15 Jacques Derrida, *Archive Fever: A Freudian Impression* (Chicago: University of Chicago Press, 1996).

16 Mario H. Ramirez, "Being Assumed Not to Be: A Critique of Whiteness as an Archival Imperative," *The American Archivist* 78, no. 2 (2015): 339–56, https://doi.org/10.17723/0360-9081.78.2.339; Flinn, Stevens, and Shepherd, "Whose Memories, Whose Archives?"

17 Haritaworn (2015); Jinthana Haritaworn, Ghaida Moussa, and Syrus Marcus Ware, eds. *Marvellous Grounds: Queer of Colour Formations in Toronto* (Toronto: Between the Lines Press, 2018).

18 Debbie Douglas, Courtnay McFarlane, Makeda Silvera, and Douglas Stewart, eds., *Má-Ka Diasporic Juks: Contemporary Writing by Queers of African Descent* (Toronto: Sister Vision Press, 1997).

19 Started by Blackness Yes! in 1998, Blockorama is a day-long arts festival at the city's annual Pride celebrations that has developed over seventeen years of resistance to whitewashing within queer organizing. An explicitly political space run by an independent committee of grassroots organizers (Blackness Yes!), the arts programming spans twelve hours and centres the narratives of Black and African diasporic trans, disabled, deaf, and queer people.

20 Omise'eke Natasha Tinsley, "Black Atlantic, Queer Atlantic: Queer Imaginings of the Middle Passage," *GLQ: A Journal of Lesbian and Gay Studies* 14, no. 2-3 (2008): 191–215, https://doi.org/10.1215/10642684-2007-030; Rinaldo Walcott, *Black Like Who? Writing Black Canada* (Toronto: Insomniac Press, 2009); Rinaldo Walcott, "Reconstructing Manhood; or, the Drag of Black Masculinity," *Small Axe: A Caribbean Journal of Criticism* 13, no. 1 (2009): 75–89, https://doi.org/10.1215/07990537-2008-007; Rinaldo Walcott, "Outside in Black Studies: Reading from a Queer Place in the Diaspora," in *Queerly Canadian: An Introductory Reader in Sexuality Studies*, eds. Maureen FitzGerald and Scott Rayter (Toronto: Canadian Scholars' Press, 2012), 23–34; OmiSoore Dryden, "Canadians Denied: A Queer Diasporic Analysis of the Canadian Blood Donor," *Atlantis: Critical Studies in Gender, Culture & Social Justice* 34, no. 2 (2010): 77–84; R. CasSandy Lord, "Making the Invisible/Visible: Creating a Discourse on Black Queer Youth," master's thesis, University of Toronto, 2005; R. CasSandy Lord, "Performing Queer Diasporas: Friendships, Proximities and Intimacies in Pride Parades," PhD diss., University of Toronto, 2015.

21 Eve Tuck. "Suspending Damage: A Letter to Communities," *Harvard Educational Review* 79, no. 3 (2009), 416.

22 Monica Forrester, transcribed audio interview, Marvellous Grounds Project, 2015.

23 The Pin Button Project featured a campaign to solicit the donation of his-

toric activist buttons from Toronto queer and trans people. The project had some content that reflected a racialized history, but largely reflected a white queer history. For more information, see http://www.clga.ca/pin-button-project-launch-party, accessed May 31, 2016.

24 BLM—TO was named Pride Toronto's Honoured Group and as a result was asked to lead the Toronto Pride parade. During the parade, BLM-TO held a twenty-five-minute sit-in during which they presented the Pride Toronto executive director a list of demands co-written with two other Black queer and trans groups: Black Queer Youth (BQY) and Blackness Yes!. The groups collectively demanded that Pride Toronto do better by Black, Indigenous, racialized, trans and disabled people, and refused to restart the parade until the Pride executive director agreed to address their concerns. There was tremendous backlash by white festival attendees, with many throwing water bottles at Black activists, screaming racial slurs, and yelling that they were being "selfish." In the days that followed, many of the BLM—TO organizers received death threats and hate mail in response to this direct action.

25 Toronto Caribbean Carnival, known by most as Caribana, is the largest annual festival in the city of Toronto. Held over several weeks and culminating in a day-long parade and carnival celebration, the festival is heavily policed and the site of the festival has been moved from a prominent location down to the edge of the city's waterfront.

26 Miss Major is a lifelong activist and community organizer well known for her role in the Stonewall Riots and for helping to set up supportive programming for black trans women across the United States. Annalise Ophelian and Florez, StormMiguel, creators, *Major! A New Documentary Film*, San Francisco: Floating Ophelia Productions, 2016.

27 Assata Shakur, *Assata: An Autobiography* (London: Zed Books, 1987).

REFERENCES

Butler, Octavia E. *Parable of the Sower.* New York: Open Road Media, 2012.

———. *Kindred.* Boston: Beacon Press, 2004.

Dadui, Kusha. "LGBT Refugees and Canadian Border Imperialism." In *Marvellous Grounds: Queer of Colour Histories of Toronto*, edited by Jinthana Haritaworn, Ghaida Moussa, and Syrus Marcus Ware. Toronto: Between the Lines Press, 2018.

Derrida, Jacques. *Archive Fever: A Freudian Impression.* Chicago: University of Chicago Press, 1996.

Douglas, Debbie, Courtnay McFarlane, Makeda Silvera, and Douglas Stewart, eds. *Má-Ka Diasporic Juks: Contemporary Writing by Queers of African Descent*. Toronto: Sister Vision Press, 1997.

Dryden, OmiSoore. "Canadians Denied: A Queer Diasporic Analysis of the Canadian Blood Donor." *Atlantis: Critical Studies in Gender, Culture & Social Justice* 34, no. 2 (2010): 77–84. http://journals.msvu.ca/index.php/atlantis/article/view/334/315.

Flinn, Andrew, Mary Stevens, and Elizabeth Shepherd. "Whose Memories, Whose Archives? Independent Community Archives, Autonomy, and the Mainstream." *Archival Science* 9, no. 1-2 (2009): 71–86. https://link.springer.com/article/10.1007/s10502-009-9105-2.

Gan, Jessi. "'Still at the Back of the Bus': Sylvia Rivera's Struggle." *CENTRO: Journal of the Center for Puerto Rican Studies* 19, no. 1 (2007): 124–40. http://www.redalyc.org/articulo.oa?id=37719107.

Haritaworn, Jinthana. *Queer Lovers and Hateful Others: Regenerating Violent Times and Places*. Chicago: University of Chicago Press, 2015.

Haritawon, Jinthana, Adi Kuntsman, and Silvia Posocco. "Murderous Inclusions." *International Feminist Journal of Politics* 15, no. 4 (2013): 445–52. https://doi.org/10.1080/14616742.2013.841568.

Haritaworn, Jinthana, Ghaida Moussa, and Syrus Marcus Ware. *Marvellous Grounds: Queer of Colour Formations in Toronto*. Toronto: Between the Lines Press, 2018.

Haritaworn, Jinthana, Tamsila Tauqir, and Esra Erdem. "Gay Imperialism: Gender and Sexuality Discourse in the 'War on Terror.'" In *Out of Place: Interrogating Silences and Queerness/Raciality*, edited by Adi Kuntsman and Esperanza Miyake. York: Raw Nerve Books Ltd, 2008.

Hartman, Saidiya. *Lose Your Mother: A Journey along the Atlantic Slave Route*. New York: Farrar, Straus & Giroux, 2008.

Lord, R. CasSandy. "Making the Invisible/Visible: Creating a Discourse on Black Queer Youth." Master's thesis, University of Toronto, 2005.

Lord, R. CasSandy. "Performing Queer Diasporas: Friendships, Proximities and Intimacies in Pride Parades." PhD diss., University of Toronto, 2015.

"Marvellous Grounds and the Belated Archive." Roundtable plenary at the Trans Temporality Conference, University of Toronto, Toronto, ON, April 1, 2016.

McFarlane, Courtnay. Speech given at Blockorama town hall meeting, The 519 Church Street Community Center, Toronto, ON, April 16, 2007.

Oparah, Chinyere/Sudbury, Julia, and Margo Okazawa-Rey, eds. *Activist Scholarship: Antiracism, Feminism, and Social Change*. Boulder, CO: Paradigm Publishers, 2009.

Ophelian, Annalise and Florez, StormMiguel, creators. *Major! A New Documentary Film*, San Francisco: Floating Ophelia Productions, 2016.

Palacios, Lena, Rosalind Hampton, Ilyan Ferrer, Elma Moses, and Edward Lee. "Learning in Social Action: Students of Color and the Québec Student Movement." *JCT: Journal of Curriculum Theorizing* 29, no. 2 (2013): 6–25. http://journal.jctonline.org/index.php/jct/article/view/469.

Ramirez, Mario H. "Being Assumed Not to Be: A Critique of Whiteness as an Archival Imperative." *The American Archivist* 78, no. 2 (2015): 339–56. https://doi.org/10.17723/0360-9081.78.2.339.

Rivera, Sylvia. "Sylvia Rivera's Talk at LGMNY, June 2001 Lesbian and Gay Community Services Center, New York City." *CENTRO: Journal of the Center for Puerto Rican Studies* 19, no. 1 (2007): 116–23. https://www.redalyc.org/pdf/377/37719106.pdf.

Said, Edward. *Culture and Imperialism*. New York: Vintage Books, 1994.

Shakur, Assata. *Assata: An Autobiography*. London: Zed Books, 1987.

Snorton, C. Riley and Jinthana Haritaworn. "Trans Necropolitics." In *The Transgender Studies Reader*, vol. 2, edited by Aren Aizura and Susan Stryker, 66–76. New York: Routledge, 2013.

Stoler, Ann Laura. *Along the Archival Grain: Epistemic Anxieties and Colonial Common Sense*. Princeton: Princeton University Press, 2010.

Taylor, Diana. *The Archive and the Repertoire: Performing Cultural Memory in the Americas*. Durham, NC: Duke University Press, 2003.

Tinsley, Omise'eke Natasha. "Black Atlantic, Queer Atlantic: Queer Imaginings of the Middle Passage." *GLQ: A Journal of Lesbian and Gay Studies* 14, no. 2–3 (2008): 191–215. https://doi.org/10.1215/10642684-2007-030.

Tuck, Eve. "Suspending Damage: A Letter to Communities." *Harvard Educational Review* 79, no. 3 (2009): 409–28. https://doi.org/10.17763/haer.79.3.n0016675661t3n15.

Walcott, Rinaldo. Foreword to *Disrupting Queer Inclusion: Canadian Homonationalisms and the Politics of Belonging*, edited by OmiSoore H. Dryden and Suzanne Lenon, vii–x. Vancouver: University of British Columbia Press, 2015.

———. "Outside in Black Studies: Reading from a Queer Place in the Diaspora." In *Queerly Canadian: An Introductory Reader in Sexuality Studies*, edited by Maureen FitzGerald and Scott Rayter, 23–34. Toronto: Canadian Scholars' Press, 2012.

———. "Reconstructing Manhood; or, the Drag of Black Masculinity." *Small Axe: A Caribbean Journal of Criticism* 13, no. 1 (2009): 75–89. https://doi.org/10.1215/07990537-2008-007.

———. *Black Like Who? Writing Black Canada.* Toronto: Insomniac Press, 2009.

Ware, Syrus Marcus, Joan Ruzsa, and Giselle Dias. "It Can't Be Fixed Because It's Not Broken: Racism and Disability in the Prison Industrial Complex." In *Disability Incarcerated: Imprisonment and Disability in the United States and Canada*, edited by Angela Y. Davis, Chris Chapman, and Alison C. Carey, 163–184. New York: Palgrave Macmillan, 2014.

Yaszek, Lisa. "Afrofuturism, Science Fiction, and the History of the Future." *Socialism and Democracy* 20, no. 3 (2006): 41–60. https://doi.org/10.1080/08854300600950236.

21

INDIGENOUS AND BLACK SOLIDARITY IN PRACTICE: #BLMTOTENTCITY

SANDY HUDSON

On Friday, March 21, 2016, Ontario's Special Investigations Unit (SIU) announced that no charges would be laid against the Toronto police officers involved in the homicide of Andrew Loku. The SIU released a bare-bones public report justifying their decision to safeguard the police officers responsible for the death of Andrew Loku.[1] As briefly described earlier in this anthology, activists responded by erecting a "tent city" in front of the Toronto Police Service Headquarters, an encampment occupation that lasted over two weeks. The context under which this action takes place may come as a surprise to those who have been deceived by Canada's denial of racism, but data reveals an anti-Black, racist landscape that Canada's very construction is meant to deny. Though less than 3 percent of the Canadian population is Black, we make up over 10 percent of Canada's incarcerated population. In Toronto the SIU has never recommended a criminal investigation of a police officer who has killed a Black person, though at least half of all people killed by the Toronto police since the 1980s are Black.[2] This context results from the enduring, continued interlocking of white supremacy and colonization in which policing in the colonies of the Americas was birthed (never forget that the police were created for the purpose of capturing Black enslaved people who had liberated themselves).

Through what we called #BLMTOTentCity, Black Lives Matter—Toronto reimagined possibilities for creating a transformative community where members were truly cared for through interdependence and revolutionary ideals of justice. The creation of this space was truly anti-colonial and strengthened solidarity between Black and Indigenous community members. Though the action was an occupation of space, we were careful and deliberate in ensuring that the occupation did not recolonize and render invisible Indigenous communities.

Described crudely, colonization in a Canadian context is typically understood to be a process concerning the theft of land from Indigenous people by white settlers and the accompanying crimes of genocide and cultural erasure committed by these white settlers. But we also understand colonization as the process by which Black people have been stolen from our lands and enslaved by these same settlers, also enduring genocide and cultural erasure. With this theoretical underpinning, a crucial solidarity was built between Black and Indigenous Torontonians through resistance.

BLACK LIVES MATTER—TORONTO AND POLICE VIOLENCE: A BRIEF HISTORY

In Canada, Black activists are often confronted with demands to prove the claims we make in respect to anti-Blackness. Whereas in the United States statistics are readily available to quantify the ways in which anti-Black racism interrupts the lives of Black people below the forty-ninth parallel, such data is scantily available in Canada. In fact, a major form in which anti-Blackness operates in Canada is the active and passive refusal to collect and provide information. Despite calls throughout the years to collect race-based data with respect to education and policing, governments have consistently refused, while simultaneously challenging activists to prove their claims.

As Black people throughout Canada can attest, there is no magic barrier at the forty-ninth parallel that has evaporated anti-Blackness from the white supremacist society of the north. Despite pervasive cultural myths, the anti-Black genocidal history of the British Empire with respect to African people has continued and evolved in contemporary imperialist Canada in much the same way as it has in the contemporary American empire. And though we lack the statistics and transparency that our kinfolk to the south often have access to, academics and community organizers continue to expose Canada's brand of anti-Blackness.

There is a long history of police violence against Black people in the city of Toronto. Despite years of protest and resistance from the Black community, the decision makers in charge of addressing these issues have avoided implementing scores of recommendations and submissions made by various groups, including the Black Action Defence Committee (BADC), the Ontario Human Rights Commission, and the Ontario Ombudsman.[3] In recent years, these issues have become underscored with the surge of Black community resistance to carding and police brutality. When Toronto police killed Andrew Loku, Black Lives Matter activists were told by the Canadian Mental Health Association (CMHA) executive director to trust in the process of Ontario's SIU. He had seen video footage of the incident (which occurred in CMHA housing) and, based on this, suggested was that there was absolutely no way the SIU could do anything other than recommend that the officers involved be charged.

Over six months later the SIU quietly released their decision to the media after business hours on a Friday night. They determined that the officers involved should not be charged. Shortly thereafter, Black Lives Matter—Toronto activists convened a meeting and decided that we would camp outside of Toronto City Hall and create a tent city. After the first night, heavy-handed police repression led to the action moving from Toronto's City Hall to the Toronto Police Headquarters. After the police attacked protesters and confiscated our tents, the action, originally intended to last twelve hours, became an indefinite expression of what a community could look like.[4]

Though the majority of the inhabitants of Black Lives Matter—Toronto's Tent City were Black, there was space made for allies, and all inhabitants were supported and valued. Of our allied participants, the solidarity and support of Indigenous communities was key to our action. The organizers' ability to recognize the resistance action as a site of possibility was transformative.

FROM TIME: SETTLER COLONIALISM AS A SITE OF BLACK AND INDIGENOUS GENOCIDE IN CANADA

In order to fully appreciate the possibilities for transformative change through Black and Indigenous alliance, one should have an appreciation for the ways in which the white supremacist colonial history of this land enacted intertwined violence on both Black people and Indigenous communities. British settler colonialism enacted (and continues to enact) a brutal centuries-long genocide on Indigenous populations across the world. The Dominion of Canada was an active participant in these genocides, benefitting from the destruction of Indigenous societies from South America to West Africa. It is useful here to invoke Andrea Smith's concept of the logics of white supremacy.[5] For Smith, white supremacy operates within logics, two of which are Disappearance and Slaveability. To these logics, I will add the logic of One True History.

DISAPPEARANCE

With respect to communities indigenous to the land, white supremacy enacted a logic of disappearance.[6] White colonizers created a persisting mythology that they are "native" to this land, despite its obvious impossibility. Presence and visibility of Indigenous communities challenge the notion of Canada as a white nation. Accordingly, white settlers violently "disappeared" Indigenous communities. In addition to intentionally isolating and diminishing reserve communities throughout the years, white colonizers created a racist understanding of indigeneity predicated on a constructed primitivity dependent upon "blood purity." Under the Indian Act, only when children with Indigenous ancestry are born to Indigenous women are they recognized by the state as Indigenous. Over the years, miscegenation, often through sexual violence, contributed to the gradual "disappearance" of Indigenous communities in the eyes of the British, French, and subsequently Canadian state. Through residential schools, strategies of disappearance were amplified, causing significant harm in Indigenous communities and resulting in cultural and biological genocide.

SLAVEABILITY

With respect to Black communities, the white supremacist colonizers enacted a logic of slaveability.[7] Certain work that built up and created profit from the colonies was seen as unfit for white colonizers, such as agriculture and housework. Despite Canada's cultural myth of innocence with respect to the enslavement of Black people in white states, Canadians not only engaged in enslavement, but Canada was also built upon the profits the British Empire gained through its use of enslaved labour.[8] Additionally, traders who took part in the trade of sugar, cotton, salt, and other plantation goods all benefitted from and engaged in the enslavement of Africans and contributed to the logic of slaveability.

The logic of slaveability resulted in a different genocidal process than the logic of disappearance, in that the colonizers benefitted from multiplying their labour supply. Instead of using purity as a marker of slaveability, this white supremacist logic enacted the "one drop" rule: so long as one had a veritable "drop" of African ancestry, one was unfit to be considered fully human. The result of such a process was to exclude African people from humanity in the eyes of the colonizers.[9] Enslavement was a permanent condition that literally stripped tens of millions of African people of their right to live. Watching our killings through lynching became a leisure activity for white settlers.

ONE TRUE HISTORY

I add to Andrea Smith's three identified logics the additional white supremacist logic of one true history. Anti-Blackness, anti-Indigeneity, and other forms of racism persist in part because of the idea that there is one version of history, which white people have exclusive dominion over. It is expressed through the Eurocentric dismissal of oral histories and the reliance on the written word as irrefutable truth. It is expressed through an almost scientific reliance on the "white encoders of history" to tell us "truths," even when we accept that there are obvious reasons as to why we should not rely on white supremacist historians to teach us Black or Indigenous history. Despite what Canada has constructed for itself as myth, Yvonne Brown makes it abundantly clear that Canada cannot escape the truth once one digs below the superficial veneer:

> Daniel Defoe, writing in 1713 about the slave trade . . . summed up the tangled web of total exploitation of Africa and Black people as follows: "No African trade, no Negroes, no sugar, no sugar islands, no islands, no continents, no continent, no trade: that is to say farewell to your American trade, your West Indian trade."[10]

The logic of one true history results in the denial of Canadian enslavement because officials responsible for census data did not include Africans in their accounts.[11] Such logic also results in the history of the Underground Railroad in the public and contemporary imagination being dreadfully incomplete. Canada is mythologized into a promised land for escaped slaves because the history of Canada's enslaved population crossing the forty-ninth parallel into the United States for freedom is unwritten. The first large-scale flows of escaped enslaved people that could be deemed as an "underground railroad" movement journeyed from the Canadian towns of Amherstberg and Sandwich to Detroit. This piece of Canadian history is virtually unknown in Canadian popular consciousness.[12] This movement of enslaved people was sparked by the brutalization of an African woman by a Canadian slaver, a fact that is also virtually unknown, as are Canada's attempts to recover its lost "property."[13] Canadian whiteness imagines borders representing a significant shift in principles, despite the colonial and imperialist history of Canada. It also mythologizes all Black people living in Canada as recent immigrants, despite our presence on this land dating back to the 1600s.

One true history also allows the other logics to continue unchallenged, despite their obvious contradictions. In what whiteness wants to imagine as a postcolonial and post-racial present, the logics of disappearance and slaveability persist, despite superficial liberal rejections of the current manifestation of these social harms in popular consciousness. And, the one drop rule continues to define Blackness, and the pure blood rule continues to define Indigeneity. It also leads to a situation where contemporary state leaders, such as former Prime Minister Stephen Harper, are able to absurdly claim without irony that Canada "has no history of colonialism."[14]

One true history also allows for a society in which white supremacy can continue without widespread challenge. If Black and Indigenous folks are seen to lack the ability to participate and advance politically and economically due to their own socio-economic faults, divorced from a history of violence, then whiteness has no responsibility for its continued marginality and oppression. The one true history convinces society, including Black and Indigenous people, that we are entitled to life, dignity, and "freedom" if we adhere to dominant notions of acceptability and social norms; historical and social locations be damned.

A careful contemplation of these concepts reveals that all people, even those who are not white, can be implicated in the logics of white supremacy. Whether white, Black, Indigenous, or non-Black racialized people, white supremacy's hegemonic status is dependent upon mass buy-in. Indigenous people can (and have) contributed to the logic of slaveability—at their own peril. Black folks can (and have) contributed to the logic of Indigenous disappearance—at their own peril. In order to truly tackle white supremacy, each of these pillars must be attacked without reinscribing or strengthening another pillar. A failure to do so runs the risk of turning Black and Indigenous people against one another, thereby contributing to the logic of white supremacy.

BLACK LIBERATION AND INDIGENOUS SOLIDARITY IN PRACTICE

An alliance between Black and Indigenous people has powerful possibilities for resistance against colonialism and anti-Blackness. Given our contemporary context in Canada, the movement against police brutality was an ideal issue with which to create a coalition. The state targets Black and Indigenous people for policing, incarceration, and surveillance like no other people in existence on this land. Black and Indigenous populations are chronically overrepresented in prisons and in communities regularly under surveillance by police officers.

When Indigenous allies joined us at the camp, a relationship that respected our specific and linked histories developed. Through waking hours, a Mohawk Warrior flag, a Six Nations Iroquois Confederacy flag and a photo of Andrew Loku were held high at the centre of #BLMTOTentCity. Space was carved out specifically for Indigenous communities and Indigenous medicines were brought to the site every day. Indigenous communities entered into conversation with us so that we could establish a respectful process for using the space that we intended to honour in the ways that the Indigenous caretakers requested of us. Indigenous activists cleansed the space each day with sage and other medicines and established expectations for interactions with police officers should they arise. Similarly, upon entering the space, members from Indigenous communities respected our goals and our plans for using the space. We made clear that our community project would accept all allies and that we had measures in place for interactions with the police for Black participants. Each day that we extended our action we furthered dialogue with our Indigenous allies. Processes for food distribution, diverse spiritual practices, and health were negotiated together. Our Indigenous allies always respected our decision-making and leadership. Once established, our partnership was very visible and intentional.

This partnership felt natural, but it is a partnership that must be intentional and continually renewed. Black communities can be anti-Indigenous, and Indigenous communities can be anti-Black. It is crucial for both our communities to resist the myths sold to us by the state, lest we end up tacitly supporting white supremacist logics. If Black communities buy into the logic of disappearance, white supremacist settler-colonial logics are upheld within Blackness. If Indigenous communities buy into the logic of slaveability, white supremacist settler-colonial logics are upheld within Indigeneity. If either community buys into the one true history logic, we are tacitly supporting white supremacist settler-colonial logics at the cost of erasing our own shared histories. Showing the power of Indigenous people as essential caretakers, lawmakers, and spiritual leaders in #BLMTOTentCity was an anti-colonial and revolutionary act that rendered the settler-colonial state as impermanent.

CONCLUSION AND POTENTIALITIES FOR MOVEMENT-BUILDING

Shortly after the close of Black Lives Matter—Toronto's Tent City, a state of emergency was announced in the Northern Ontario First Nation of Attawapiskat.[15] The community has been devastated by Canada's continued colonial project, leading to a spate of suicide attempts by youth as young as nine years of age. The declaration of a state of emergency came as Black Lives Matter—Toronto was holding a private healing and debriefing session for participants of Tent City. The Indigenous participants notified us, letting us know that they had been inspired by Tent City and might need our solidarity in the coming days. Shortly after, an Indigenous activist group called upon us to support another occupation action: #OccupyINAC.[16] Toronto and Indigenous organizers in coalition with Black Lives Matter—Toronto occupied the Indigenous and Northern Affairs Canada (INAC) office. Once again, our mutual solidarity was impossible to ignore. The presence in the media made it clear that Black activists would be using their own resources, contacts, and tools to benefit Indigenous communities.

During these actions, both groups acted with respect for and solidarity with each other that led to our ultimate success in mobilizing our respective communities and forcing powerful decision makers to act. The potential for both groups to enact transformative change by continuing to work in coalition is boundless. We should roundly reject white supremacist logics that see us competing with each other for scraps at the bottom of the white supremacist lowerarchy. We should never forget that, in some ways, we are the most dangerous groups to the white supremacist state structure. Our very existence reveals its injustices and attacks its legitimacy. The possibilities stemming from our solidarity and coalition are nothing short of revolutionary.

The potential for decolonizing, Black-affirming futurities inherent in the coalition between Black and Indigenous communities is exciting. White supremacy has historically attempted to prevent these communities from coming together and has benefitted from the genocide of these groups, as well as from the particular ways Black and Indigenous people have been implicated in particular logics of white supremacy. The strategic unity between these groups and their inherent ability to dismantle deception in the logics of slaveability, disappearance, and one true history necessarily creates possibilities for futurities we have yet to truly theorize. My hope is that strategies like the one taken through #BLMTOTentCity will open up possibilities for creating alternative futures that effectively and radically dismantle the white supremacist present.

NOTES

1 "Investigation Finds No Grounds for Criminal Charges in Fatal Shooting of Andrew Loku," Special Investigations Unit, March 18, 2016, http://www.siu.on.ca/en/news_template.php?nrid=2578.

2 Anthony N. Morgan and Darcel Bullen, *Civil and Political Wrongs: The Growing Gap between International, Civil, and Political Rights and African Canadian Life – A Report on the Canadian Government's Compliance with the International Covenant on Civil and Political Rights* (Toronto: African Canadian Legal Clinic, 2015), https://tbinternet.ohchr.org/Treaties/CCPR/Shared%20Documents/CAN/INT_CCPR_CSS_CAN_20858_E.pdf. Since the writing of this piece, the SIU charged police officer Daniel Montsion with manslaughter, aggravated assault, and assault with a weapon in the killing of Adirahman Abdi, a Black man in Ottawa. In this case, thousands of activists across the country demonstrated, demanding justice for the Somali man, who was beaten by Montsion. Montsion was later revealed to be wearing knuckle-plated gloves during the beating.

3 Law Union of Ontario, *Submission to Toronto Police Service Board Re: The CAPP Report on Police Carding* (Toronto: Law Union of Ontario, 2014), http://www.lawunion.ca/wp-content/uploads/2014/12/2014-12-15-LUO-Submission-to-TPSB-re-CAPP-FINAL.pdf; Urban Alliance on Race Relations, *Saving Lives: Alternatives to the Use of Lethal Force by Police* (Toronto: Urban Alliance on Race Relations, 2000), https://urbanalliance.files.wordpress.com/2012/05/savinglivesreport.pdf; Ontario Human Rights Commission, *Paying the Price: The Human Cost of Racial Profiling – Inquiry Report* (Toronto: Ontario Human Rights Commission, 2003), http://www.ohrc.on.ca/sites/default/files/attachments/Paying_the_price%3A_The_human_cost_of_racial_profiling.pdf; André Marin, *Oversight Unseen: Investigation into the Special Investigations Unit's Operational Effectiveness and Credibility* (Toronto: Ombudsman of Ontario, 2008), http://www.siu.on.ca/pdfs/marin_report_2008.pdf; Ombudsman of Ontario, *2014-2015 Annual Report* (Toronto: Ombudsman of Ontario, 2015), https://www.ombudsman.on.ca/resources/reports-and-case-summaries/annual-reports/2014-2015-annual-report.

4 S. Hudson and R. Diverlus, "Toronto Police attack peaceful Black Lives Matter—Toronto protestors," news release, March 21, 2016, http://www.newswire.ca/news-releases/toronto-police-attack-peaceful-black-lives-matter-toronto-protestors-573027871.html.

5 Andrea Smith, "Indigeneity, Settler Colonialism, White Supremacy," *Global Dialogue* 12, no. 2 (2010): 1–14.

6 Ibid.

7 Ibid.

8 David Austin, "Narratives of Power: Historical Mythologies in Contemporary Quebec and Canada," *Race & Class* 52, no. 1 (2010): 19–32.

9 Afua Cooper, "Acts of Resistance: Black Men and Women Engage Slavery in Upper Canada, 1793–1803," *Ontario History* 99, no. 1 (2007): 5–17.

10 Yvonne Brown, "Ghosts in the Canadian Multicultural Machine: A Tale of the Absent Presence of Black People," *Journal of Black Studies* 38, no. 3 (2008), 385.

11 Brown, "Ghosts in the Canadian Multicultural Machine."

12 Cooper, "Acts of Resistance."

13 Cooper, "Acts of Resistance."

14 T. Fontaine, "What did Justin Trudeau say about Canada's history of colonialism?" CBC News, April 22, 2016, http://www.cbc.ca/news/aboriginal/trudeau-colonialism-comments-1.3549405.

15 J. Forani, "Attawapiskat in state of emergency following rash of suicide attempts." *Toronto Star*, April 10, 2016, http://www.thestar.com/news/canada/2016/04/10/attawapiskat-in-state-of-emergency-following-rash-of-suicides.html.

16 C. Da Silva, "Idle No More, Black Lives Matter protesters demand action on Attawapiskat suicide crisis," CBC News, April 13, 2016, http://www.cbc.ca/news/canada/toronto/protesters-occupy-indigenous-northern-affairs-office-1.3533662.

REFERENCES

Amadahy, Zainab, and Bonita Lawrence. "Indigenous Peoples and Black People in Canada: Settlers or Allies?" In *Breaching the Colonial Contact: Anti-Colonialism in the US and Canada*, edited by Arlo Kempf, 105–36. Toronto: Springer, 2009.

Austin, David. "Narratives of Power: Historical Mythologies in Contemporary Quebec and Canada." *Race & Class* 52, no. 1 (2010): 19–32.

Brown, Yvonne. "Ghosts in the Canadian Multicultural Machine: A Tale of the Absent Presence of Black People." *Journal of Black Studies* 38, no. 3 (2008): 374–87. https://doi.org/10.1177/0021934707306572.

Churchill, Ward. "Marxism and the Native American." In *Marxism and Native Americans*, edited by Ward Churchill, 183–204. Cambridge, MA: South End Press, 1983.

Cooper, Afua. "The Fluid Frontier: Blacks and the Detroit River Region." *Canadian Review of American Studies* 30, no. 2 (2000), 129–50. https://doi.org/10.3138/CRAS-s030-02-02.

———. "Acts of Resistance: Black Men and Women Engage Slavery in Upper Canada, 1793–1803." *Ontario History* 99, no. 1 (2007): 5–17.

Lawrence, Bonita, and Enakshi Dua. "Decolonizing Antiracism." *Social Justice* 32, no. 4 (2005): 120–43.

Marin, André. *Oversight Undermined: Investigation into the Ministry of the Attorney General's Implementation of Recommendations Concerning Reform of the Special Investigations Unit.* Toronto: Ombudsman of Ontario, 2011. Retrieved from: http://www.siu.on.ca/pdfs/ombudsmans_report_2011_oversight_undermined.pdf.

———. *Oversight Unseen: Investigation into the Special Investigations Unit's Operational Effectiveness and Credibility.* Toronto: Ombudsman of Ontario, 2008. Retrieved from: http://www.siu.on.ca/pdfs/marin_report_2008.pdf.

Morgan, Anthony N., and Darcel Bullen. *Civil and Political Wrongs: The Growing Gap between International, Civil, and Political Rights and African Canadian Life – A Report on the Canadian Government's Compliance with the International Covenant on Civil and Political Rights.* Toronto: African Canadian Legal Clinic, 2015. Retrieved from: https://tbinternet.ohchr.org/Treaties/CCPR/Shared%20Documents/CAN/INT_CCPR_CSS_CAN_20858_E.pdf.

Ombudsman of Ontario. *2014–2015 Annual Report.* Toronto: Ombudsman of Ontario, 2015.

Paying the Price: The Human Cost of Racial Profiling – Inquiry Report. Toronto: Ontario Human Rights Commission, 2003. Retrieved from: http://www.ohrc.on.ca/sites/default/files/attachments/Paying_the_price%3A_The_human_cost_of_racial_profiling.pdf.

Saving Lives: Alternatives to the Use of Lethal Force by Police. Toronto: Urban Alliance on Race Relations, 2000. Retrieved from: https://urbanalliance.files.wordpress.com/2012/05/savinglivesreport.pdf.

Sharma, Nandita, and Cynthia Wright. "Decolonizing Resistance, Challenging Colonial States." *Social Justice* 35, no. 3 (2009): 120–38.

Smith, Andrea. "Indigeneity, Settler Colonialism, White Supremacy." *Global Dialogue* 12, no. 2 (2010): 1-14.

Submission to Toronto Police Service Board Re: The CAPP Report on Police Carding. Toronto: Law Union of Ontario, 2014. Retrieved from: http://www.

lawunion.ca/wp-content/uploads/2014/12/2014-12-15-LUO-Submission-to-TPSB-re-CAPP-FINAL.pdf.

Trask, Haunani-Kay. "Coalition-Building between Natives and Non-Natives." *Stanford Law Review* 43, no. 6 (1991): 1197–213. https://heinonline.org/HOL/P?h=hein.journals/stflr43&i=1214.

Walcott, Rinaldo. "The Book of Others (*Book IV*): Canadian Multiculturalism, the State, and Its Political Legacies." *Canadian Ethnic Studies* 46, no. 2 (2014): 127–32. http://muse.jhu.edu/article/548141.

Wigmore, Gregory. "Before the Railroad: From Slavery to Freedom in the Canadian-American Borderland." *Journal of American History* 98, no. 2 (2011): 437–54. https://doi.org/10.1093/jahist/jar256.

Wolfe, Patrick. "Settler Colonialism and the Elimination of the Native." *Journal of Genocide Research* 8, no. 4 (2006): 387–409. https://doi.org/10.1080/14623520601056240.

22

BLACK LIVES MATTER—TORONTO FREEDOM SCHOOL

PHOTO ESSAY BY ANIQUE JORDAN

The Black Lives Matter—Toronto Freedom School, or Freedom School, began as a three-week pilot program in the summer of 2017. The school was born out of a desire to support our young people in caring ways. We created the Black Lives Matter—Toronto Freedom School within the context of disproportionately high push-out rates, Eurocentric curriculum, suspensions, expulsions, and streaming of Black kids. We created the school at a time in which police were in schools criminalizing our children, when the news of another young person killed by police flooded our television screens.

Deeply inspired by the Black Panther Party for Self-Defense and the Oakland Community School, Freedom School was provided to the community free of charge and quickly became a central project of Black Lives Matter—Toronto. The initial program included children aged four to ten, a number that was subsequently expanded. Freedom School was a response to a lack of humanizing, self-affirming, and queer- and trans-inclusive educational opportunities for Black children in the Greater Toronto Area (GTA). The school provided an alternative setting for parents who do not feel their children are being taught self-love and a passion for social justice through their formal education. Working with local Black educators, the program was designed to teach children about Black Canadian and diasporic history, to engage children in political resistance to anti-Black racism and state violence through a trans-feminist lens.

At the core of the program is preserving Black children's dignity, giving them space to be affirmed of their Blackness and all the things that come with it. We see this program as an antidote to the historical and present-day erasure of Black resistance history in Canadian curriculum. Freedom School is grounded in providing children with information on their shared history as the children of the diaspora, filling the gaps where traditional educational institutions fail. The school's students learn a critical curriculum currently absent in mainstream formal education, from Marsha P. Johnson to the Haitian Revolution, Queen Nanny Maroon and the Maroons in Canada to the Bussa Revolution in Barbados and the Soweto Uprisings. Each year, we engage local artists and educators in the creation of child-friendly resources such as claymation, video animation, puzzles, games, and workbooks.

Children have been present since the origins of BLM—TO; we have parents among our steering team, our volunteer base, and in our community. When we are protesting, it's often about the death of a young person killed by police, or detrimental policies and practices that have or will have profound impacts on our children's lives. But what is often not seen are the moments of tenderness, of our children playing and laughing, making signs, colouring, and living in joy. The beautiful intergenerational exchanges between our children, our youth, and our elders, between our collective and communal parents, and between our children and our adolescents—these are the true moments of revolution.

What was perhaps the most exciting part of Freedom School was witnessing young people expressing agency and thirst for a better world. These young people were very active in #BLMTOTentCity, the 14-day durational protest at Toronto Police Headquarters, and some were unfortunately present when Toronto Police inflicted violence on peaceful protestors. They've hosted their own actions and demonstrations, and were the cornerstone of our #NOSROs campaign, in which Black Lives Matter—Toronto worked with the Latinx, Afro-Latin-America, Abya Yala Education Network and Education Not Incarceration to force police officers out of the Toronto District School Board. Our youth joined 100 teachers, parents, and community educators to walk out of their schools for #BLMTOFreedomDay to protest issues faced by Black youth in schools across the GTA, including their criminalization and surveillance by armed police officers in schools. With our children by our sides, we pushed and won the removal of School Resource Officers from the largest public school board in North America. Our children have always been there, and creating spaces for them to thrive has been our priority and focus.

We do this not only for each other, but for those who will come after us.

Thank you to the initial team who supported the children in Freedom School, including the Black Lives Matter—Toronto Steering Team: Leroi Newbold, Nauoda Robinson, Naomi Bain, Galme Mumed, Emmanuel Ruta, Kike Otuije, and many more. It took a village to create this school year after year, including many cooks, bus drivers, chaperones, speakers, presenters, volunteers, content creators, and of course, all the parents.

—The Editors

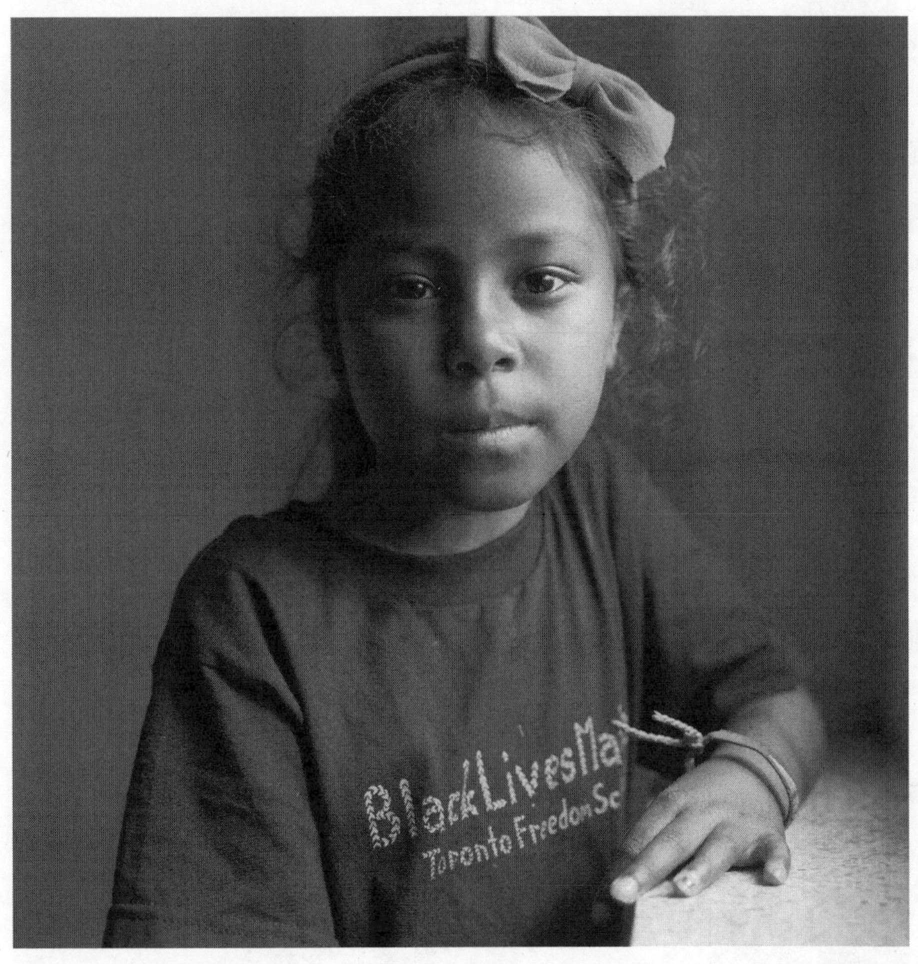
BlackLivesMa
Toronto Freedom Sc

JORDAN

For the past two years I have been asked to document the student body and faculty of Black Lives Matter—Toronto's Freedom School. As I go through these images, I think about what it means to photograph a Black child. What angles do we choose? What visual languages take precedence? What symbols and body language do we note and how are they read? As a Black photographer I realize how sensitive I become to guarding the practice of photographing our children as an act of protection.

This series is not solely a documentary or archival work, but also a contemplative one, asking, How do we see the Black child?

—Anique Jordan

CONCLUSION

THE PALIMPSEST

Indeed, freedom is still beyond us.

We are often asked what this freedom will look like. "What is it that you are fighting for?" liberal detractors might ask. The question, a deflection at best, suggests that we have no business demanding a global reorganization—a revolutionary abolition—if we cannot fully articulate a system design—as though capitalism itself was a fully articulated system when the sugar cane plantations in the Americas yielded their first millionaires. As though the systems that we currently struggle to survive under are not of themselves processes that shift and morph to the needs of those in power. Systems are processes. In fighting against such processes we reveal what new processes might look like. In refusing white supremacist constructions of time and instead relying on Black feminist constructions of time to guide us, we reveal what new processes might look like and what the Afrofuture might hold.

In her masterpiece *In the Wake*, Christina Sharpe wrestled with how to "articulate a method of encountering a past that is not past." She references Dionne Brand's *A Map to the Door of No Return* as "an unscientific method" of "blackened knowledge" that comes from the "historical rupture" of Blackness.[1] Jacqui Alexander, as quoted in Tiffany Lethabo King's thesis, seeks a palimpsestic methodology. This palimpsestic approach removes the requirement to rely on a white -supremacist, colonial construction of time. Instead of seeing our history as a series of connected events that occur in a linear fashion, as dominant, conventional wisdom expects from us, Alexander brings time and space together from different eras, recognizing that the past is still with us, and refuses to distance the historical and the contemporary, creating a tesseract-like methodology she refers to as "the palimpsest:—a parchment that has been inscribed two or three times, the previous text having been imperfectly erased and remaining and therefore still partially visible . . . The idea of the 'new' structured through the 'old' scrambled, palimpsestic character of time, both jettisons the truncated distance of linear time and dislodges the impulse for incommensurability, which the ideology of distance creates. It thus rescrambles the 'here and now' and the 'then and there' to a 'here and there' and 'then and now.'"[2]

In search of this Blackened knowledge, we employ the palimpsest by considering the history of the Black Lives Matter movement in Canada, this present anthology and the work it does, and the futurespace below.

THEORIZING THE PRESENT IN MAPPING THE FUTURE: WHO, HOW, AND WHAT WE'VE WRITTEN

We came into this project looking to bring together people in struggle and creation all over Canada to honour the work that we've done, the work that we're doing, and where we want to go as a broad Black movement community. We have not yet lived in liberation, but our theorizing of the present and our reflection on the past in the present gives us a theoretical space in which we can map the future.

It was important for us to collect the words of activists, artists, change-makers, and practitioners of all sorts.

Through these pages we ruminated on carceral violence, front-ending and prioritizing incarceration as one of the most urgent issues in our community, in addition to imperialist border policies. We've considered a variety of voices and spaces, from incarcerated people to refugees, from Nova Scotia to the Yukon, to the Mediterranean Sea. With verve, we express our commitment to abolition: in a liberated future there is no carceral violence. There are no prisons. There are no police. There is no colonization. There is no imperialism.

We considered our creative selves, visually, musically, poetically, and physically. We lean into our artistic sensibilities with intentionality, ensuring there is space for the injection of art into our construction of our future. From the pulse that carries us through a chant, to the breadth of imagery from the visual artists who lend their work to our movements, to the choreography of a demonstration, art is our modality and our message, is central to the generation of action. Our ancestors used art to survive, to educate, to communicate, and to build: a legacy sown into our movement culture.

We asked questions about Blackness and the intersectionality of our identities. Being Black above the forty-ninth parallel is an experience in erasure, one we reject when we discuss the complexities of our identities in the colonial state of Canada. We insisted on considering our Muslim identities, our trans identities, our disabled identities, and our northern geography.

Who are we as defined through our full selves, outside of the gaze of the colonizer? Who can we be in a liberated future? We must be ready to articulate who we can be in a fully liberated future: a daunting task that begins with a consideration of who we were, and who we are.

Finally, we considered the future through the past and present. Yes, we have not yet lived a liberated Blackness, but we are well on our way to creating that future. This compendium is a documentation of generative from-the-ground work that is Black-affirming, Black-loving. Work that is global, intergenerational, anti-capitalist, and trans-feminist in nature. We may not know exactly what its final form is, but we've imagined bits and pieces of it. We've felt the edges of it and even tasted it. We know what it doesn't look like, and we know what it will feel like. And we know that we will create it, in the palimpsest.

In the Blackest of knowledge. We know.

We will win.

NOTES

1 Christina Sharpe, *In the Wake: On Blackness and Being* (Durham, NC: Duke University Press, 2016), 13.

2 Tiffany Lethabo King, "In the Clearing: Black Female Bodies, Space and Settler Colonial Landscapes" (PhD dissertation, University of Maryland, 2013), 219.

POSTSCRIPT

THE YEAR 2092 C.E.—AN IMAGINED FUTURE, PART 2

We did eventually find ways to emerge from our underground safety. In the early part of 2070 we figured out how to redirect the jet stream, to remove carbon from the oceans and atmosphere in a rapid way, and to restore much of Earth's natural cycles. We had lost more than a quarter of Earth's population and most of its biodiversity, but we were on the road to healing and rebuilding. I still visited the water treatment plant, now turned into a public graffiti gallery, the toxic spray paints of yesterday aimed through aerosol containers now made of natural dyes and computerized mechanisms that kept our Earth's air safe.

I remembered the long days walking from the water station to the underground collecting pools, and me sitting to read whenever I could. Those old tattered pages have now been retyped, preserved in small but growing libraries in our newly sun-filled, above-ground homes.

When we began writing these texts we were gathered in huddled activisms, whispering the chant We Will Win, our voices growing louder and louder until they became a worldwide cacophony and we did in fact win. Our timing was hard, and the climate realities provided challenges to our new way of living—beyond our wildest dreams—but we worked through them, together. Using collective brilliance, social justice frameworks, and ways of working that ensured that we embraced the Adinkra tenet of Sankofa, to learn from and remember our past, we grew and changed together. Sankofa. So that we may never have to repeat the worst of it, and so that we can build on and grow from the most wonderful parts.

We are steadily rebuilding our communities, and they are centred around Black and Indigenous knowledges. We truly are living in the free.

We won.

CONTRIBUTORS

SILVIA ARGENTINA ARAUZ is a Nicaraguense Latina with African and Indigenous roots. She/they is/are Mother, Writer, Educator, and Ancestor. Silvia Argentina has dedicated much of her youth and adult life to the incubation and amplification of pro-liberation models coming out of kick-ass grassroots organizing in order to disrupt mainstream narratives and centre the voices of those most marginalized by dumb-ass colonial systems.

LEANNE BETASAMOSAKE SIMPSON is a Michi Saagiig Nishnaabeg scholar, writer, and artist. She is on the faculty at the Dechinta Centre for Research and Learning in Denendeh. She is author of *As We Have Always Done*, *Dancing on Our Turtle's Back*, *The Gift Is in the Making*, *Islands of Decolonial Love*, and *This Accident of Being Lost*. Leanne is a member of Alderville First Nation in Ontario, Canada.

Artist, organizer, educator, and popular public speaker, **PATRISSE KHAN-CULLORS** is a Los Angeles native, co-founder of the Black Lives Matter Global Network, and founder of the grassroots Los Angeles–based organization Dignity and Power Now. In 2013 Patrisse co-founded the global movement with the viral twitter hashtag #BlackLivesMatter, which has since grown to an international organization with dozens of chapters around the world fighting anti-Black racism. In January 2016 Patrisse Khan-Cullors published her memoir, *When They Call You a Terrorist: A Black Lives Matter Memoir*, which became an instant *New York Times* Best Seller. Patrisse has been honoured with various awards, including: the Sydney Peace Prize Award (2017), Black Woman of the Year Award from the National Congress of Black Women (2015), named an emerging civil rights leader for the 21st Century by the *Los Angeles Times* (2015), Community Change Agent Award from BLACK GIRLS ROCK!, Inc. (2016), Women of the Year Award: The Justice Seekers by Glamour (2016), and ESSENCE's first-ever Woke Award. Patrisse recently received her MFA from the University of Southern California.

GISELLE DIAS (NIIGAANII ZHAAWSHKO GIIZHIGOKWE, LEADING BLUE SKY WOMAN) is a mixed-race, Metis woman from the Red River; she is a community organizer and activist who has been working on issues related to prisoners' rights, penal abolition, and transformative justice for twenty-five years. Her recent work is considers how to decolonize and indigenize anti-prison work through her relationship with her land and Creation.

OMISOORE H. DRYDEN, PhD, is the James R. Johnston Chair in Black Canadian Studies and associate professor in the Department of Community Health and Epidemiology, Faculty of Medicine, at Dalhousie University. Dryden is an interdisciplinary scholar who examines the symbolics of blood and the "social life" of blood donation while engaging with Black, queer, diasporic analytics, and health and medical humanities. Dryden co-edited the collection titled *Disrupting Queer Inclusion: Canadian Homonationalisms and the Politics of Belonging* (UBC Press, 2015). Dryden is the principal investigator of a research project that seeks to identify the barriers African/Black gay, bisexual, and trans men encounter to donating blood in Canada.

Haitian, activist, and feminist, **PAIGE GALETTE** is passionately involved in political movements fighting for social justice: the labour movement, women's movement, queer movement, and the Black liberation movement. She is president of Les Essentielles, a francophone women's organization in Yukon, and is serving as an elected director of the Community Midwifery Association of Yukon, which works towards the regulation and funding of midwifery in Yukon. Paige Galette resides in Whitehorse with her English bulldog, Totoro.

Since 1985 **DANA INKSTER** has worked in the education and cultural sectors and is proud to recognize storytelling as a tool that shapes our communities. Her 1999 film *Welcome to Africville* was the first of many experimental films and videos exploring love and place and states of heart and mind. Dana has been profiled by numerous publications, and journalists and cultural theorists from around the world have lauded her documentary film work. She continues to make independent documentaries that explore personal and cultural histories.

Her documentary *24 Days in Brooks* (2007) was co-produced by the National Film Board of Canada and CBC Newsworld. She has served as faculty and played key roles in development for a number of institutions, including the Calgary Stampede, the University of Lethbridge, and Lethbridge College.

SARAH JAMA is a community organizer from Hamilton, Ontario. She is co-founder of the Disability Justice Network of Ontario (DJNO), is a current board member with the Hamilton Transit Riders Union, and is working with the Hamilton Wentworth District School Board to create curriculum around combating anti-Black racism. She has given over 100 lectures, presentations, and keynote speeches on issues surrounding leadership, diversity, and justice, and she works at the Hamilton Centre for Civic Inclusion as a program coordinator.

EL JONES is a poet, educator, journalist, and advocate. She was the fifth Poet Laureate of Halifax, and currently holds the fifteenth Nancy's Chair in Women's Studies at Mount Saint Vincent University. El is a co-founder of *The Black Power Hour*, a radio show developed collectively with prisoners. Her advocacy and work fights anti-Black racism in Canada, walking in the path of our great-grandmothers, who resisted relentlessly.

Award-winning artist, writer, and curator, **ANIQUE JORDAN** looks to answer the question of possibility in everything she creates. Principally interested in Canadian histories that speak to Black Canada, women, and working-class communities, and exploring the relationships between Black and Indigenous peoples, Jordan's work ultimately questions the authority of the Canadian state.

DR. NAILA KELETA MAE is an assistant professor at the University of Waterloo whose areas of research and teaching expertise are race, gender, and Black expressive cultures. Keleta-Mae is also a published playwright, a published poet, and a recording artist. Her research and art are funded by grants from the Social Sciences and Humanities Research Council of Canada, the University of Waterloo, and the Canada Council for the Arts. She has commentated for the BBC, CBC, CTV, The Canadian Press, and *The National Post*, among others, and written for *The Globe and Mail*, *VICE*, and *The Fader*.

JANAYA KHAN is a lecturer, author, and co-creator of Black Lives Matter Canada. Known as 'Future in the Movement for Black Lives,' Janaya is a firm believer in local organizing for national and global change. They have had the pleasure of doing public speaking that has taken them around the world and have been featured in Vogue, The Cut, and Love Magazine. Janaya currently serves as program director for Color Of Change and resides in Los Angeles, California.

GILARY MASSA is a proud Afro-Panamanian Muslim who lives in Toronto, Canada, with her husband and two young children. She has a long-standing history in community engagement, public education, and activism related to equity, human rights, and social justice. With roots in both the labour movement and student movement, Gilary spent her last three years working as the Advocacy Coordinator for the National Council of Canadian Muslims (NCCM), where she spearheaded their efforts in engaging school communities on issues related to better supporting the needs of Muslim students and their families. Prior to working at NCCM, she was the Executive Director of Communications and Outreach at the Ryerson Students Union and now works as the Human Rights Outreach and Engagement Officer at the Toronto District School Board. Gilary sits as a founding board member of both the Parkdale Centre for Social Innovation and the Black Muslim Initiative, and is the co-founder of the Sisters' Retreat—a Muslim women's wellness retreat in her home country of Panama.Gilary is currently pursuinga master's degree in Leadership and Community Engagement at the Faculty of Education at York University in Toronto.

ROBYN MAYNARD is a Toronto-based writer and author of the award-winning national bestseller *Policing Black Lives: State Violence in Canada from Slavery to the Present* (2017). She has published writing in a wide variety of academic, trade, and activist publications and is currently a PhD student and Vanier Scholar at the University of Toronto. Her writing can be found at www.robynmaynard.com, and she tweets at @PolicingBlack.

QUEENTITE OPALEKE is a Nigerian/Jamaican Hybrid of the African Diaspora™, the co-founding director of Prosthetics For Foreign Donation (PFFD), and the owner/master stylist of Natty Hair. This former international model and spoken -word poet led chants for the Winnipeg Women's March on Washington, 2017, was guest speaker for the Black History Month Committee Luncheon 2018, and was awarded the African Community Awards Humanitarian Award, 2019. QueenTite earned a diploma in Disability and Community Support from Red River College in 2011 and is now pursuing her BA (Honours) in behavioural sciences at Humber College. Queen is a black light in the darkness of the night. Melanin sight.

RANDOLPH RILEY is a prison activist, writer, and community leader from Cherrybrook, Nova Scotia. He led the Black August prison strike in 2018, and his work has been published with CBC, *Halifax Examiner, Nova Scotia Advocate* and other venues. He is a co-founder of the *Black Power Hour* radio show on CKDU 88.1FM, and his work on prison abolition has been presented at national and international conferences.

CAMILLE TURNER, an artist and explorer of race, space, home, and belonging, recovers silenced voices and conjures life from archival fragments that whisper stories from another dimension. Driven by curiosity, outrage, and fierce belief in a better world, Turner looks for gaps in places where the unresolved past haunts the present. Her interventions, installations, and public engagements have been presented throughout Canada and internationally, and she is currently a PhD candidate in York University's Faculty of Environmental Studies.

RAVYN WNGZ is a co-founder of ILL NANA/DiverseCity Dance Company, the founder of O.V.A. Collective, and a member of Black Lives Matter—Toronto's steering committee, Wngz's vision is to create work/art/conversations that open the minds and the hearts of all people, and encourage self-reflection and force fundamental change. As an empowerment-movement storyteller, Wngz aims to challenge mainstream arts and dance spaces by sharing her stories as a Tanzanian, Bermudian, queer, two-spirit, transcendent, Mohawk individual. She aims to create opportunities, positive representations, and platforms for marginalized LGBTTIQQ2S communities with a focus on people who are Black, Indigenous, and people of colour.

EDITORS

RODNEY DIVERLUS is a Port-au-Prince-born and Toronto-based organizing strategist, contemporary artist, and consultant. Rodney is co-founder of Black Lives Matter—Toronto and is co-leading the development of Black Lives Matter Canada. An ardent artivist, Rodney toggles between worlds; his multidisciplinary artistic practice weaves in contemporary movement, physical theatre, protest, and performance art. His work has taken him across the globe, performing, speaking, or presenting throughout Canada, the United States, Australia, Europe, and the Caribbean community. Visit rodneydiverlus.com for more information.

SANDY HUDSON is a community organizer, political strategist, wand scholar. An award-winning public intellectual, Sandy has been honoured as one of *Toronto Life*'s 50 Most Influential Torontonians, one of Post City Magazines' Most Inspiring Women, and one of Canada International Black Women's 100 Black women to watch. Sandy serves as the founding vice-chair of the Black Legal Action Centre and co-hosts the Canadian political podcast *Sandy and Nora Talk Politics*. Sandy is the founder of the Black Lives Matter movement presence in Canada and Black Lives Matter—Toronto. She is currently studying law at the University of California in Los Angeles.

SYRUS MARCUS WARE is a Vanier Scholar, a visual artist, community activist, researcher, youth advocate, and educator. For twelve years, he was the coordinator of the Art Gallery of Ontario Youth Program. Syrus is currently a facilitator/designer for the Cultural Leaders Lab (Toronto Arts Council; the Banff Centre). He was the inaugural artist-in-residence for Daniels Spectrum (2016/2017) and was awarded the MayWorks Labour Artist of the Year award and the TD Diversity Award, both in 2017. Syrus is also a core team member of Black Lives Matter—Toronto.